高等学校试用教材

建筑类专业英语

建筑学与城市规划

第三册

李明章 　　　　主编

王天发

娄作友　潘龙明　　编

黄天琪 　　　　主审

中国建筑工业出版社

前　言

经过几十年的探索，外语教学界许多人认为，工科院校外语教学的主要目的，应该是："使学生能够利用外语这个工具，通过阅读去获取国外的与本专业有关的科技信息。"这既是我们建设有中国特色的社会主义的客观需要，也是在当前条件下工科院校外语教学可能完成的最高目标。事实上，教学大纲规定要使学生具有"较强"的阅读能力，而对其他方面的能力只有"一般"要求，就是这个意思。

大学本科的一、二年级，为外语教学的基础阶段。就英语来说，这个阶段要求掌握的词汇量为 2 400 个（去掉遗忘，平均每个课时 10 个单词）。加上中学阶段已经学会的 1 600 个单词，基础阶段结束时应掌握的词汇量为 4 000 个。仅仅掌握 4 000 个单词，能否看懂专业英文书刊呢？还不能。据统计，掌握 4 000 个单词，阅读一般的英文科技文献，生词量仍将有 6％左右，即平均每百词有六个生词，还不能自由阅读。国外的外语教学专家认为，生词量在 3％以下，才能不借助词典，自由阅读。此时可以通过上下文的联系，把不认识的生词猜出来。那么，怎么样才能把 6％的生词量降低到 3％以下呢？自然，需要让学生增加一部分词汇积累。问题是，要增加多少单词？要增加哪些单词？统计资料表明，在每一个专业的科技文献中，本专业最常用的科技术语大约只有几百个，而且它们在文献中重复出现的频率很高。因此，在已经掌握 4 000 单词的基础上，在专业阅读阶段中，有针对性地通过大量阅读，扩充大约 1 000 个与本专业密切有关的科技词汇，便可以逐步达到自由阅读本专业科技文献的目的。

早在八十年代中期，建设部系统院校外语教学研究会就组织编写了一套《土木建筑系列英语》，分八个专业，共 12 册。每个专业可选读其中的三、四册。那套教材在有关院校相应的专业使用多年，学生和任课教师反映良好。但是，根据当时的情况，那套教材定的起点较低（1 000 词起点），已不适合今天学生的情况。为此，在得到建设部人事教育劳动司的大力支持，并征得五个相关专业教学指导委员会同意之后，由建设部系统十几所院校一百余名外语教师和专业课教师按照统一的编写规划和要求，编写了这一套《建筑类专业英语》教材。

《建筑类专业英语》是根据国家教委颁发的《大学英语专业阅读阶段教学基本要求》编写的专业阅读教材，按照建筑类院校共同设置的五个较大的专业类别对口编写。五个专业类别为：建筑学与城市规划；建筑工程（即工业与民用建筑）；给水排水与环境保护；暖通、空调与燃气；建筑管理与财务会计。每个专业类别分别编写三册专业英语阅读教材，供该专业类别的学生在修完基础阶段英语后，在第五至第七学期专业阅读阶段使用，每学期一册。

上述五种专业英语教材语言规范，题材广泛，覆盖相关专业各自的主要内容：包括专业基础课，专业主干课及主要专业选修课，语言材料的难易度切合学生的实际水平；词汇以大学英语"通用词汇表"的 4 000 个单词为起点，每个专业类别的三册书将增加 1000～1200 个阅读本专业必需掌握的词汇。本教材重视语言技能训练，突出对阅读、翻译和写作能力的培养，以求达到《大学英语专业阅读阶段教学基本要求》所提出的教学目标："通过指导学生阅读有关专业的英语书刊和文献，使他们进一步提高阅读和翻译科技资料的能力，并能以英语为工具获取专业所需的信息。"

《建筑类专业英语》每册 16 个单元，每个单元一篇正课文（TEXT），两篇副课文（Reading Material A&B），每个单元平均 2 000 个词，三册 48 个单元，总共约有十万个词，相当于原版书三百多页。要培养较强的阅读能力，读十万词的文献，是起码的要求。如果专业课教师在第六和第七学期，在学生通过学习本教材已经掌握了数百个专业科技词汇的基础上，配合专业课程的学习，再指定学生看一部分相应的专业英语科技文献，那将会既促进专业课的学习，又提高英语阅读能力，实为两得之举。

本教材不仅适用于在校学生，对于有志提高专业英语阅读能力的建筑行业广大在职工程技术人员，也是一套适用的自学教材。

建设部人事教育劳动司高教处和中国建设教育协会对这套教材的编写自始至终给予关注和支持；中国建筑工业出版社第五编辑室密切配合，参与从制定编写方案到审稿各个阶段的重要会议，给了我们很多帮助；在编写过程中，各参编学校相关专业的许多专家、教授对材料的选取、译文的审定都提出了许多宝贵意见，谨此致谢。

《建筑类专业英语》 是我们编写对口专业阅读教材的又一次尝试，由于编写者水平及经验有限，教材中不妥之处在所难免，敬请广大读者批评指正。

《建筑类专业英语》
编审委员会

Contents

UNIT ONE

Text   What a Building Is

[1]　　A building does not express its meaning in the same way as a picture or a sculpture, because it is by nature much more complex. It demands a prior effort of analysis. In the first place, we never see a building in its totality: we can never obtain more than partial views both of the exterior and interior, with the result that we are always obliged to relate what we can see to what we cannot see to form a clear picture of the whole. ①It is impossible simply to indulge the pleasure of the eye: one has to think as well as look. To help us in this intellectual exercise we have an important tool to hand, the plan, which informs us simultaneously about exterior and interior, the whole and the part. Together with the cross section, which reveals the structure, it gives in abstract form a composite image of the building which photographs-in whatever number-could never give. ②It is therefore necessary, before anything else, to learn to read a plan and to familiarize oneself in a general way with the various means of graphic expression used in architecture (cross section, elevation, axonometric plan).

[2]　　The transformations to which buildings are subject constitute a second difficulty. ③ Very often we can no longer see today what the builders would have wished: projects are abandoned or modified before completion, parts that were complete are demolished, others, added later, are of a different character. Time, it is true, alters all works of art, but its effect on architecture is more noticeable because the construction of a major building takes a long time, and because buildings—always intended for use-must be adapted to the changing needs of men. We should not, therefore, look at a building completed at one stretch and still more or less intact, such as Salisbury Cathedral, in the same way as we regard an incomplete chateau, such as Brissac, or a building that has been continuously altered, such as Versailles. In the first unusual case, we are immediately in a position to appreciate the work of the builders; in the second, we have to imagine what was intended; and in the third case, we have to discover the successive stages of building to interpret correctly what we see, and not attribute to the intention of a single architect what was the product of several building campaigns. ④

[3]　　Finally, it should never be forgotten that even the most magnificent buildings were never intended simply as works of art, and that they are incomprehensible if one is unaware of their purpose, whether utilitarian or symbolic. The particular forms of religious buildings, houses and palaces, are always a reflection of the demands of religious cult, of everyday life, or of the exercise of power in any given society. Less independent than other artists, the architect exercises his powers of invention within a framework strictly defined by the society to which he belongs and the individuals to whom he owes each commis-

sion. Such constraints, compelling to a degree dependent on the particular age and social level (the Greek temple, the urban dwelling, are highly standardized types), impose limits on invention, but also confer on architecture an important social significance: buildings are a unique embodiment, the most durable, the most manifest—of the needs and dreams of men.

[4]   We take an interest in a building to the degree to which we see in it "effects" of volume, space, rhythm and colour that please us. In certain cases—an urban dwelling or rural architecture, for example—these effects are very simple and result above all from harmony between a building and its environment. In other cases—the most interesting—these effects are extremely complex and can be attributed to one or more creative individuals who have deliberately contrived them. Between these two extremes-architecture without architects and the architecture of great masters—there are numerous degrees, but it would be pointless to distinguish them. It is more worthwhile to identify the various means of expression available to architecture: only in this way can we enrich our perception of the buildings we encounter.

[5]   This perception should not be equated with aesthetic appreciation, but it is a necessary precondition. Without it, spontaneous judgments which appear to be expressions of personal opinion do no more than repeat preconceived ideas—on the "bareness" of the Romanesque, the "excesses" of the Baroque, the "frigidity" of classical churches···. Thus we could not recommend to the reader too strongly to forget such prejudices and to look with a fresh eye and open mind in order to appreciate the objectives peculiar to each style. ⑤

[6]   All these observations lead to the same conclusion: a work of architecture is too complex to be understood at first glance: one has simultaneously to be aware of all its elements, to imagine its successive states (including those that were never completed), and to know what it signified to those who built it. This initial analysis must precede aesthetic appreciation. It enables one to form a clear picture of the building and to differentiate between what is due to constraints (structural necessity, existing buildings, stylistic conventions, demands of the client), and what is the product of purely artistic creation, the play of forms. ⑥

New Words and Expressions

sculpture ['skʌlptʃə]	n.	雕刻，雕塑
totality [təu'tæliti]	n.	整体，总体
indulge [in'dʌldʒ]	v.	满足，沉溺
plan [plæn]	n.	平面图
composite* ['kɔmpəzit]	a.	合成的，混合的
graphic ['græfik]	a.	图（解）的，用图表示的
elevation [ˌeli'veiʃən]	n.	正视图

axonometric [ˌæksənəˈmetrik]	a.	三向投影的
demolish [diˈmɔliʃ]	v.	拆毁，推翻
intact* [inˈtækt]	a.	完整的，未受损的
Salisbury Cathedral		索尔兹伯里主教堂
chateau [ˈʃɑːtəu]	n.	〔法〕城堡
Palais de Versailles		凡尔赛宫
incomprehensible [inˌkɔmpriˈhensəbl]	a.	不可理解的，不易领会的
utilitarian [ˌjuːtiliˈtɛəriən]	a.	功利主义的；实用的
symbolic [simˈbɔlik]	a.	象征主义的
cult [kʌlt]	n.	信仰，崇拜
constraint* [kənˈstreint]	n.	限制，约束
confer [kənˈfəː]	v.	授与
manifest [ˈmænifest]	a.	直观的，明白的
contrive [kənˈtraiv]	v.	发明，设计
aesthetic [iːsˈθetik]	a.	美学的，审美的
differentiate* [difəˈrenʃieit]	v.	区别，区分
stylistic [staiˈlistik]	a.	风格的，文体的
perception [pəˈsepʃən]	n.	理解（力）
precondition [ˈpriːkənˈdiʃən]	n.	前提，先决条件
preconceive [ˈpriːkənˈsiːv]	vt.	预想，预先想到
Romanesque [ˌrəuməˈnesk]	n.	罗马式建筑
Baroque [bəˈrəuk]	n.	巴罗克式建筑
frigidity [friˈdʒiditi]	n.	索然无味，冷淡
to hand		手边
cross section		剖面图
axonometric plan		三向投影图
at one stretch		一口气，连续地
confer sth. on sb		授与某人某物

Notes

①本句 that 从句中包含句型 relate sth.（what—从句）to sth.（what—从句）

②主句中的主语 it 指代上文中的 the plan。主句部分的结构为 give sth. in abstract form。由于宾语 sth. 部分太长而后置。

③be subject to sth. 易受到……的。

④attribute to the invention…several building campaigns 原句句型为 attribute A to B，"将 A 归于 B"。直接宾语是从句 What was the product of several building campaigns。由于太长而后置。

⑤…could not…too ……并不过分；越……越好。

⑥本句结构 It enables one to from…and to differentiate between A (what—从句) and B (what—从句)。句末的 the play of forms 为 purely artistic creation 的同位语。

Exercises

Reading Compre hension

I . Say whether the following statements true (T) or false (F) according to the text.

1. To understand a building in its totality, one must learn to read a plan and other various means of graphic expression used in architecture.　　　( )

2. Though time alters all works of art, the graphic expressions can be transformed to buildings without much difficulty.　　　( )

3. Buildings are special works of art, and one can not understand them without the realization of their purpose.　　　( )

4. Some buildings are results of the demands of the clients while some are products of purely artistic creation.　　　( )

5. In order to appreciate the objectives peculiar to each style, one should forget the prejudices but keep in mind the ideas concerned with each style.　　　( )

II . Read the text carefully and then complete each of the following statements with your own words.

1. _____ and _____ give in abstract form a composite image of the building.

2. To appreciate such a building as Versailles, one should not _____ the product of several building compaigns to a sing architect.

3. The architect's powers of creation are confined within _____ defined by the society and his client.

4. Architecture is of an important social significance in that it is a _____ of the needs and dreams of men.

5. _____ or _____ bears the pleasing _____ that result from the harmony between a building and its environment.

6. We should not look at a building completed in the _____ way as we regard an incomplete chateau or a building that has been continuously altered.

7. Buildings are _____ if one is unaware of their purpose.

Vocabulary

I . Match the words in Column A with their corresponding definitions in Column B.

　　　Column A　　　　　　　　　　Column B
　　1. cross section　　a. of an system of literature or art which uses a sign, shape or object to represent a person, idea, value, etc.

4

2. elevation   b. a graphic expression formed by a plane cutting through an object, usually at right angles to an axis.

3. symbolic   c. a flat upright side of a building

4. Romanesque   d. an artistic style current in about 1550—1700, marked by massive forms and elaborate decoration.

5. Baroque   e. the style of building with round arches and thick pillars, common in Western Europe in about 11th century.

6. sculpture   f. the art (or the work by this art) of shaping solid figures out of stone, wood, clay, metal, etc.

Ⅱ. Fill in the blanks with words or expressions given below, changing the form where necessary.

> aesthetic   indulge   composite   confer
> contrive   constraint   manifest   preconceive

1. A building which has undergone successive alterations could have been _____ by more than one architect.

2. The initial analysis can not take the place of _____ appreciation but it is a necessary precondition.

3. If one intends to understand a building in its totality, it is impossible simpiy to _____ the pleasure of the eye.

4. An architect is different from other artists in that he has to perform his creative work under various _____ .

5. The author of the passage has _____ three difficulties in the understanding of an architecture.

6. A building may be a _____ result of various social and environmental considerations as well as of the efforts of many people.

7. A building should be a _____ expression of human needs; otherwise it would be simply a play of forms.

8. It is not only aesthetic value but also practical purpose that is _____ onto architecture.

Writing   Selecting the Key Words

Key words are informative words that can give the information about what a piece of writing is mainly talking about. They are often nouns and verbs, etc.

For example:

Read the following text and find out the key words

With the rapid industrialization of the States, air pollution is posing a problem. Fertilizer and steel plants, cement industries, thermal power plants and paper mills are among the units which cause an air pollution.

Automobiles also cause air pollution as they emit smoke which contains such pollutant as hydro carbon nitrous oxide and carbon, monoxide.

The Air Act was passed in Congress 1982 and came into effect in 1983.

Key words:

Air pollution, Pollutant, Air Act

Directions: Read the text of this Unit and find out five to six key words.

Reading Material A

Facades

No architectural volume, except for a pyramid, has completely smooth and "blind" surfaces. Facades are always animated by openings, by recessed or projecting features, or by contrasts of colour. The elements which are thus brought together can be of many types, but it is possible to divide them into three groups—relating to the wall, to the structure, and to decoration.

Solids and voids

The number, shape and distribution of openings to a large degree determines the character of a facade. Italian Palazzi appear massive because their windows are relatively small, whereas houses in northern Europe are more open, and appear lighter.① At the Hotel Matignon, for example, the architect has incorporated a great number of windows·whose tall, narrow proportions contrast happily with the horizontality of the mass of the building; by slightly modifying their spacing he has varied the rhythm and given greater "weight" to the lateral pavilions that terminate the facade.②

The solid areas themselves appear more or less weighty depending on the physical surface of the wall: smooth, shiny or colored surfaces lighten a building whereas rusticated surfaces (roughened and marked by sunk joints) give an effect of solidity.③Rustication is often used on the ground floor to form a base, or in the form of quoins, to emphasize the corners. Modern architects are also aware of the effects that can be obtained through materials alone—or, rather, through their appearance: rough concrete and faceted claddings emphasize the strength of a wall, while glass walls give buildings an insubstantial character— an effect well known to Gothic architects.

Lines of force

Most facades are articulated by some kind of membering, standing out either in relief or in color, to provide accents and set up rhythms. Members are generally horizontal or vertical; they can even be free—standing and independent when the wall becomes simply a row of supports (in a colonnade, for instance). The facades of cathedrals clearly show the importance of membering: Reims Cathedral appears taller, more slender and more rhythmic than Notre—Dame, Paris, because its vertical members are thinner, more numerous and set closer together, and because they rise uninterrupted to the top of the towers. ④Architecture in antiquity and the Renaissance had no sense of this dynamic linearity: classical buildings emphasize the horizontal mouldings dividing the storeys and the topmost cornice—a sharply projecting feature that clearly defines the upper limit of the volume. ⑤The two traditions, Gothic and classical, came into conflict when Italian forms penetrated northwards in the 16th century: such hybrid features as windows cut through the main entablature and extending into the roof created a new, animated effect.

By adjusting the horizontal and vertical members (especially secondary ones, since the primary members are always more or less bound by the storeys), by moving them closer together or further apart, by giving them different emphasis, interesting and varied rhythms can be obtained. Architects from the Renaissance onwards have systematically explored these possibilities; using the classical system of pilasters, columns and entablatures in all manner of combinations, developing numerous kinds of bay unit and interpenetrating the Orders. ⑥

Members can also be accentuated or attenuated in relief. Gothic architects used progressively finer and more ductile mouldings which seemed endowed with a life of their own on the surface of the wall, while Renaissance and later architects employed heavier, fuller members which were integral with the wall and were able to express its internal strength and tensions. Somerset House in London or the example of the Louvre indicate the varying effects that can be produced by slight alterations of relief or rhythm. ⑦

Ornament

Ornament can be natural or geometric, coloured or in relief, consisting in mouldings or developed across a flat surface, confined within a frame or freely disposed. Formed of small—scale and disparate elements, ornament sets up a subtle play of light and shade, or of colour, very different from the bolder architectural effects. When it reproduces animal, vegetable, or human forms, it also brings a literal animation into the abstract world of architecture. ⑧It plays very different roles, in different times and places: it can proliferate, obscure the structure or underline it. In all cases it creates its own effects which reinforce, elaborate or oppose the strictly architectural effects.

Notes

①Palazzi［意大利］府邸。

②Hotel Matignon 马提格伦府邸；pavilion *n.* 侧楼。例如，马提巴格伦府邸的建筑师配置了大量的窗户，其既高 又窄的比例与建筑物厚重的水平状态形成了和谐的对比。通过略微 改变间距他改变了节奏，使位于正立面两端的侧楼更具重实感。

③墙体本身是否显得厚重取决于墙体表面的处理：光滑、泛光或有色 的表面使建筑显得纤巧，而粗砌的（包括有粗糙表面或有明显排水管接头的）表面则给人以坚实感。

④Reims Cathedral 兰斯市主教堂；Notre—Dame, Paris 巴黎圣母院。大教堂的正立面清楚表明构件的重要性。兰斯市主教堂比起巴黎圣母院更高，更修长，更有节奏感，因为它的垂直构件更细，数量更多，配置更紧凑，而且还由于这些构件一直向上，直达塔顶。

⑤moulding *n.*（装饰）线条；cornice *n.* 檐口。

⑥entablature *n.*（柱式的）檐部；bay *n.* 间距，架间；order *n.* 柱式（同古希腊 Ordine）

⑦Somerset House 索莫塞特大厦 Louvre 卢浮宫。

⑧literal *a.* 实在的（与下文 abstract 相对）

Reading Material B

Internal Space

Volumes and facades determine the external appearance of a building. It remains to discover what is enclosed behind those walls, that "reverse space" which is unique to architecture: "in giving definitive form to this spatial void architecture is in truth creating its own world" (Henri Focillon). ①No, photograph, unfortunately, can reproduce the impression made by a space that completely envelops the spectator and which he discovers gradually as he moves around and explores a building.

Anyone who has entered a great Gothic church has experienced the dynamic quality of its space—the predominance of vertical members, the virtual disappearance of walls, the lightness of the vaults, the rapid succession of bays; all these direct our gaze both upwards and towards the apse without any intervening obstruction. ②This taste for dynamic space recurred in another form in the domed churches of the Renaissance and the Baroque (in contrast with the internal space of the Pantheon in Rome, which is strictly static). At St. Peter's in Rome the immense space becomes ever more vast as one moves up the nave, and the broadening out at the crossing (achieved by the use of cut-away piers) and the prodigious volume of the dome (made to seem still larger by the handling of light) are gradually revealed. ④Far from weighing down on its supports, the dome appears suspended, held up by an irresistible force. The sense of movement is not the product of uninterrupted lines, but of the skillful coordination of increasingly large spaces.

The forms of St. Peter's are perfectly clear, with the result that the spaces, however vast, are always exactly defined. In German Baroque churches, on the other hand, space appears elusive and subject to continuous movement: the walls lose all solidity, articulation disappears, lines undulate, and an all—pervasive light sets stucco and paintings aglow: we are transported into an insubstantial, animated, vibrant world, with undefined limits. [5]

Thus each major style has its own spatial qualities that can stimulate sensations beyond those of everyday experience. In the West, the most important examples are in religious architecture because it commandeered the largest spaces, but spatial effects were also created in secular architecture—by successions of rooms of different shapes and by the elaboration of staircases. What an extraordinary sequence of this kind is afforded by the Paris Opera! After passing through two relatively low entrance foyers, the visitor suddenly finds himself in the immense space of the staircase, open to further space on three sides. As he climbs the steps and follows the staircase round, he is made aware of all that is around him, and he perceives more and more clearly the secondary spaces that extend the principal space beyond the screen of columns: before he has even entered the auditorium, he is already in the magic world of theater.

External space

Streets and squares are open—air spaces enclosed by architecture in much the same way as internal spaces. In some cases—once rare, now common—an architect uses the elements of a city to create an urban composition: he calculates his effects, places the elements in relation to one another and, if he is capable of it, contrives surprises—in compositions of this type the danger is always monotony and overstatement. In older cities, on the other hand, the layout is generally the product of many years of history. Made up of small—scale elements and disposed in a very haphazard fashion, the streets and squares give rise to a constant succession of spatial experiences—quite independent of the interest of the buildings that border them. Rather than impose an artificial regularity on such spaces, architects have often drawn inspiration from them: they have kept the site and existing buildings in mind when building anew. In this way the most interesting urban compositions have been built up gradually over the centuries—for example, the Piazza and Piazzetta of Venice, perfectly disposed around the campanile. [6]

Notes

①尚待发现墙体之后所包容的空间，即在赋予这种具有内部空间的建筑以特定形体方面对于建筑来说是独一无二的"反转空间"，确实正在创造它自己的世界。

②apse 教堂东端（或东西两端）的半圆开龛。

③Baroque 巴洛克（文艺复兴末期十七世纪的一种建筑风格）；Pantheon，Rome 罗马，万

神庙。

④St. Peter's 罗马，圣彼得大教堂（意大利文艺复兴盛期的杰出代表）nave *n.*（早期教堂的）中殿，中厅。

　　当人们循着罗马圣彼得大教堂的中殿深入内部时，它那巨大的空间变得更加广阔。由于使用切角方柱而在交叉拱下拓宽的空间和通过光线的处理而显得似乎更大的穹顶之下宏大的空间逐渐展现出来。

⑤另一方面，在德国巴洛克式的教堂里，空间显得难以捉摸，使人感到连续不断的运动。墙体失去了坚实感，所要表达的意义不明朗，线条波浪起伏，无所不在的光线使灰泥和绘画泛光。这一切使我们置身于一个无明确界定的极富活力的虚幻世界。

⑥Piazza and Piazzetta of Venice：即 Piazza and Piazzetta San Marco，Venice. 威尼斯，圣马可广场；campanile *n.*（独立的）钟楼

UNIT TWO

Text   Making Architectural Judgements

[1]   How should an architect, a client, a citizen, or a government agency or commission judge designs for new buildings? This question is especially pertinent if the new structures are to be erected in historic districts. How does one decide whether the proposed new building will enhance or detract from its surroundings, and whether it promotes the kind of further development that will benefit the historic area? What criteria can be used as a basis for such judgements? Do the answers lie in adhering to some 'correct' architectural ideology derived from a classical, a modernist, or a post-modernist point of view to be handed down by 'experts'? Does the task require studied connoisseurship, group consensus growing out of broad publi participation, or some combination of these positions?

[2]   The need for a more rational approach to these questions is evident from the nature of the discussion that has surrounded recent controversial buildings, in which reasonable differences of opinion have often devolved into vituperative confrontations. The differences among opposing groups often hinge on passionately held beliefs about aesthetics, politics, or such vague notions as the demands of the Zeitgeist, the 'spirit of the times'. The focus on subjective questions of taste, ideology, and personality tends to discourage constructive debate and to ignore more complex and pertinent questions of how to protect the public interest.

[3]   The depth of this problem may be seen by reviewing the weak and conflicting statements of problems that are presented within transcripts of hearings before boards and commissions with purview over architectural projects, and by reading their subsequent reports.[1] Anyone who has attended juries evaluating students' work at schools of architecture will be familiar with the subjective criteria that often pass for considered, objective judgements. Because decision-making bodies cannot evade their responsibilities, this haphazard, emotion-laden way of defining architetcural standards has created the incoherently planned cityscape, the suburban sprawl, and the suburbanised countryside we see aroundus[2].

[4]   This contemporary dilemma should be considered in its proper historical context. The generations of architects since 1945 are the first in the history of architecture who have not been able to fulfil two expectations that society has taken for granted since the ancient Greeks created cities: that architects are able to creat both the competently designed background architecture that forms the bulk of building in a town or city, as well as noble foreground buildings, the monumental architecture of civic and religious structures that embodies a society's highest aspirations. It was in this way that architects of the past arranged their designs in city plans so as to make the new as beautiful, or better than, what

was there before. ③Remarkable examples of this abound: Jacopo Sansovino's inspired 're-creation' of the Piazza di San Macro and the Piazzetta, accomplished by transforming the Campanile into a free-standing tower and fulcrum to connect Piazza with the Piazzetta, and the brilliant design of the new Library; ④JF Blondel's classical facade of the medieval Metz Cathedral, sadly destroyed, and new adjacent buildings; Mnesicles' Propylaea at the Acropolis; and Wren's buildings at Oxford and Cambridge. To revitalise contemporary practice to meet the standards of the past is an urgent responsibility.

[5]　　Architecture is a liberal art that is taught at our great universities, and is a discipline that should be amenable to rational discourse. The aim here is not to decide on the ultimate artistic worth of a proposed building, for this requires the kind of considered assessment that, ultimately, only the distance of time can provide. Instead, it is to suggest a process that may assist us in evaluating the quality of proposed designs for new architecture in a variety of historic areas, a way of deciding whether the proposal at hand will add to or detract from the beauty and character of the place. The process offers a set of criteria which can help to make distinctions between the architectural characteristics of a proposed building and to relate them to those of the buildings which exist around its site. Once articulated, these distinctions provide a common basis for concerned citizens, critics, decision-making bodies and architects to debate the drawbacks and virtues of the design and to prepare a solid foundation for a decision to accept or to improve or otherwise modify the design or programme.

[6]　　Architecture is a public art. It is the building block of the city, a compound work, realised over centuries. Cities are always changing, growing and being altered, being destroyed and being rebuilt, all in response to social and political change, to the demands of commerce and industry, and to the rhythms of technological innovation. Villages and rural areas are subject to the same pressures. Each time a new building is proposed it must be studied, not in isolation, but evaluated as a part of the increasingly complex whole that forms all regions.

New Words and Expressions

detract* [di'trækt]	vt.	减损；降低
adhere [əd'hiə]	vt.	坚持；粘附（常跟 to）
ideology [aidi'ɔlədʒi]	n.	思想体系；意识形态
connoisseurship [kɔni'sə:ʃip]	n.	鉴赏能力
consensus [kən'sensəs]	n.	一致
participation [pɑːtisi'peiʃən]	n.	参与
devolve [di'vɔlv]	v.	转移，退化
vituperative [vi'tjuːpəreit]	vt.	责骂
confrontation* ['kɔnfrʌn'teiʃən]	n.	对抗，对立

hinge [hindʒ]	v.	依……为根据
	n.	铰链
zeitgeist ['tsaitgaist]	n.	〔德〕时代精神
transcript ['trænskript]	n.	副本；文字记录
hearing ['hiəriŋ]	n.	意见听取会；听力
purview ['pə:vju:]	n.	权限；眼界
jury ['dʒuəri]	n.	评审员；陪审团
evade [i'veid]	vt.	逃避，避开
subjective* [səb'dʒektiv]	a.	主观的
haphazard [hæp'hæzəd]	a.	任意的，杂乱的
emotion-laden [i'məuʃən-'leidn]	a.	带情绪的
incoherently [inkəu'hiərəntli]	ad.	前后矛盾的，支离破碎的
sprawl [sprɔ:l]	n.；v.	（无规划的）漫延
suburbanise [sə'bə:bənaiz]	v.	市郊化，（使）变为市郊
dilemma [di'lemə]	n.	困境，进退两难
civic ['sivik]	a.	城市的；市民的
campanile ['kæmpə'ni:li]	n.	钟楼
abound [ə'baund]	vi.	大量存在
fulcrum ['fʌlkrəm]	n.	支点
propylaeum [prɔpi'li:əm] (pl. -laea [-li:ə])	n.	（神殿等）入口
revitalise ['ri:'vaitəlaiz]	vt.	使新生，使恢复元气
discourse [dis'kɔ:s]	n.；v.	论说，谈论
amenable* [ə'menəbl]	a.	经得起检验的
articulate [ɑ:'tikjuleit]	vt.	表现（思想）；明确表达
drawback* ['drɔ:bæk]	n.	欠缺；障碍

Notes

①The depth of this problem may be seen by …and by…两个由 by 引出的介词短语做方式
状语。"with purview over" 在这里意思是 "有……权限"。
②Decision-making bodies. 决策机构（关）。
③as beautiful, or better than, what was there before 在 beautiful 后省去了 as。在 as…as
结构中第二个 as 引出的比较状语从句可省部分或全部，包括 as 本身。
④Jacopo Sansovino 雅各布·桑索维诺（1486—1570），意大利建筑师，雕塑家，主张保持
文艺复兴盛期风格，主要作品有雕像《酒神巴克斯》，威尼斯的圣·马可教堂图书馆等。

Exercises

Reading Comprehension

I . Skim the text and match each of the following ideas with its appropriate paragraph
   number or numbers in the brackets.

1. People hold different opinions about how to evaluate designs for new buildings.
                                                                              ( )
2. Architecture in history is still of great significance today.   ( )
3. Subjective criteria are often adopted for objective judgements.   ( )
4. Architectural judgements should be made in accordance with the overall development.   ( )
5. The paragraph that tells us the purpose of the author in writing this essay. ( )

II . Read the text carefully and then choose the best answer among the four choices given
   to complete each statement.

1. From the first paragraph, we can see _____ .
   A) many problems have been solved about how to judge designs for new buldings
   B) there are lots of questions to be answered about evaluating designs for new build-
      ings
   C) everyone has his own idea about a new building
   D) different buildings should be judged with different criteria.
2. According to the author, which of the following is more important in judging a new
   building?
   A) Public interest.
   B) Aesthetics and demands of the zeitgeist.
   C) Taste, ideology, and personality.
   D) Environmental protection.
3. The incoherently planned cityscape and the suburban sprawl are caused by _____ .
   A) carefulness of the decision-making bodies
   B) the assessment commissions
   C) the construction contractors
   D) conflicting arbitrary standards
4. Architects of today are less able to fulfil the two expectations that the society has
   taken for granted because _____ .
   A) the two expectations are no longer held by public
   B) people of today have different expectations
   C) today's architects have ignored the standards of the past
   D) the monumental civic and religious structures have been transformed

into free standing towers

5. In paragraph 4, the "Piazza di san Marco" and the "piazzetta" are _____.
   A) names of architects in the past
   B) names of two buildings
   C) names of two cities
   D) names of places in a city

6. According to paragraph 5, what should people do first before deciding whether a proposed building goes along well with its surroundings?
   A) Find out the distinctions between them.
   B) Debate the drawbacks and virtues of the design.
   C) Improve or modify the design.
   D) Ask both the experts and the public for their opinions.

7. The quality of proposed designs for new buildings in historic areas is determined by
   _____.
   A) how much priority is given to the overall development there
   B) whether they can embody a society's highest aspirations
   C) whether they will promote the further development of the areas
   D) whether they will enhance or detract from their surroundings

8. If the distinctions between the architectural characterics of a proposed building and those of the historic one around the site are great, the proposed building _____.
   A) can be accepteal and built
   B) should be redesigned or can not be accepted
   C) will add much to the beauty and character of the place
   D) will promote the further development of the area

9. The anthor may agree with all of the following except that _____.
   A) architecture is a precise discipline, all of whose principles should be strictly observed
   B) architecture is a public art that is always changing
   C) the contemporary practice of architecture is not very satisfactory
   D) architectural designs must be carefully examined before they are put into construction

10. The purpose of the author in writing this text is to _____.
    A) introduce various points of view in architecture
    B) criticize the contemporary practice in architecture
    C) put forward some ways to help judge designs for new buildings
    D) offer a complete set of criteria to evaluate architectural designs.

Vocabulary

I. Match the words in column A with their corresponding definitions in Column B.

    Column A   Column B

    1. detract   a. disadvantage or shortcoming

    2. confrontation   b. point of support

    3. amenable   c. range of control or sight

    4. drawback   d. take away or diminish something desirable

    5. fulcrum   e. open opposition

    6. Purview   f. able to undergo testing

II. Complete each of the following statements with one of the four choices given below.

1. As a law-abiding citizen, nobbody should _____ paying his taxes.

    A) evade   B) extrude

    C) eliminate   D) intercept

2. Owing to population explosion in recent decades, urban _____ has become an increaslingly irritating problem.

    A) extension   B) deviation

    C) sprawl   D) shrinkage

3. Their argument _____ on whether the proposed project can satisfy the demands for further development.

    A) protrudes   B) hinges

    C) disputes   D) interacts

4. Rather than _____ the differential variations between elements into an invariant static type, Lavater employs a continuous, differentiated system of transformation.

    A) subtract   B) resolve

    C) upgrade   D) devolve

5. To _____ the stand-still economy, measures are being considered to increase capital investment and improve industrial performance.

    A) refine   B) reclaim

    C) revitalize   D) retract

6. In the process of design, climatic forces must be taken into full consideration in the area where wind and rain _____ all the year round.

    A) abound   B) converge

    C) activate   D) scatter

7. The symbolic content of carpenter centre appears to have nothing in common with other buildings on Harvard campus, which makes it a _____ paradigm for other architects.

    A) interactive   B) haphazard

C) orthogonal   D) integral

8. The municipal government decided to withdraw its _____ in financing the new power plant, leaving it entirely to private enterprises.

    A) objection   B) adhesion

    C) texture   D) participation

Writing Selecting the Key Words

Directions: Read the text of Unit Two and find out five to six key words.

Reading Material A

Criteria for Evaluating Proposed Architecture

Perhaps the best place to begin to develope criteria for evaluating new designs for historic areas is with working definition of architecture. The one that follows is a synthesis of the ideas of Geoffrey Scott and Le Corbusier, as well as those gleaned from my own practice: 'Architecture, simply and immediately perceived, is a combination, revealed through light and shade, of spaces, of masses, and of lines,' which embody the meaning and significance of the institution housed within its walls. ①It should enhance its environs and serve as a paradigm for future development.

The definition suggests five criteria which may be used for guidance in assessing the relationship between a proposed new design and its context. The first is architectural language, which has two components: forms and grammar. Forms are the orders of architecture: the columns and entablatures of the Doric, Ionic, Corinthian, composite, and Tuscan orders, and the mouldings. ②The latter are a set of specific forms which have a precisely determined geometric shape and a name. Grammar is the set of conventions by which these elements are arranged to form coherent elements, or parts, of buildings. These may be conventional and compound architectural forms such as cornices, pediments, architraves, serliana, dadoes, baseboards and plinths. Grammar also determines specific conventions governing the use of planning devices such as grids and axes. The classical language of architecture contains the most highly developed grammar, which uses forms to create plans, sections, and elevations of buildings, rooms, streets (which may be considered as walls of exterior rooms) and groups of buildings. Gothic, Byzantine, and Romanesque architecture use many of the elements and aspects of the grammar of classical architecture. Like the less complex and elaborate architectural language of Japan or of the Maya, classical architecture is tied to a particular time, place, culture and geography. Thus the architectural language of the 17th century in Venice is different from that of France or of England, although all three are classical and contemporary. Modernistic architecture has its own forms—piloti, horizontal window bands—and grammar. Both are derived from the work of Le Corbusier,

Mies van der Rohe, Auguste Perret and Walter Gropius, and they are newer and therefore much less developed than classical or Gothic architecture.

The second criterion, architectural syntax, consists of organising systems that are fundamental to the perception of architectural form and space. These include rhythm, sequence of spaces, differentiation of scale, notions of order, reflection, translation, superimposition, the tension between interior and exterior, the relationship of solid and void or of mass and volume, inflection, and ideas of unity. All are properties of form, and they transcend the particularities of style and culture.

The third criterion, that of context, which may be urban, suburban, village or rural, posits the character of the relationship between the new building and the neighbourhood. This should be analysed in terms of formal characteristics and of relationships to physical infrastructure of public works, as well as of questions which transcend architectural form and encompass relevant law and ordinances, as well as custom and tradition (mores).

In exploring these concerns, it is sometimes easy to slough off custom and tradition as a mere collection of arbitrary value judgements. Yet it is precisely these elements that are often crucial to the success of any project. The history of the many failures of subsidised housing projects in England and the United States illustrates the folly of ignoring the most basic consideration of our human need for dignity and respect, as well as how easily noble intentions can blight communities and create human misery. [3]

The fourth criterion is symbolic content, the articulation of meaning and significance projected by architectural forms through their language, syntax, and relation to their context. Like customs and traditions, it has been ignored for the past 50 years by architects. For example, the beautiful door of the Hammond-Harwood House (1770-74) in Annapolis is framed by an arch set within attached columns and a pediment. It is a unique feature of the facade and clearly marks the entrance. Its large scale within the facade diminishes the building's scale in order to mediate between the size of the building and a human being. The symmetrical and obvious location of the beautiful door, as well as its superb scale and proportion, makes a gracious gesture of welcome.

The fifth criterion is the idea that new buildings should serve as paradigms for what other buildings, to be erected at some future time on adjacent parcels of land, should be like. For architects, the implication of this principle is obvious: gauge any new architectural or planning idea by assessing what would happen if everyone around you followed your example. It is an architectural version of the biblical injunction not to do to others as you would not have them do to you. The principle was well understood by the architects and developers of Georgian London and Dublin, or 19th-century Boston. It is not so well understood in recent times by those planning authorities in Europe and the United States who have permitted the indiscriminate construction of high-rise buildings in and adjacent to districts that contained only low buildings, or by those leaders of universities who have allowed their campuses to lose their architectural cohesion by permitting construction that lacks any relationship in form or meaning to the existing context. ④That some of these new buildings were designed by distinguished architects makes the irony sadder still.

Notes

①下面这个定义是杰弗里·斯科特,勒·柯布西耶以及我自己在实践中悟出的思想的综合: "建筑学,明白无误地说,就是透过光线的明暗反映空间、质量和线条的组合"。这体现了建筑学府存在的意义和重要性。which 引出定语从句修饰前面的 ideas.

②建筑形态是指建筑物的不同风格式样。仅圆柱和柱顶饰就有:陶立克式(纯朴、古老的希腊建筑风格),爱奥尼式(小亚细亚风格),科林斯式(古希腊带叶形饰钟状柱顶的建筑),混合式,托斯卡纳式(意大利中西部风格)等等。

③在英国和美国,受到补贴的住房计划所遭受的诸多挫折表明,忽视了人类对尊严的需要这一最基本考虑就会做费力不讨好的蠢事。同时也表明良好的意愿反而很容易伤害公众,给人类造成不幸。

④近年来,那些欧洲和美国的规划当局没有深刻领会这一原则,他们不加区别地允许在只有低层建筑的地区和相邻地区修建高层建筑。那些大学的领导人也没能很好地领会这一原则,他们允许在校园里修建无论在形态上还是在意义上都与现存校园环境毫不相称的建筑,从而使校园建筑风格失去一致。

句中第一个由 who 引出的从句修饰 authorities。在一个名词同时受介词短语和定语从句修饰的情况下,应介词短语在前,定语从句在后;第二个 who 引出的定语从句也是这样。

Reading Material B

The Midland Bank and Carpenter Center

In order to test the validity of this series of critical categories for assessing the merits of building proposals, let us explore two case studies of buildings of widely differing character on historically important sites.

Sir Edwin Lutyens, the Midland Bank (1992) .①

The forecourt of St James, Piccadilly②, a church by Sir Christopher Wren (1676-84), is defined by another building: the Midland Bank by Sir Edwin Lutyens.

Lutyens orients his bank building to Piccadilly, but also recognises its crucial role defining one side of the space of the forecourt. In order to suggest a relationship between the bank building and the church, he uses similar design features—brick, with stone trim at the windows and doors, and rustication. All three buildings—church, bank and rectory—

use red brick, while their immediate neighbours are built of white or cream-coloured stone. This establishes the family of buildings defining the forecourt. Lutyens designed the bank's side elevation with two rows of three high windows. These are the only elements punctuating the brick wall facing the forecourt. There is no articulation at forecourt level, and visitors sense the lack of any functional relationship between bank and forecourt, aware that the latter relates exclusively to the church.

The bank's street facade suggests continuity with the church, for both use arches and rustication, and are built of brick and stone. The bank's design appears overly elaborate next to Wren's austere and monumental side elevation of St James'; Lutyens does this purposely. He followed the example of most of the adjacent commercial buildings on Piccadilly, which vie with each other in their abundance of detail. In this way, he unequivocally, relates his design to the life of the street, and away from the forecourt.

Thus Lutyens successfully uses contrast of both architectural language—a richly articulated and Italian-inspired version of Wren's simpler and more monumental 17th-century English classicism—and of syntax. The pronounced vertical rhythm and three-dimensional character of the rustication are very different from the simpler and flatter elevation of the church. The expression of similar elements—windows, doors and architraves is carefully orchestrated to relate Lutyens' building to the street, while balancing its role as the definer of the space of the forecourt. So we see how contrast plays upon differences between various 'dialects' of classical architecture while allowing for the continuity of some elements of syntax.

Le Corbusier, Carpenter Center for the Visual Arts[3] (1960—63).

Le Corbusier uses the Five Points as the basis of his design for Carpenter Center which is set on the Harvard University campus in Cambridge, Massachusetts. The expression of these aesthetic ideals in built form effectively divorces the building from the classical colonial, federal, colonial revival, Victorian, Romanesque revival and American Renaissance buildings which are nearby. The main cubic mass is situated on a diagonal in relation to Quincy Street, on one side, and Prescott Street on the other. An elevated ramp cuts through the centre of the building to connect the sidewalks of both streets. Two curved, sculptural forms on piloti, housing studios, bulge out on either side of the cube. [4]The Carpenter Center's monolithic concrete construction no longer celebrates Le Corbusier's technological aesthetic of the 1920s. The concrete is brutal in its purposeful lack of any concession to human tactile sensibility.

Carpenter Center's design makes it a unique structure on the campus. It disrupts the continuity of street line and its main mass is perceived on the diagonal, pulling the viewer's eye away from the street and focusing it on the building. It has no front or rear facade, no obvious designated entrance, or even an entry door. The elevated walkway, which cuts right

through the centre of the building, lacks definition as part of the public realm—the street—
or the private. Although the two curved, concrete masses on either side of the building elo-
quently try to mediate between its diagonal cubic core and the adjacent orthogonally sited
buildings, they also emphasise its isolation from the fabric of the university. ⑤

The Harvard Yard is a series of spaces defined by buildings, many of which are modest
and of indifferent architectural quality. It is the space formed by these background buildings—more than the buildings themselves—which gives the Yard its memorable character.

The lack of relationship among the disquieting forms and the coarse materials employed at Carpenter Center with those of other buildings on the Harvard campus inhibits or
even precludes any effective dialogue between Carpenter Center and it neighbours. On the
grounds of an institution dedicated to rational discourse and exchange of ideas, this purposeful lack of dialogue projects a singularly inappropriate and discordant message to fac-
ulty and students.

These two case studies of building on an urban street speak to very different general
notions of the appropriateness inherent in reliance on tradition. Both teach that this should
be violated only in unusual circumstances. Lutyens strove to ensure that Piccadilly was enhanced by their new buildings, while preserving the integrity of the forecourt to St
James'. Carpenter Center's design and symbolic content, on the other hand, make it a building that becomes more difficult to admire with the passage of time. These buildings offer
very different sorts of paradigms for future development. One lesson to be derived from
study of Carpenter Center is that while it may be acceptable to experiment with intensely
personal architectural ideas on sites which are removed from visual contact with neighbours, to do so on a city street or on a university campus may be destructive of urban environments and offensive to many of the citizens and students who must live and work in
it. A change in any aspect of an urban architectural paradigm, especially if the building is
in a specific setting like a university or a residential square, demands substantial justification.

Notes

①Sir Edwin Lutyens 埃德温·勒琴斯爵士，伦敦米德兰银行大厦的设计师。
②St James Piccadilly 圣·詹姆斯·皮卡德利教堂，由克里斯托弗·雷恩爵士设计。
③Carpenter center for the Visual Arts 卡彭特视觉艺术中心，由勒·科布西耶设计，位于
　马萨诸塞州剑桥的哈佛大学校园内。勒·科布西耶，建筑师，立体派画家和建筑规划专
　家，"现代建筑"倡导者之一。本世纪 20 年代初提出"住房是居住的机器"和"新建筑
　五点"(Five Points Toward New Architecture) 的理论。50 年代后提出以混凝土可塑性、
　粗糙感和沉重感为特征的新建筑风格，如马赛公寓和朗香教堂等。著有《走向新建筑》。
④piloti 底层架空柱；bulge out 突出。
⑤虽然大楼两边的两个弯曲的混凝土构造物试图尽量使其对角布局的立方体核心与直交布
　局的邻近建筑相协调，但是它们仍然使整个大楼与校园里的其他建筑格格不入。

UNIT THREE

Text   The Legacy of Modernism in New Classicism

[1]   The revival of classical architecture has been accompanied by a crusading fervour similar to that of the early Modern Movement. The relationship between the opposites goes further. The attitudes of many of the New Classicists themselves can be seen as a direct product of Modernism, the reverse side of the same coin, sharing an obsession with progress, technology and modernity. It is an obsession that could lead to the destruction of New Classicism.

[2]   New Classical architecture is only one aspect of the break up of the Modernist monopoly in the early 70s. Attempts to use history to liven up architecture such as Post-Modernism, Regionalism and the Neo-Vernacular generally did little more than add ill-digested bits of past buildings to essentially Modernist structures. Serious classical revivalists were only an isolated part of this great revolution and were at first dismissed as an irrelevant aberration.

[3]   Fierce conviction backed by genuine scholarship and a number of important commissions backed by public support have finally established a small body of New Classical architects as significant contributors to the development of contemporary architecture. ②

[4]   This combination of isolation and hostility, growth in the face of adversity, and the background of educational censorship have had a profound influence on the development of Classicism.

[5]   In antiquity and from the Renaissance until the 19th century, classical architecture was all there was. Even in the 19th century it was one of two dominant styles and it became the dominant style again in the first 40 years of this century.

[6]   The last 15 years of classical architecture have been a period of consolidation. From a base-point of zero, not seen since the 15th century, practitioners and theorists had to justify their existence in an atmosphere of professional ridicule which had never been seen before. The success of this consolidation was based on a growing public hostility to the excesses of the Modern Movement, and it is not surprising that the ideology of New Classicism should be based on a negative response to all that the Modern Movement represented.

[7]   In particular classical theorists have vigorously denied the two founding principles of Modernism: the theory of artistic advance through the avant-garde, and the supremacy of technological innovation.

[8]   A negative stance to all aspects of Modernism is, however, in danger of throwing out the baby with the bathwater. ③ In practice the denial of the importance of the avant-garde has, in the hands of more extreme traditionalists, become the denial of any desire to be modern; the denial of technological supremacy has become a sort of constructional fun-

damentalism where all forms of post-1820 structure and construction have been dismissed as un-classical; and the concentration on pre-1820 architecture has cut classical architecture off from its natural course of development so abruptly interrupted by post-war Modernism. ④

[9]   The quite reasonable idea that some avant-garde artists might produce work yet to be recognized by the public has, since the war, been exaggerated to the ridiculous idea that any form of popular appreciation of new art makes it automatically bad. ⑤This does not, however, mean that the desire to be modern, different and even shocking is unknown in the history of classical architecture. The idea that society is carried along by a sort of technological juggernaut driven by blind progress can be demonstrated to be incorrect. This does not alter the fact that classical architecture from the Roman arch onwards has adapted itself to new requirements. ⑥While it is hard not to admire the beauty of the various Georgian forms of Classicism, it is unrealistic to deny any validity to classical architecture produced in the 19th and early-20th centuries. ⑦

[10]   Although an appreciation of Georgian architecture cannot be a bad thing, the rejection of the concept of modernity (not rejected in the Georgian period itself) drives away much potential young talent. Constructional fundamentalism turns its back on genuinely useful technological developments and frightens off many of the commercial interests that lie behind many architectural commissions. If New Classical architecture does not look beyond a negative attitude to all things associated with the modern world—good or bad—it is defined to be a side show for ever and will fade into the oblivion predicted by its modernist detractors. As one of the small body of practising Classicists, this is a future I would like to avoid.

[11]   If classical architecture is both to develop and expand it must adopt both technology and architecture to produce something both new and recognizably classical. It must not use its enormously fertile past as a deadweight in a futile attempt to prevent progress but as a springboard into the excitement of the future.

New Words and Expressions

crusading [kruːˈseidiŋ]	a.	改革的，讨伐的
fervour [ˈfəːvə]	n.	热情，炽热
modernism [ˈmɔdənizəm]	n.	现代派，现代主义
monopoly [məˈnɔpəli]	n.	垄断（局面）
obsession [əbˈseʃən]	n.	着迷，缠住
liven [ˈlaivn]	v.	（up）使活跃
post-modernism [ˈpəustˈmɔdənizəm]	n.	后现代派
regionalism [ˈriːdʒənəlizm]		地方色彩派
neo-vernacula [niəu-vəˈnækjulə]		新地方色彩派

ill-digested ['ildai'dʒestid]	a.	消化不良的
revivalist [ri'vaivəlist]	n.	复兴者
aberration [æbə'reiʃən]	n.	偏离常轨，离开正道
adversity [əd'vəːsiti]	n.	逆境，不幸
censorship ['sensəʃip]	n.	审查，检查
antiquity [æn'tikwiti]	n.	古代，古风
renaissance [rə'neisəns]	n.	文艺复兴（时期）
practitioner [præk'tiʃənə]	n.	实践者，开业者
ridicule ['ridikjuːl]	n.	嘲笑，嘲弄
founding ['faundiŋ]	a.	基本的
avant-garde ['ævɑːŋ'gɑːrd]	n.	前卫派，先驱
supremacy [sju'preməsi]	n.	至高无上
stance [stæns]	n.	态度，姿态
fundamentalism ['fʌndə'mentlizm]	n.	原教旨主义
juggernaut ['dʒʌgənɔːt]	n.	不可抗拒的力量
oblivion [ə'bliviən]	n.	忘却；淹没
detractor [di'træktə]	n.	毁损者
deadweight ['dedweit]	n.	重负，自重
springboard ['spriŋkɔːd]	n.	跳板，出发点

Notes

①…the reverse side of the same coin… 同一硬币的反面。喻指新古典主义与现代派本质相同。

②本句结构…conviction…and …commissions…（主语）have… established a small body…as…contributors…确立了这一小批建筑师作为重要的贡献者。

③throwing out the baby with the bathwater 不分精华糟粕一律抛弃。

④…and the concentration…by post-war Modernism. 这个并列分句有两层意义：战后现代派使建筑艺术的自然发展进程突然中断；专注于1820年以前的建筑艺术将古典建筑艺术与此进程割裂开来。此句表明，作者认为古典建筑艺术应看作是一直在发展，直到战后现代派的出现。

⑤本句结构 The reasonable idea（that 从句）has been exaggerated to the ridiculous idea（that 从句）。本句表明了作者对于完全弃绝任何与现代感有联系的事物这样一种极端态度的批评。

⑥Roman arch 罗马拱。

⑦Georgian a. 乔治时代的，乔治王朝的。指1714—1810年间乔治一世、二世、三世统治时期。乔治时代的建筑非常严谨，有着平衡的比例。

⑧a side show 不重要的部分。

Exercises

Reading Comprehension

I. Say whether the following statements are true (T) or false (F) according to the text.

1. The author warns that a simple combination of classical architecture with Modern Movement would result in the destruction of New Classicism.   (   )

2. It is understandable that the New Classicists are obsessed by progress, technology and modernity but meanwhile base their ideology on a negative response to all that the Modern Movement represented.   (   )

3. The author approves of the inheritance of classical architecture but flatly denies the theory and practice of Modernism.   (   )

4. As a practising classicist, the author disapproves the present stance and practice of the New Classicism or of the constructional fundamentalism.   (   )

5. According to the author, Classicism has always denied anything modern, different and even shocking from the very beginning.   (   )

II. Read the text carefully and then choose the best answer among the four choices given to complete each statement.

1. When the author says "the reverse side of the same coin", he means that.

   A) the attitudes of many New Classicists are nearly the same in nature as those of the Modernists.

   B) the Classicists should turn against the Modernists

   C) no classicists should share the obsession with progress, technology and modernity.

   D) anyone obsessed with progress, technology and modernity is not classicist at all.

2. The New Classicists have had significant contributions to the development of contemporary architecture because of.

   A) the fierce conviction

   B) the important commissions

   C) the isolation, hostility, adversity and educational censorship

   D) Both A and B

3. The success of classical architecture in the last fifteen years was due to.

   A) the consolidation of Classicism in the period

   B) the justification of its existence

   C) a growing public hostility to the excesses of Modernism

   D) a negative response to all that the Modern Movement represented

4. When the author says "throwing out the baby with the bathwater", he means we should.

   A) deny any desire to be modern

B) deny technological supremacy

C) dismiss all forms of post-1820 structure and construction

D) concentrate on pre-1820 architecture

5. The author believes that.

   A) some avant-garde artists can not produce work of value

   B) any form of popular appreciation of new art makes it automatically bad

   C) classical architecture has adapted to new requirements because of technological progress.

   D) the beauty of the various Georgian forms of Classicism contributed to the validity of classical architecture in the 19th and early-20th centuries.

6. The author suggests that.

   A) one should not regard only architecture before 1820 as classical archi-tecture.

   B) pre-1820 architecture had cut off the natural development of classical architecture.

   C) the denial of technological supremacy is a sort of constructional funda-mentalism.

   D) the traditionalists deny any desire to be modern.

7. The author argues that.

   A) classical architecture has nothing to do with technological progress.

   B) classical architects should not try to create anything shocking.

   C) we may also find something modern, different and even shocking in the history of classical architecture.

   D) one can never find anything modern, different or shocking in the history of classical architecture.

8. The author advises that for the future development the New Classical architects.

   A) should stick to the negative attitude to all things associated with the modern world.

   B) should combine technology and architecture to produce something new and recognizably classical.

   C) should get rid of the deadweight of the fertile past.

   D) should take technological progress as a springboard into the future.

Vocabulary

I. Match the words in Column A with their corresponding definitions in Column B.

   Column A   Column B

   1. monopoly   a. the belief in the exact truth of Bible, now also referring the belief in the original exactly as opposed to anything new and modern.

   2. censorship   b. the group of people who produce the newest ideas, esp. in the arts

3. aberration   c. exclusive ownership or control

4. avant-garde   d. an oppressive burden or difficulty

5. fundamentalism   e. the action or policy of examining printed material to prevent unacceptable ideas, etc.

6. deadweight   f. deviation or departure from the normal, the typical or the expected

Ⅱ. Fill in the blanks with the given words.

> crusading fervour obsession ideology
> supremacy stance oblivion liven

1. They devoted to their work with such a kind of _____ that nothing could distract them.

2. They are under the _____ with technology to such a degree that they believe only technology can make architecture adapt to the modern requirements.

3. Either technological _____ or constructional fundamentalism is beneficial to the natural and healthy development of contemporary architecture.

4. The author criticizes the _____ and practice of both New Classicism and Modernism and offers his opinions as to what may be the correct attitude.

5. Any works of art, as long as they are of genuine artistic value, would never fall into _____ .

6. They believe that technology may _____ up the development of classical architecture.

7. In 1970, they carried out a _____ movement in order to break up the situation of the Modernist monopoly in the world of architecture.

8. He believed that all the theories and practices should have a place in history and we should hold a correct _____ to them.

Writing Outline Writing (1)

To write an outline of an article, you must first of all identify the main ideas in the paragraphs and then express them by using noun phrases (topic outline) or simple sentences (sentence outline).

Topic outline is one that uses incompletesentences, e. g. nouns, noun phrases, etc. while sentence outline uses complete sentences.

For example:

The Topic Outline:

a) Three Main Groups of Oil

b) Uses and Importance of Mineral Oil

c) History and Origin of Mineral Oil

The Sentence Outline

a) Oil falls into three categories: animal, vegetable & mineral.

b) Of them mineral oil is the most useful and has changed our life.

c) The oil originated in the distant past and has formed from living things in the sea.

Directions: Now read the text of Unit Three again and then complete the outline by matching the paragraph numbers in Column A with their proper topic outline in Column B:

Column A

1. Paragraph 1.
2. Paragraph 2-4
3. Paragraph 5-6
4. Paragraph 7-8
5. Paragraph 9-10
6. Paragraph 11

Column B

a. Factors related to the development of Classicism
b. Criticism of the negative stance of Classicism to Modernism
c. Conclusion
d. The necessity of Classicism's adaptation to modern requirements
e. Close relation between New Classicism and Modernism
f. Brief introduction of the history of Classicism

Reading Material A

The Classical Reality

The Classical Revival in architecture began in earnest a decade ago. The first serious exhibition of Quinlan Terry's work (in 1981 at our own galleries) marked the start of what was to become a crusade to remake British architecture. There had, of course, been more senior traditionalist architects who survived the Modernist triumph of the post-war years and went on building in their own fashion. It mattered little to any of them that housing estates, shopping centres, City of London office blocks and comprehensive schools were designed in a manner which they found repugnant, derived from Le Corbusier, Mies, and Gropius. [1]They had their clients—mostly a landed elite which scorned Modernism—and they could simply ignore the rest of the world. [2]

They were an isolated minority, entirely marginal to the practice of architecture. [3]An eminent figure in their ranks—for he appeared to be just another regional traditionalist— was Raymond Erith, Quinlan Terry's mentor and partner. After Erith's death (in 1973) Terry carried on the practice. At first, he was tolerated—insofar as anyone took an interest in his work—as his late partner had been. Richmond Riverside marked him, in some people's eyes, as a dangerous subversive, but he soon had the support of the Prince of Wales for his efforts. [4]

Leon Krier, whose work had been extensively published in Britain by AD, remained an influential theorist whose connection with practical building had ceased, it appeared, when he quit the office of James Stirling. [5]But he was not content to be a theorist.

The Paternoster Square project, which forms the core of this issue, has brought to-gether all key figures in the 'revival of architecture' (as Erith put it) in Britain. [6]In addi-tion, as a result of the way in which commercial development is funded, it has involved some of the leading American Classicists, heirs to a tradition with its own complex histo-ry. [7]

Prince Charles lashed the proposals for the area by Arup Associates, Norman Foster, Richard Rogers, Arata Isozaki and others as mean-minded and arrogant: 'Market forces', he declared, 'are not enough'. Leon Krier's criticism of the various competition schemes and his support for the unofficial rival drawn up by John Simpson was less about style than about content. [8]It is hardly surprising therefore that Krier has not been a vocal supporter of the current proposals—for they do not provide for the mix of uses which he advocates.

Paternoster Square provides a considerable dilemma for supporters of traditional ar-chitecture. The proposed buildings are—apart from those by Terry, Simpson and Green-berg facing the Cathedral—essentially large modern blocks, dependent on artificial servic-ing and constructed on nontraditional lines. [9]Yet the form of the scheme is, superficially at least, 'classical' and there is every prospect of a picturesque townscape which builds on the popular success of Richmond Riverside. What was never explored—and perhaps now never will be—was the application of a classically inspired masterplan in a pluralist way. [10]

Paternoster Square could yet be a dead—end for Classicism. In any case, the very defi-nitions of the 'classical' or 'traditional' urgently require rethinking. In Britain, Demetri Porphyrios has increasingly demonstrated his scorn for simplistic style—mongering and his recent projects at Belvedere Farm and Magdalen College, Oxford, underline his lively view of tradition and the positive force of convention. [11]The Oxford scheme, in particular, shows him bending to the context in a way that the individualistic Quinlan Terry, interestingly, was not prepared to do when he added to Downing College, Cambridge. For Porphyrios, Magdalen is the embodiment of a living tradition which no architect should seek to per-vert.

If Classicism in Britain has not entirely escaped from the old milieu of landed wealth and political conservatism, its connotations in the United States are very different. Thomas Beeby has been working towards a new civic style with his great library in Chicago—stylis-tically a blend of a Chicago and New York motifs from the first decades of this century but at heart a big, rational building—and with his Rice Building at the Art Institute of Chica-go. The latter is oddly but appealingly spare, almost stripped in style——like an internal version, one might suggest, of the public manner of Arup Associates in their Paternoster Square scheme. [12]

The work of Beeby and Greenberg, Simpson and Adam, Terry and Porphyrios, exem-plifies the central issue for classical architecture in Britain and America in the 1990s. How far can it continue to be an expression of a narrowly conceived view of tradition, a reworking of stylistic motifs necessarily applied to new buildings types？If Classicism is to make inroads into urban planning—and such is the ambition of Leon Krier——precedent is not enough. In this light，Paternoster Square，as presently conceived，is not the climax of a crusade but a stage in a continuing dialogue.

Notes

①comprehensive school 综合学校。区别于 grammar school（相当于普通中学）和 secondary modern school （相当于职业中学）。
②landed elite 拥有土地的重要人物。
③marginal *a.* 微不足道的，少量的。
④marked him…as a dangerous subversive 把他当作危险的破坏分子。
⑤AD＝Architectural Design，《建筑设计》，英国建筑刊物。
⑥this issue （据上下文应指）古典主义建筑艺术。全句意为：帕坦诺斯特广场是目前古典主义建筑艺术的核心工程。这一工程吸引了英国建筑艺术复兴运动（照埃里斯的话说）的所有关键人物。
⑦另外，由于古典主义的商业化建筑实践有了资金作后盾，这一工程也 吸引了一些主要的美国古典主义建筑师，他们继承了有着自己的复杂历史的传统。
⑧利昂·克莱尔对各种参赛方案的批评和对约翰·辛普森的非正式参赛方案的支持都较少注重风格，而更多地注重内容。
⑨servicing *n.* （全套）设施，设备。
⑩从未探索，也许将永远不会探索的是，以一种多元的方式去实施具有真正古典主义精神的总体规划。masterplan *n.* 总（平面）图。
⑪style-mongering *n.* 卖弄风格。
⑫ （be）stripped in style 缺乏风格。

Reading Material B

What the Classical Can Do for the Modern

Many of us have come to value Classicism anew because of a historical Modernism's failure to provide satisfactory built responses to the very critical social，environmental and cultural demands from which its proponents claimed to derive their theories. ①Modernism emphasised innovation over invention，disruption over continuity，interior monologue over public discourse. ②In arbitrarily rejecting the time-honoured forms that resonate with a cul-ture we have taken such pains over time to create，it introduced a kind of tyranny of the present （the 'eternal present' was Sigfried Giedion's chilling phrase）that stripped away the rich historic complexities of street ensembles，neighbourhoods and sometimes entire cities，as it revelled in the very personal and self-important thrill of isolated invention. ③As we turn away from a reductive Modernism and search for more culturally inclusive and more physically satisfying ways to build, Classicism again demonstrates its validity and vitality, enabling architects to carve as well as to extrude, to construct and not merely assemble forms that go beyond the mere exemplification of extra-architectural social or literary ideals. ④ This renewed invocation of Classicism, and beyond it of traditional building as a whole, is not intended to substitute one form of cultural absolutism—the imposition of the new— with another, the oppression of the old. ⑤Rather, it is intended to affirm the architect's role as a conservator of values; to call for invention rather than the too—easy innovation of 'me- too' shape making; to plea for a 'present-and-future-oriented' materialism infused with the ideal of cultural memory. ⑥ It is precisely Classicism's timeless otherness that makes it so germane to a culture that simultaneously and contradictorily celebrates explorations in outer space while it searches for its roots in the ethnic cultures of the pre-industrial past. ⑦

How an architect approaches Classicism today varies as much as thetradition itself but the intrinsic struggle to protect and project its values is shared by all who recognise artistic creativity as a process of recollection and invention. Why an architect proposes Classicism today is also worth asking: for so long the target of modernist contempt, Classicism was made to serve as a symbol of social and political dysfunction and of a troubled status quo. ⑧ Is not an adherence to the classical canon—to the discipline of its methods and the richness of its vocabulary—an optimistic undertaking for architects who operate in a culture that in other aspects equally values measure and bravura, computers and rock and roll?⑨Classicism offers the architect a canon, but what a liberal and tolerant canon it is. It proposes models of exellence in composition and detail. It does not set out on a singular route but points out various ways to participate in a continuum yet contribute to its evolution, to be fresh without resorting to self-indulgent iconoclasm, to celebrate the ideals and the fundamental discourse that bind people together rather than search for the cultural rifts that pull us apart, to reaffirm the communalties amidst the chaos which everywhere all too easily makes its own way without our help. With its deep cultural ties, its innate hierarchy of form and detail, and its capacity for purity and hybridisation, Classicism still seems, after nearly a century's struggle to overthrow it, perhaps not inevitable and certainly not God-given, but surely much more than merely viable: taken in its broad sense, a classical approach to architecture seems to offer a fresh stimulus to modern architects seeking to recapture the act of building as a reconciliation of individuality and community, to reaffirm enduring,even timeless values in a dynamic culture continuously challenged by bold and often disturbing political and technological innovations. Classicism has flexibility and built-in tolerance, but do our architects have the skill and scholarship, the art and wisdom to work within its great canon? Isn't it easier to hide behind the head-lines and profess the hopelessness of a world in holocaust? Or to claim that nothing humanly noble can be done in a world dominated by machines? Isn't it just easier to fling a pot of paint in the public's face?⑩

Notes

①我们许多人开始重新评价古典主义，因为现代派未能针对至关重要的社会、环境和文化的需求提供令人满意的建筑，尽管现代派的拥护者们声称正是根据这些需求得出他们的理论。

②现代派强调革新而忽视创造，专注于对传统的破坏而忽视连续性的保持，醉心于自我的内心独白而忽视公众的评论。

③在现代派从闭门造车的创造中去着迷地寻求表现自我、妄自尊大的刺激之时，曾一度通过武断地弃绝与我们经过长期艰苦努力而创造的文化相呼应的、经过时间考验的建筑形式，而对现实（Sigfried Giedion 令人冷战哆嗦地称为"永恒的现实"）采取了一种专横的态度。这就丧失了整条街道、居民区，有时甚至整座城市所拥有的具有丰富历史意义的各种复杂的表现形式。

④当我们抛弃日渐没落的现代派而寻求文化内涵更广的，实实在在地更令人满意的建筑方式的时候，古典主义又一次展现出它的时效性和生命力。它使建筑师们能够去雕塑、去创造、去构筑各种建筑形式，而不是仅仅将各种形式组合起来，从而超越了那种仅仅对建筑艺术之外的、社会或文学的理念解释说明的做法。

⑤使古典主义，或者更广泛地说整个传统建筑艺术东山再起，并非想要将一种形式的文化专制主义（将新生事物强加于人）用另一种形式（用传统事物来压制人）取而代之。substitute…of the other 句型 substitute one with another.

⑥相反，这样的意图是要确立建筑师保留传统价值的作用，号召创造发明而不是草率从事模仿他人造型的所谓革新，呼吁充满着文化传统理念的"注重现实和未来的"写实主义。present-and-future-oriented…memory 充满着文化传统理念的"注重现实和未来的"写实主义。

⑦恰好是古典主义的永恒的不同使它与这样一种文化密切相关。在这种文化中，两种现象同时发生却又紧密相连：一方面欢呼人类在外层空间的探索活动，另一方面又在工业化以前的不同人类文化中去寻找自己的根。

⑧for so long…contempt 因为古典主义长期以来一直是现代派冷嘲热讽的对象。status quo ［拉丁］现状。

⑨建筑师们正处于这样一种文化形态：它在其他各个方面既重视标准，又重视出色技艺，既重视计算机，又重视摇滚乐。对于这些建筑师来说，坚持古典主义的原则，坚持古典主义设计方法的原理，保护古典主义设计语言的财富，这样的做法难道不是令人乐观的事业吗？本句基本结构为 Is not an adherence to sth. an optimistic undertaking for sb.？

⑩fling a pot of paint 表示责难或抗议。

UNIT FOUR

Text   The Skyscraper

[1]   It has been stated that the skyscraper and the twentieth century are synonymous and there can be no doubt that the tall building is the landmark of our generation. It is a structural marvel that reaches to the heavens and embodies human goals to build ever higher. The skyscraper is this century's most stunning architectural accomplishment.

[2]   But the question of how to design the tall building still continues to taunt, disconcert, and confound practitioners. The swing in taste and style is as predictable as night and day, and we are at this very moment busy rewriting the rules of skyscraper design. In the process we are not sure that the right lessons we have learned are not being discarded for the wrong ones. ①

[3]   A successful skyscraper solution and the art of architecture itself depends on how well the structural, utilitarian, environmental, and public roles of the tall building are resolved. Style, any style, must be intrinsic to, and expressive of, these considerations. Architecture is, above all, an expressive art.

[4]   The skyscraper has totally changed the scale, appearance, and concept of our cities and the perceptions of people in them. No doubt it will continue to do so. But it is more important today than ever that the builder and architect consider all the factors associated with the design of a tall building and how it is incorporated into its urban setting.

[5]   Looking at the whole historical spectrum of skyscraper design, four significant phases can be identified: the functional, the eclectic, the modern, and what is currently called the postmodern, a term coined more by the media, for surely our references to modernism have not changed but have merely broadened. ②

[6]   It is significant that all of the most important structural solutions came early in the development of tall buildings and in a very short space of time. Because these structures were concentrated in Chicago in the two decades at the end of the last century, it was quickly acknowledged and referred to as the Chicago style.

[7]   The period from 1890 to 1920 was considered the golden age of architecture, and there have been few more masterful and original tall buildings produced than those by the architect Louis Sullivan. ③Running as counter current to the already emerging eclecticism, Sullivan believed that the design of the skyscraper was the translation of structure and plan into appropriate cladding and ornament and that the answers were not to be found in the rules of the past.

[8]   The eclectic phase produced some most remarkable monuments, employing many of the styles and ornamentation from the temples of Greece to the Italian Renaissance. The best examples displayed skilled academic exercises, composed with ingenuity and drama to

answer the new needs and aspirations of the twentieth century. These designs so beautifully compiled by architects like Raymond Hood and Cass Gilbert culminated in the famous international competition for the Chicago Tribune Tower in 1922. This competition, which called for "The Most Beautiful and Distinctive Office Building in the World", drew more than 200 entries. The selection of the Gothic revival design by Howells and Hood prolonged the eclectic style against the concepts of the modern. For ten years modernism as pioneered by a relatively few European architects, paralleled a style that would better be termed modernistic. This style was neither pure nor revolutionary, but fused the end of the decorative eclectic style with the modernist theories and has become popularly known today as Art Deco.④

[9]   The early modern or international style skyscrapers are small in number because of lack of courage on the part of the builder and a reluctance to invest in a style not yet accepted.⑤But after the Second World War the descendants of these early modern skyscrapers, such as the McGraw-Hill Building in Manhattan, came to make up the high modern corporate style, the flat top glass boxes that have been the focal point of criticism over the past ten years.

[10]   These big buildings have taught us a hard lesson. But it is wrong that so much has been blamed on the esthetics, for such problems owe just as much to investment patterns and social upheavals. Unfortunately the minimalism of the modern esthetics let itself to the cheapest corner cutting. Since this is the most profitable route for the builder to take, it is an elegant and refined vocabulary that was quickly reduced to bottom line banality. Many are already grieving the passing; for it is structure in its purest form, enclosed in a sheer curtain of shaped and shimmering glass, that has produced some of the most innovative designs of our time.

[11]   These ideas should not be abandoned in a search for ideal answers. After all, the history of the skyscraper—which is also the history of the century—is a search for identity.

New Words and Expressions

skyscraper ['skaiskreipə]	n.	摩天大楼
synonymous [si'nɔniməs]	a.	同义（语）的
landmark ['lændmɑːk]	n.	里程碑；界标
marvel ['mɑːvəl]	n.	奇迹
stunning ['stʌniŋ]	a.	令人吃惊的
accomplishment [ə'kʌmpliʃmənt]	n.	成就，成绩
taunt [tɔːnt]	vt.	嘲弄，辱骂
disconcert [diskən'səːt]	vt.	挫败；使窘迫
confound [kən'faund]	vt.	使困惑；混淆

* intrinsic [in'trinsik]	*a.*	内在的，固有的
spectrum* ['spektrəm]	*n.*	光谱，领域
acknowledge* [ək'nɔlidʒ]	*vt.*	承认；感谢
masterful ['mɑːstəful]	*a.*	名家的；巧妙的
counter ['kauntə]	*a.*	相反的
eclecticism [ek'lektisizəm]	*n.*	折衷主义
cladding* ['klædiŋ]	*n.*	涂层；敷层
Italian Renaissance		意大利复兴运动（时期）
drama ['drɑːmə]	*n.*	戏剧（性）；戏剧效果
compile [kəm'pail]	*vt.*	汇集；编辑
culminate ['kʌlmineit]	*vi.*	达到顶点
revival [ri'vaivəl]	*n.*	复兴，复活
modernistic [mɔdə'nistik]	*a.*	现代派的；现代主义（者）的
fuse* ['fjuːz]	*vt.* ; *n.*	熔合；熔断；保险丝
prolong* [prə'lɔŋ]	*vt.*	延长，拉长
descendant [di'sendənt]	*n.* ; *a.*	弟子；后代；祖（遗）传的
reluctance* [ri'lʌktəns]	*n.*	不情愿，勉强；磁阻
upheaval [ʌp'hiːvəl]	*n.*	动乱，剧变
minimalism ['miniməlizəm]	*n.*	极简抽象派艺术
banality [bə'næliti]	*n.*	平庸，陈腐
profitable ['prɔfitəbl]	*a.*	有利的；有益的
grieve [griːv]	*vt.*	使悲伤，使痛心
sheer [ʃiə]	*a.*	透明的；极薄的；纯粹的
shimmering ['ʃiməriŋ]	*a.*	闪闪发光的

Notes

①discard…for 舍去（抛弃）……取……

②Looking at the whole historical spectrum…，此为垂悬分词短语，其逻辑主语并非下文的 four significant phases，在科技文献中，这种用法很常见。

③Louis Sulivan 路易斯·沙利文（1856—1924），美国建筑师，芝加哥学派的代表人物之一，主张"功能决定形式"，主要作品有芝加哥会堂大厦，圣路易斯的温顿特大厦等。

④Art Deco 装饰派艺术起源于本世纪 20 年代末，流行于 30 年代，60 年代中再度兴起，以轮廓和色彩明朗粗犷，呈流线型和几何形为特点。

⑤International Style 国际式建筑风格，指由功能主义建筑思想倡导的一种建筑风格，首见于 20 世纪 20 年代，其特色是强调实用性，具有大窗户、宽门廊及强固的屋基建筑。

Exercises

Reading comprehension

I. Skim the text and match each of the following ideas with its appropriate paragraph number or numbers in the brackets.

1. Present situation of skyscrapers and questions to be considered and answered.   (   )

2. A brief trace-back of the history of skyscrapers.   (   )

3. Conclusion.   (   )

II. Choose the best answer for each of the following:

1. What is the main idea of the first two paragraphs?

   A) Great achievements have been made in building skyscrapers.

   B) How skyscrapers have become the landmark of our time.

   C) People are faced with the problem of how to design tall buildings.

   D) Both A and C.

2. Which of the following is the accomplishment people have made in architecture?

   A) The tall building has become the symbol of the achievements in the twentieth century.

   B) People have set up their goal to build higher.

   C) The skyscraper has changed everything in the twentieth century.

   D) Great changes have taken place both in cities and rural areas.

3. What plays the major role in building the skyscrapers?

   A) Design methods.

   B) People's perceptions.

   C) Progress in structure.

   D) Changes of our cities.

4. Which of the following is the problem affecting the development of the skyscraper?

   A) Roles of the public in it.

   B) Rules of design.

   C) Its environmental effect.

   D) All of the above.

5. According to the text, functional phase is represented by _____ .

   A) a building with beautiful decoration

   B) Chicago Style

   C) Raymond Hood and Cass Gilbert

   D) Art Deco

6. Designs in the competition for the Chicago Tribune Tower belong to _____ .

   A) the modernism

B) the postmodernism

C) the eclectic phase

D) the functional phase

7. It can be learned that modernism came from _____ .

A) European countries

B) the United States

C) the end of the eighteenth century

D) the late twentieth century

8. In paragraph 10, "vocabulary" refers to _____ .

A) words and expressions of any language

B) an aesthetic language in architecture

C) a written and spoken form of a language

D) a word list of an essay or a text

9. Which of the following will the author agree with?

A) The skyscraper may cause a lot of problems therefore it is unnecessary.

B) Functional phase has contributed most to the development of the skyscraper.

C) Eclecticism attaches special importance to the structure of the skyscraper.

D) There is still much that we can learn from those that have been widely criticised.

10. What is the thesis statement of the whole text?

A) The skyscraper is this century's most stunning architectural accomplishment.

B) Architecture is, above all, an expressive art.

C) It is more important today than ever that the builder and architect consider all the factors associated with the design of a tall building and how it is incorporated into its urban setting.

D) These big buildings have taught us a hard lesson.

Vocabulary

I. Match the words in Column A with their corresponding definitions in Column B.

Column A	Column B
1. reluctance	a. a layer of material covered on structure
2. cladding	b. unwillingess in mind to do sth
3. acknowledge	c. recognize or appreciate
4. prolong	d. a continuous range or entire extent
5. fuse	e. melt or break as a result of melting
6. spectrum	f. lengthen or extend in time or space

II. Complete each of the following Statements with one four Choices given below.

1. We need art, but the _____ value of art is determined by whether it responds to humen needs.

A) intrinsic   B) incompatible

C) intricate   D) intact

2. The war has done a lot of damage to the country but the reconstruction work is going on at _____ speed.

A) spontaneous   B) restrictive

C) stunning   D) ultraviolet

3. The fact needs further clarifying as it _____ everyone with common sense.

A) encompasses   B) confounds

C) fascinates   D) actuates

4. "Participate in" and "take part in" are _____ in meaning.

A) counter   B) synonymous

C) Obscure   D) implicit

5. The Concise Oxford Dictionary of Current English is _____ by H. Fowler and J. sykes.

A) integrated   B) comprised

C) formulated   D) compiled

6. Recently finacial and environmental constraints have _____ in the abandonment of many ambitious proposals in the world.

A) cultivated   B) advanced

C) culminted   D) evaculated

7. Political or social _____ will inevitably prevent the development of economy.

A) upheaval   B) stagnation

C) exploitation   D) speculation

8. People are _____ to see that their living space is being endangered by industrial pollution.

A) tensile   B) grieved

C) salient   D) relieved

Writing Dutline Writing (2)

Dire ctions: Read the text of Unit Four again and write a topic outline of the text.
The Topic Outline The skyscraper

a) _____

b) _____

c) _____

d) _____

Reading Material A

GOING TALLER

We are now in a period of reaction to all of this. Respect for the street wall is coming back, as well as respect for scale and texture, factors that are absolutely critical to the esthetic success of any tall building, and which are vastly more important than style. But we are only beginning to understand that the problem really is one of background and foreground, one of making cities which are wholes and not merely disparate, competing parts. In any good city the whole is something much more than the sum of the parts, but in too many of our cities, the whole is not more at all. It is vastly less.

There is no better example of this than the first scheme for the Upper West Side of Manhattan, the project called Television City, which included six 76-story towers and one 150-story tower which, if built, would have been the tallest skyscraper in the world. It has a certain excitement to it. Who could fail to be moved, even today, by the words "the tallest building in the world"? For the entire history of skyscraper construction, height has had a power over architects, builders, everyone. To build taller seemed, for so long, to be the goal, like winning a race, and not only like winning it, but like winning it better than anyone had won it before. One generation could produce the four-minute mile, the next could produce a miler who could run it in 3'50" and so it would go, from 80 stories to 110 now, isn't the logical thing to go on to 150, just as we keep trying to run the mile faster and faster, keep on shooting for the moon, keep on trying to do everything?①

For if architecture and the building of cities mean anything, they have to do with making civilized places for people to live in, use, be inspired by, be uplifted by. ②The proposed 150-story building for New York does cause the heart to beat faster for a moment, and granted credit is due for that. But Ifail to see where building 150 stories worth of condominium apartments in a tower that, by virtue of its vast bulk, must contain 2,600 separate apartment units will be anything other than a Buck Rogers fantasy. ③And while Buck Rogers may be fun to contemplate for amusement, in real life—which the middle of New York City all too certainly is—it would be more of a science fiction nightmare.

It would seem like a nice leap—a wonderful way, in fact, to commemorate the beginning of the skyscraper's second century——to be able to make this jump in magnitude to an entirely different kind of building. And Helmut Jahn's plan, which would put the building on a large, relatively open site, makes more sense than many earlier schemes for buildings of this great height in denser parts of Manhattan. ④But these things provide only momentary appeal; in real life, such a building would be otherwise, a case of technology ability completely and entirely outpacing common sense. Because we would build it, I am not convinced that it would deepen and enrich the experience of urban life at all.

But now that we can go high, far higher even than this 150-story proposal, perhaps the real issue that must be faced is not all the way up in the sky 488m (1,600ft) versus 518m (1,700ft) versus 549m (1,800ft) Perhaps it is colser to the ground—back to the whole question of making a civilized city, of trying to see the tower not as an isolated object, but as a part of a larger whole, as something that seems to grow organically from everything around it, enriching its surroundings and in turn being enriched by them.

The best architecture comes always out of specific circumstances, not out of ideological predisposition. We are looking to advance the art of skyscraper design by looking not only at the tallest and most technologically advanced, but also at the buildings that seem to emerge out of the cities of which they are a part and, in turn, enrich those cities. It is encouraging that Rockefeller center is turned to constantly as a model for admiration by architects today; so is Carrere & Hastings's splendid 26 Broadway in lower Manhattan, or Holabird & Root's Board of Trade in Chicago, or Van Alen's Chrysler or McKim, Mead & White's Municipal Building or Hood's Chicago Tribune.

These are all buildings of strong personality, of strong image and character, yet they are all buildings that exist to make a statement about the life of the cities of which they are a part, and they are not isolated objects. Some connect to their surroundings more than others, but it is impossible to imagine any of them existing anywhere except precisely where they are—on pieces of land in the midst of cities with which they have come, by now, to have a deeply symbiotic relationship. ⑤

And so it should be with every tall building. The skyscraper has, in the end, a special responsibility. Its image is powerful, and if handled well, it can be among the most compelling visual experiences architecture can provide us with. The Monadnock, the Wainwright Building, the Woolworth Building, the Chrysler Building, Rockefeller Center, Seagram—these greatest of tall buildings belong on any list of the greatest of all American buildings. But as we have lived with tall buildings for a century, we by now should know that they alone, for all their glory and power, do not in and of themselves make a city.

Notes

①一代人可能培养出四分钟跑完一英里的人，下一代人可能培养出三分五十秒跑完一英里的人。以此类推，楼房从八十层已建到现在的一百一十层，进而再建到一百五十层难道不顺理成章吗？就像我们千方百计用越来越短的时间跑完一英里，又在力争到达月球，还想无所不能一样。

句中 "the four-minute mile" 可以理解为 a man who could run a mile in four minutes. "a miler"：善跑的人。"so it would go"：it 指人们想修建越来越高的建筑的愿望。

②如果城市的建筑和建设就是一切的话，就必须要解决好为人们造就一个能在其中生活，有便利的设施供人们使用，使人受到启迪和振奋精神的、文明的地方这一问题。

不定式符号"to"有四个动词，一起构成不定式短语修饰 places.

③建造一幢一百五十层高的公寓大楼，其庞大的建筑面积是可容纳二千六百套独立的单元，但是这除了是巴克·罗杰斯的一个奇思妙想以外，我看不出其中还有什么别的意义。

by virtue of＝because of 由于，因为。

④make sense 有意义。

⑤其中一些建筑与其环境的结合比另一些建筑更为紧密。然而，除了它们现在所处的环境——位于城市中心地带的一片片土地上，已与城市形成根深蒂固的共生关系——外，很难设想它们中的任何建筑还能在别的什么地方生存下去。

Reading Material B

The Impact of Tall Buildings——Pedestrian Needs

The development of a tall building can either aggravate problems of pedestrian movement or, perhaps, be part of the solution. Because of the scale of ameliorating measures that it can support, a tall building could be more acceptable in some situations than a much smaller one.

One key to the generation of a positive impact from a tall building is its location. In most situations, the lack of specialized pedestrian and/or transit facilities can be traced at least in part to a lack of concentration, focus, or organization in patterns of movement. In some instances, the volumes of movement simply may not be high enough to support the required investment in transit or pedestrian facilities. A tall building, strategically located to reinforce present patterns of movement or to create new movement in an appropriate corridor, may provide the impetus required to produce the needed access investment. This may be true whether the building is located within or near an intensive concentration of business activity.

However, if pedestrian benefits are to be achieved, several conditions must be met. First, priority must be given to developing a good system for movement *within* the existing activity core. This may consist of some combination of transit, grade-separated pedestrian ways, or pedestrian precincts or malls. ①The important condition is that existing functions be strongly linked to each other. New development can later connect via this linkage, and the access to markets and services will make location within or near the central area or activity center valuable.

Second, the ability of a movement system to provide access to lower-cost peripheral land accommodating parking and/or development should be exploited. A large building or complex may be able to utilize effectively and justify the development of a movement system extending outside of the present pattern of intensive activity. Such an extension may reduce costs, minimize pollution and access problems, and bring attractive but less accessi-

ble sites into use. Still, with a strong connection, the advantages of proximity and intercon-
nection can be maintained.

Third, existing core development and/or the proposed new development must include
a variety of uses——office, retail, and services. Unless a mix of uses is available, the need
for interaction between areas will probably not be large enough to generate the level of interchange required to sustain a useful linkage. Excluding the home-work trip, over 70% of
pedestrian trips are for non-business purposes. Thus the availability of shopping, restaurants, and consumer services is important to the extended use of pedestrian or related facilities.

To achieve these conditions, and to assure that the access needs of large concentrations
of development can be met, a three-part strategy should be employed.

*The improvement of facilities for pedestrians in existing areas of concentrated activity
should receive first priority.* Even if extensive investments can be made in transit and peo-
ple-movement systems, good pedestrian facilities will be required (most trips are too short
for transit) One of the most effective ways to improve the environment for pedestrians is to
create auto-restricted or auto-free zones involving precincts of several blocks in which
pedestrian movements are given preference. Additional techniques include the provision of
pedestrian and transit malls and the redesign of streets to improve pedestrian amenities. Quantified justification of such improvements in the United States is not readily available. However, the success of such improvements is readily observable in many situations,
particularly in Europe.

The provision of grade-separated walk ways represents still another level of investment to improve pedestrian movement systems. Ideally, such walkways should be provided
as part of a system which extends through many blocks of an area or which connects several auto-restricted precincts. A large, intense development frequently can provide the basis
for initiating or extending the development of such a system. Relatively modest volumes of
movement can justify the construction of a typical bridge. Assuming a benefit of 10¢ per
use, less than 3 000 crossings per business day would pay for the span across a normal
street, plus the costs of stairs and other vertical connections to grade. [2]

Plan a people-mover system and reserve a location and right-of-way. [3] This is most important in providing a transit facility. Once a right-of-way is established, buildings, streets,
pedestrian facilities, and other features can be adjusted gradually to reflect and reinforce
the transit plan. These adjustments will help assure the success of the transit facility when
it is provided, and should help reduce its cost.

*Large developments should be located and planned to help implement plans for both
pedestrian systems and transit.* Large developments at least should help to create, extend
and provide continuity to pedestrian movement systems. They should also be located and
designed to connect into any transit system, planned or existing. And consideration should
be given to using such systems as an integral part of development, to meet the need for es-

sential connections between the development and other features of the area, parking, and the like. A large, mixed-use development can be expected to generate 40 000 or more pedestrian trips per day. About 60% or 24 000 of these, are in movement between home and work. Sixteen thousand involve other origins or destinations. If no more than 10 000 of these trips were to use transit each business day with a benefit per ride of 30¢, this would generate annual revenues (or benefits) of over $660, 000. If half of this were available to cover debt service, this could support a capital investment of up to $4 million. An investment at this level would pay for a significant extension of a trolley or street car line, which could not only meet movement needs but open up lower cost land for parking or for development.

The opportunity to build a portion of transit or people-mover system in connection with a major development may seem remote. However, as cities and developers struggle with problems of access, parking, and pollution, they may find that the type of coordination of land and transportation planning described above may be a solution. Certainly additional study of this approach and application of the principles described above are warranted.

Notes

①grade-separated pedestrian ways 立交式人行道；pedestrian precincts 人行区；mall 林荫道。
②假设每人使用一次能产生 10 美分的效益，每个工作日有不到三千人的使用率，修建一座跨越一般街宽的立交人行道，连同上下阶梯及平整地面的费用，都是合算的。
③people-mover system 短程快速载客交通系统；right-of-way（铁路、公路、管线等）公用事业地（或称交通用地）。

UNIT FIVE

Text   Safety in Design

[1]   The concept of safety in the context of current design is complex. The danger or risks inherent in structural design arise from the designer's limited knowledge of the exact environment in which the structure may have to operate and also of the material properties and performance of the structure itself. ① In the context of building design and construction, safety is sought by using the best design and construction techniques available, the best materials and construction expertise and the best environmental data. With the design calculations, margins are ensured more specifically by the use of appropriate numerical factors. For the purpose of this discussion, it is accepted that all practical controls on material properties, workmanship, details, and so forth, are exactly as specified by the designer. Such an assumption is necessary to establish any analytical (or more properly, synthetic) process of design in which formal controls over safety are incorporated.

[2]   Consider the limit state or the Load and Resistance Factor Design (LRFD) approach to design. These methods appear to place equal importance on meeting serviceability requirements as on meeting those for ultimate limit states. It is arguable, however, that the principal objective of design is to produce serviceable structures and further, that completed structures complying with serviceability requirements are ipso-facto safe. The question arises therefore: what function does the establishment of ultimate limit states perform vis-a-vis the security of structures? It can be said that the requirement of stability under extreme load states provides a specific security margin over the serviceability condition for the explicitly considered load cases. The evaluation of margin does not, within the conventional meaning of such a factor, result in a partial safety factor. Indeed, this part of the safety control mechanism is more akin to design requirements in that it affects primarily the nature of structural behavior.

[3]   The explicit use of numerical factors in the design process is to circumvent the differences between the design model and its assumptions and the real structure and its environment. ②Factors in this class reflect ignorance of the real world. Consider the ideal "perfectly safe" building. Such a building would be one for which the material and structural properties were known exactly and could be maintained throughout its life and also for which environmental, loading, and support conditions were known and controlled within the prescribed levels. No factors would be required in the design of this building.

[4]   Traditionally, designers have incorporated factors into their analyses by assuming pessimistic values of basic variables, by the use of conservative analytical models and quasi-global factors at appropriate stages of a design. In such an approach to design, it is only possible to decide qualitatively whether the method is successful or not by a study of the

44

nature and rate of failure in the population of buildings constructed according to its principles. There is no practical way of evaluating the actual factor for any given load case.

[5]　　The introduction of a partial safety factor system into the design process requires the possession of a significant body of data related to the basic variables to be considered in a design. This data should allow the assessment of ignorance of each variable independently. Each factor can only reflect the state of knowledge of one specified parameter. The many other factors known to affect design, such as modeling errors, cannot be evaluated individually; allowance for them has to be made by some lumped or global design factor. This class of factor differs from those associated directly with particular variables in that determination of magnitude involves evaluation by some form of calibration in relation to existing design practice. ③Thus the introduction of partial factors of safety requires two following conditions to be satisfied: a large body of well-chosen data related to each basic variable, and clear and unequivocal rules to quantify individual partial factors of safety.

[6]　　For pragmatic reasons, where data for a particular variable is not available, realistic values of basic variables must be used whether chosen intuitively or by some analytical process.

[7]　　The partial factor of safety systems incorporated into some modern codes or standards do not comply with the second condition. The use, for example, of pessimistic load values defeats the object of a partial factor of safety approach.

[8]　　The justification for changing the format of code must be that it becomes more self consistent and conforms more properly with the design process and that new data and methods can be introduced in the future without requiring modification of the factors; also, ideally it should be easier to use.

New Words and Expressions

expertise* ['ekspəti:z]	n.	专门技能，专门知识
numerical* [nju (:) 'merikəl]	a.	数字（值）的，用数表示的
margin ['mɑ:dʒin]	n.	安全系数
workmanship ['wə:kmənʃip]	n.	工艺，技巧
serviceability ['sə:visəbiliti]	n.	适用（性）；耐用（性）
arguable ['ɑ:gjuəbl]	a.	可争辨的，可论证的
comply* [kəm'plai]	vi.	应允；遵照（常跟with）
ipso-facto ['ipsəu'fæktəu]		[L.] 照那个事实，根据事实本身
vis-a-vis ['vi:zɑ:vi:]	ad.; prep.	相对；与……相较
explicitly* [iks'plisitli]	ad.	明晰地，明确地
mechanism ['mekənizəm]	n.	机理（制）；技巧，手法
akin [ə'kin]	a.	类似的，同样的（常跟to）
circumvent [ˌsə:kəm'vent]	vt.	回避，绕过；围绕

quasi-global	[ˈkwɑːziˈgləubl]	a.	准（拟，半；类似）总体的	
analytical	[ænəˈlitikəl]	a.	分析的，解析的	
assessment	[əˈsesmənt]	n.	估计；评价	
ignorance	[ˈignərəns]	n.	不知；无知	
allowance*	[əˈlauəns]	n.	留量；容差；补助	
lumped	[ˈlʌmpt]	a.	整块的	
global*	[ˈgləubəl]	a.	整体的	
magnitude*	[ˈmægnitjuːd]	n.	大小，量，量值	
calibration*	[ˈkæliˈbreiʃən]	n.	标度；校准	
unequivocal	[ʌniˈkwivəkəl]	a.	不含糊的，明确的	
quantify*	[ˈkwɔntifai]	vt.	确定数量；用数量表示	
pragmatic	[prægˈmætik]	a.	重实效的，实际的	
realistic*	[riəˈlistik]	a.	现实（主义的）	
intuitively*	[inˈtjuː(ː)itivli]	ad.	直觉上，直观上	
justification*	[dʒʌstifiˈkeiʃən]	n.	正当理由；认为正当	

Notes

①in which 引出定语从句修饰 environment；and also of 介词短语（直到句子结束）修饰前面的 knowledge.

②between the design model and…and the real structure and…介词短语 between 在此处指 the design model and its assumptions 和 the real structure and its environment 之间的差别。

③in that 为介词宾语从句，表示"在……方面"，in relation to：与……相关。

Exercises

Reading Comprehension

Ⅰ. Skim the text and match each of the following ideas with its appropriate paragraph number or numbers in the brackets.

1. Partial safety factor system.   （ ）

2. Safety in design：a very complicated problem.   （ ）

3. Traditional design method.   （ ）

4. LRFD approach.   （ ）

5. The explicit use of numerical factors.   （ ）

Ⅱ. Read the text carefully and then choose the best answer among the four choices given to complete each statement.

1. What is the main idea of the first paragraph?

   A) Today the designers' knowledge is very limited.

   B) The best design and construction techniques are not available.

   C) Not all the controls are exercised exactly as specified by the designers.

   D) The concept of safety in present design is complex.

2. Which of the following about the limit state approach and LRFD approach is true?

   A) Both methods can satisfy the serviceability requirement.

   B) Neither of the methods can ensure that the completed works are safe.

   C) The requirement of stability under extreme load states works well in supplying security margin and it leads to a partial safety factor.

   D) There is in fact no safety control mechanism at all.

3. The sentence "The explicit use of numerical factors⋯ and its environment. "(Para. 3, Line 1—3) means _____.

   A) the use of numerical factors is not absolutely reliable.

   B) the mentioned differences are disguised deliberately by the designer.

   C) the mentioned differences are purposefully avoided.

   D) the designer who uses the numerical factors is irresponsible.

4. The word "differences" (Para. 3, Line 2) refers to _____

   A) those between A. the design model and B. its assumptions, the real structure and its environment

   B) those between A. the design model, its assumptions and the real structure and B. its environment

   C) those between A. the design model and its assumptions and B. the real structure and its environment

   D) those between the design model and its assumptions and between the real structure and its environment

5. According to the author, the "perfect/y safe " building is _____.

   A) not real

   B) an ideal one that has ever been built

   C) an absolutely safe one if it is built

   D) one that can satisfy every condition related

6. The method discussed in paragraph four is considered impractical mainly because _____.

   A) the values and factors used for analyses are groundless

   B) the analytical models are not used at all the stages of a design

   C) it is difficult, if not impossible, to determine whether the method is successful due to the data-collecting and evaluating problem

   D) there are few given load cases for evaluating the actual factor

7. What does the author think about the partial safety factor system?

A) It requires a large body of data.

B) Many factors can not be assessed.

C) The required conditions are not fully satisfied.

D) All of the above.

8. What is the author's general attitude toward the method discussed in the text?

A) Neutral   B) Negative

C) Affirmative   D) positive

Vocabulary

I. Match the words in Column A with their corresponding definitions in Column B.

Column A	Column B
1. modification	a. the act of checking or correcting
2. allowance	b. sth. that justifies
3. calibration	c. determine or measure the quantity of
4. quantify	d. the amount by which sth. is allowed to be more or less than stated
5. justification	e. partial change or correction
6. magnitude	f. size or measurable quantity

II. Replace the following underlined part with one of the four choices given below:

1. The return periods are related to an expected building life or, more explicitly, to design life.

A) precisely   C) exclusively

B) generally   D) explanatorily

2. It is arguable that completed structures complying with serviceability requirements are actually safe.

A) compromising   C) meeting

B) composing   D) involving

3. A study of comparative values associated with broad alternative solutions to a building problem is clearly part of the assessment process.

A) alternation   B) recognition

C) assumption   D) evaluation

4. Collectively, tall buildings have created a series of pragmatic problems that still confront those who plan, design and build them.

A) genuine   B) practical

C) ingenious   D) practicable

5. Flexibility in solving problems requires more intelligence and more special knowledge and skill.

A) expertise   C) perfection

B) excellence   D) prominence

6. The failure could have been <u>circumvented</u> if the properties of the material used had been better known.

   A) predicted   C)　circulated
   B) prevented   D) prohibited

7. Like many other things in the world, the expression of harmony can not be touched but can be <u>intuitively</u> felt.

   A) impulsively   B) sensitively
   C) instinctively   D) simultaneously

8. Up to new complaints have been heard about the practical functioning of the "Shell Building". But functioning alone as a leading principle will result in <u>unequivocal</u> arbitrariness.

   A) eloquent   B) unavoidable
   C) crucial   D) definite

Writing   Outline-Writing (3)

Directions: Read the text of Unit Five and match the paragraph numbers in Column A with proper sentences in Column B to form a sentence outline.

Column A   Column B

Reading Material A

Choice of Basic Variables

The choice of values for basic variables to be used in a combined limit state/partial factor of safety design method is conceptually quite different from that appropriate for a permissible stress or load factor method. ①Great care must be exercised to ensure that pessimistic values ("to be on the safe side") are rejected, since the employment of such values defeats the object of using partial factors associated with the variables. The values chosen must depend on their function in the design process and consequently on the methods used to compile the data base. Critical assessments should be made of each variable data bank in order to evaluate its potential role as a guide to the establishment of design standards② . Consider, for example, snow loading in the United Kingdom. Data in this field is limited, but it is probable the critical extreme values associated with the heaviest snow falls have not been measured because the manual techniques of depth and density assessment require the on-site attendance of a technician. This, more often than not, is prevented by the snow itself. ③

A study of the potential causes of extreme values of basic variables show that very often they are generated by mechanisms that are quite different from those that generate normal distributions. ④Whether or not these extreme values are important in design terms must depend upon the particular variable under consideration. However, two important points follow from this discussion: (1) Measurement techniques designed to gather data in the normal range will often not be appropriate to record extreme values of basic variables that may be generated by quite different mechanisms; (2) Where extreme values are generated by abnormal mechanisms, the probability of their occurrence cannot be deduced by extrapolation from distributions representing normal variations.

It is necessary to choose the "best" figure to represent the variable, in other words, one that does not implicitly include a safety margin, and also, in the case of loads, to choose a figure from the appropriate distribution.

Data on material properties are collected from a variety of sources and over considerable periods of time. These data represent the variability that has existed in the material properties manufactured and supplied by the industry. ⑤ For use to be made of this information, it must be accepted first, that material specified for a new construction would be produced in the same general environment and consequently be legitimately included in the same data distribution, and second, that the designer makes a statement along these lines:

a value has been chosen for material strength that, it is possible, might occur with current practice and that only a small percentage has been weaker than this. Therefore should this building be manufactured from the material specified, it will function properly under the prescribed loads.

It is irrelevant that should the actual material used be nearer to the average strength met in practice, the completed structure may be stronger than the designer aimed for. ⑥A difference between assumed and actual strength so generated cannot be treated as a safety factor for design purposes since it is unknown at the time of design and, until the construction is completed, indeterminate. This strength difference has, of course, great importance in the reassessment of the performance of existing structures and is the source of many problems of rationalizing the apparent high strength of structures as deduced from load tests, which cannot be simply correlated with the lower values generated by the substitution of low measured material strength in current design methods.

Notes

①permissible stress 许用应力；load factor 载荷系数。

②variable data bank 变量数据组（库）。

③more often than not＝as often as not, very frequently 常常，经常。

④extreme value 最大值，极限值。

⑤这些数据代表的是在厂商生产和运输过程中就已存在的材料特性的变率（变异性）。

⑥认为实际使用的材料强度越接近于施工要求的平均强度，完工的结构就会比设计人员要

求的更坚固，这一看法不恰当。

should 放在主语之前，是省略了 if 的倒装句，表示假设。

Reading Material B

Loads

The choice of loading values is constrained by an extra consideration not included in the general analysis given above. This constraint arises because each principal limit state can be defined basically by a loading condition. The choice of any particular load value must reflect its function in a limit state design. It was pointed out above that the main objective of design is to satisfy serviceability conditions, meaning that the normal loading states likely to pertain at some time during the life of the structure should be carried satisfactorily. Now, available loading data relates almost exclusively to normal loads and has been collected from a wide range of sites. It is therefore proper for the designer to choose an upper fractile and accompany his design with the implicit statement that:[1]

Loading data collected from many similar structures have shown that this high load value is possible. This structure has been designed to remain serviceable should it be subjected to this load.

In practice, many structures will never be subjected to their design loads, but as with the material values, the indeterminate difference between peak actual and design values cannot be used as a safety factor at the design stage.[2]

Very careful inspection of the nature of loading data must be undertaken before it is assumed that simple extrapolation of data gathered in serviceability conditions is appropriate to ultimate limit state conditions. Extreme floor loads may, for example, be generated by fires, floods, office parties and so on, and it is proper to choose ultimate load values from the nonnormal distribution so generated.

A further problem to be resolved before choosing a design value from the data bank of a variable load pertains to the relationship between a building life as reflected by that data bank and the prospective life of the building being designed. Considering first the floor loading data available, such data have been collected over a relatively short period (a few years) when compared with the life of a permanent building. It has, however, been collected simultaneously from many similar buildings, and the argument is propounded that the variation in loads indicated by the spatial distribution of measurements is very closely analogous to the temporal variation that might occur during the life of a single building.[3] Such an assumption is insupportable except by resort to heuristics. Fortunately, it is not necessary to follow such a difficult path. Consider the question: What significance has a standardized design load for a class of floors in the performance of a particular floor? Examine the following answers to this question:

If the design value is conservative or a high characteristic value and is used in a permissible stress design method or a load factor design method, then it can only be said to indicate a conservative lower bound for the performance of a floor.

If this design value is used in a properly constituted partial factor of safety design method, its effect is indeterminate.

These somewhat unsatisfactory responses can be resolved. The distribution of values deduced from the data bank reflect the nature of loads on a whole population of floors and that any specific value chosen to characterize this distribution and subsequently to act as a design value will serve to unify the performance of any new population of floors. Put simply, standard design values for variables control the performance of the population of structures in which they are used.

The paucity of information relating to the temporal variation in floor loads during the life of a building means that there is no logical basis to justify any variation in design load to suit an expected building life. It seems however reasonable to accept that to all intents and design purposes, floor loads are invariant with time for most structures.

Turning second to wind loading on structures, much effort has been directed towards the collection of both temporal and spatial (geographical) variations in wind speed data and to the conversion of this data into equivalent pressures on buildings. Because of the nature of this load, it has proved convenient to express characteristic values for the wind data in relation to "return periods" and to discuss 50-or 100-year winds when establishing design values for this variable. [4]In the BRE Digest on Wind Loading (HMSO, 1984) by implication and by assumption in the BS Code for the structural design of farm buildings (British Standards Institution, 1978-1981), these return periods have been related to an expected building life or, more explicitly, to design life. No simple connection exists between the two concepts even though they are expressed in an identical form. Consider the design of a one-off special building to be constructed in a known locality with an expected life of say 50 years, prudence might suggest a 95% characteristic value for the design wind load, which in turn would imply perhaps a 150-200 year return period. [5]

The design of more run-of -mill construction leads to a different problem of data interpretation. As before, the choice of a standard design value is directly related to the performance of the population of structures designed using that value. Therefore, in the case of data such as that for the wind, the period to be considered is that for the population as a whole, for example, while buildings within that population are extant. For example, if a particular form of short life structure (say two years) such as a specialized farm building is required for a particular production system, which itself might be expected to have an economic life of say 15 years, then the characteristic value should be chosen in relation to the 15 years. If this were a 95% value, then the resultant return period would be very much greater than the two-year life expected for a particular building.

Notes

①upper fractile 分位值上限。

②…the intedeterminate difference between peak actual and design values.
实际载荷峰值与设计峰值之间的不确定差别。

③…and the argument is … during the life of a single building. 争议在于：由多座类似建筑的测试数据的空间分布表明的荷载变化非常类似于单座建筑在使用期限内可能发生的瞬时变化。

④characteristic value 特征值 return period 重现期，回复期。

⑤假设要设计一幢一次性使用的特殊建筑，位置情况熟悉，预期使用寿命为五十年，为审慎起见，可以为设计风力荷载设定 95％ 的特征值，这就意味着重现期可能有一百五十至二百年。

UNIT SIX

Text On Design

[1]   For many reasons, it has become increasingly difficult in recent years to make a statement about the ground rules on which, in general, building design criteria should be based. Primarily the difficulty is that at present, there is no unified voice about style development in buildings related to our up-to-date technical opportunities, and designers face a barrage of possible structural solutions, and a great number of alternative building materials. The results are often a chaos of grouped buildings and some very poor design detailing. When, in the past, choice was much more limited, design crudity was avoided by the development, over years, of both architectural scholarship and elegance. In the 18th century Georgian domestic work in this country clearly demonstrates these qualities, and where such work survives, it remains very adaptable and usable 200 years afterwards. Certainly the Georgian terraces of houses, in large measure, meet Alex Gordon's statement of four goals at which building design should aim. ①They are:

1. To modify climate
2. To support patterns of activity
3. To add to our resources
4. To provide delight

He could have added, of course, that any design must relate to an overall financial commitment.

[2]   During the oil crisis of 1974 and the reaction of trying to save on the rapidly rising fuel bills in buildings, Gordon sponsored a design programme in which he invented the following telling directive to aim at—*long life, low energy, loose fit*—with the intention of reducing the capital turnover of buildings by making them continually viable with low fuel and maintenance costs, and easily adapted to changing uses. There are recent signs that these principles are being thought of, and some buildings can now be seen which reflect in large measure these constraints. There are considerable design advantages in working within the guide lines of limited material choices. Though there has been a startling minor revival of pseudo-Georgian housing in the last 3 years, this kind of solution provides no real answer, and no authenticity in its miniscule scale of the present day. ②Nevertheless, the last survival of the neo-Georgian of Welwyn Garden City of the 1920s, had great advantages and showed scholarship in its understanding of scale, form, colour and detail. ③

[3]   There was an available stock-in-trade in the general simple plan dignity of solutions which came from the Beaux Art traditions of axis and symmetry, and in the understanding of the standard details of windows, front doors pediments, which might have been dull and even inappropriate but were never vulgar or exhibitionists. ④The designer, within this cho-

54

sen idiom, sketched out his plan solutions on the basis of a convenient matrix of accommodation, recognising the (simple)constraints of place, usage and the standard byelaws, codes and regulations of the time. Sections and elevations nearly automatically built up from the resultant plan, and could be very accurately worked out by draftsmen wonderfully skilful in element design in detail. The whole design, measurement, specification, contract and production process were nearly universally understood and followed. It could not, of course, last, though the work of recent masters, Le Corbusier, Wright, Mies van der Rohe, and one or two others not quite so prominent, retains the vestiges of the confidence resulting from these earlier techniques.

[4]   The temptation to refer further to the more recent 20th century history of building design must be resisted because others have written with great authority about the many sided planning and architectural activities of the last 50 years. In general, the traditional vision of the scholarly architect serving the cultured client has faded, along with the confident autonomy of both. They now rely upon the additional skills of many specialists. A new world of building developed in the 1920-30s, much influenced by the world wide collapse of the economy, particularly in Germany and its neighbours. One of its manifestations was the Intermational Style. We had to build within a new framework of requirements, for which old style designs seemed inappropriate. Official clients, the public need, increasing urban populations and cost accounting were all influences. And within more rigid regulations, technical developments of light frameworks and structural facing concrete were becoming available.

[5]   Now our buildings are fashionable, speculative, and either of geometric and sculptured intricacy,or anonymous and componented. There is a multitude of structural gymnastics and immature material innovations. At one end of the spectrum the public buildings, and university and prestige commercial buildings (all very self-consciously designed)and at the other, the component assembled buildings, providing the social needs of schools, housing, offices, work and industrial buildings.

[6]   This dichotomy of basic approach to design and construction remains with us, and highlights some of the disparities of the social and technical goals of the times. We have in the world of building reached one of the great divides——straddled between contradictions:

simple tent enclosures	high indoor performance
solid walls	light frameworks
privacy	community
low density	high density
vehicle	pedestrian

In this great dilemma and confusion of interests we must now try to get our design and performance priorities right.

[7]   The acceptable logic of the process would seem to be to recognise and analyse the

very best solutions of the past, before advocating drastic change. It is essential to ask how much the far reaching changes have affected the continuing suitability of the previous solution, and what new constraints prevent its repetition. The drama of continuous change does not befit the provision of an artifact with the extended life of a building. This means the recognition of the prime requirement of shelter for an activity, the essential feature being the quality of roofing. Isaac Ware's maxim fits very seemingly the requirements of today:

"The art of building cannot be more grand than it is useful, nor its dignity of greater praise than its convenience."

[8]   To move more closely to this logic, we need to develop a new strategy of design method in order to have more confidence about the present and future answers to the many conflicts. A programme is rarely ready-made in all its aspiration to continuity. The aim must be a continuum——a satisfactory design producing an efficient and rewarding contract.

Naw Words and Expressions

barrage ['bærɑːʒ]	n.	一连串
crudity ['kruːditi]	n.	简陋，粗糙
adaptable [ə'dæptəbl]	a.	适应性强的
commitment* [kə'mitmənt]	n.	承付款项；许诺
directive [di'rektiv]	n.；a.	指示（的），指导（的）
authenticity [ɔːθen'tisəti]	n.	可靠性，真实性
miniscule ['miniskjuːl]	a.	微小的
stock-in-trade ['stɔk-in-'treid]	n.	惯用手段；存货
dignity ['digniti]	n.	真正价值；尊严
inappropriate [inə'prəupriit]	a.	不恰当的，不合适的
vulgar ['vʌlgə]	a.	粗俗的
exhibitionist [eksi'biʃənist]	n.；a.	表现狂（的）
idiom ['idiəm]	n.	风格；惯用法；习语
matrix* ['mætriks]	n.	基体；（矩）阵
byelaw ['bailɔː]	n.	细则；地方法规，附则
accommodation [ə'kɔmədeiʃən]	n.	调和；迁就；住处
resultant* [ri'zʌltənt]	a.	作为结果的；合成的
draftsmen ['drɑːftsmən]	n.	绘图员
specification* [spesifi'keiʃən]	n.	（设计，产品等）说明书，规格
vestige ['vestdʒ]	n.	残余；痕迹
autonomy [ɔː'tɔnəmi]	n.	自主权，人身自由；自治
speculative ['spekjulətiv]	a.	思辨的；纯理论的；投机性的
geometric* [dʒiə'metrik]	a.	几何（图形）的；整齐匀称的

anonymous [ə'nɔniməs]	a.	无特色的
intricacy* ['intrikəsi]	n.	错综复杂；理以理解
multitude* ['mʌltitjuːd]	n.	众多，大量
gymnastics [dʒim'næstiks]	n.	绝技；体操
immature [imə'tjuə]	a.	未成熟的；未臻完美的
dichotomy [dai'kɔtəmi]	n.	一分成二；二分法
disparity* [dis'pæriti]	n.	差异；悬殊
privacy ['praivəsi]	n.	独处，隐居；隐私
straddle [strædl]	v.	跨立于
drastic* [dræstik]	a.	激烈的；严厉的
suitability* [sjuːtə'biliti]	n.	适合，适合性
befit [bi'fit]	vt.	适合于
artifact ['ɑːtifækt]	n.	人工制品；低劣艺术品
maxim [mæksim]	n.	基本原理；格言；座右铭
continuum* [kən'tinjuəm]	n.	连续性（体）；统一体

Notes

①in large measure 在很大程度上，多半。
②pseudo-Georgian 仿乔治王朝式的。
③neo-Georgian 新乔治王朝式的
④Beaux Art 古典装饰风格。19 世纪流行于法国及欧洲，源自古典文艺思想的一种建筑装饰风格。

Exercises

Reading Comprehension

Ⅰ. Skim the text and match each of the following ideas with its appropriate paragraph number or numbers in the brackets.

1. The development of International Style. ( )
2. The difficulty in describing basic rules. ( )
3. A response in the field of architecture to the oil crisis in 1970s. ( )
4. A simple design method. ( )
5. Present situation. ( )
6. Conclusion ( )

Ⅱ. Read the text carefully and then choose the best answer among the four choices given to complete each statement.

1. It is difficult to give description to basic rules mainly because _____ .

A) it is unnecessary

B) people do not share the same idea about them

C) there are too many rules

D) the rules may cause disorder in buildings

2. What conclusion can we draw from the Georgian domestic work?

A) There are some merits that we can take from it today.

B) It can be completely introduced into the present.

C) It is the origin of today's skysrapers.

D) It was poorly designed.

3. What result has the oil crisis of 1974 brought about?

A) The life-span of building is longer than before.

B) People turn to other forms of energy.

C) Efforts have been made to reduce the consumption of energy.

D) The revival of Georgian style has come into reality on large scale.

4. In general, the design method introduced in paragraph three _____.

A) is a successful one

B) is of importance even today

C) has advantages in theory and practice

D) is no longer popular

5. The traditional vision of scholarly architect and the cultured client has faded because

_____ .

A) both of them have lost their confidence

B) both of them are bound by lots of restraints

C) an architect is no longer a scholar nor is a client cultured

D) International Style is out of date

6. Which of the following factors does not influence architecture according to paragraph four?

A) Fiancial problems.

B) The number of people in towns and cities.

C) Political changes.

D) Government leaders.

7. What do the contradictions listed in paragraph six tell us?

A) People have different interests.

B) Architects have different taste.

C) There is great chaos in the world of building.

D) Environmental protection has become a focus.

8. What conclusion can we make from the text?

A) Everything has changed now so that people have to adapt themselves to the new world.

B) Long life, low energy and loose fit should serve as the top priority.

C) Architecture has a bright future with the development of science and technology.

D) We should critically learn from the past and develop the new for the present and the future.

Vocabulary

Ⅰ. Match the words in Column A with their corresponding definitions in Column B.

Column A	Column B
1. commitment	a. sth that is continuous
2. crudity	b. consequent
3. continuum	c. roughness or lack of elaborateness
4. disparity	d. greatness of number, size or extent
5. multitude	e. inequality of difference
6. resultant	f. promise or undertaking

Ⅱ. Complete each of the following statements with one of the four choices given below.

1. "Form follows function" is Sullivan's most famous _____ .

A) maxim   B) deduction

C) formula   D) paradigm

2. In architecture, I prefer coherence rather than arbitrariness, simplicity rather than _____ , "both-and" rather than "either-or" .

A) analogy   B) intricacy

C) approximation   D) contradiction

3. A program requires definitive statement about the expected standards of the completed building fabric when it is in use over its lifetime. Such statement is called performance _____ .

A) justification   B) explanation

C) specification   D) matrix

4. "Seek colorful forms for colorfully expressed needs" . We can not imagine what the world would be like if the _____ form of laborer-dwelling and factories were applied to shopping centers and churches！

A) anonymous   B) ingenious

C) spontaneous   D) rigorous

5. The column or wall defines the length and breadth of a space, and the beam or vault its height. Any _____ change in dimension must intrude to blur the statement of how a space is made.

A) cascade   B) diagonal

C) cellular   D) drastic

6. Sicence and technology bring forward problems whose solution demands painstaking

studies before final results can be formulated. Such typical _____ act as stock exchange finds no position in this field.

    A) void   B) speculative

    C) subtle   D) prospective

7. It is believed that the upright stones in the park are _____ of an ancient palace.

    A) remarks   B) profiles

    C) vestiges   D) grids

8. Enclosure is not only required to create a suitable internal climate but also required to provide _____ to keep home a secret.

    A) elegance   B) safety

    C) convection   D) privacy

Writing   **Outline Writing** (4)

Directions: Read the text of Reading Material A of this unit and write a sentence outline of it.

Reading Material A

Design Methods

When design becomes a specialist group exercise as it must be for all complex building problems, the adoption of an acceptable and adaptable design method becomes highly desirable. The six point check list provides a valuable guide to pinpoint the development stage reached, and therefore can reveal the discrepancies of maturing solutions, but to be effective and of practical use, certain characteristics must be expected. For example, the sequence is by no means linear, particularly as the total assembly of a 'system' solution (ie the total building) involves designing within very limited parameters of components and elements. The adoption of components can return consideration of the totality back to the analysis and transformation stages—and in doing so can add or change a practical condition in the definitive programme.

The proliferation of design methodologies, all of which promise some aid at certain stages of particular design problems, has tended to make the theoretical activity an end in itself, without following with a designed technical artifact. [1]It would seem that the individual designer requires external guide lines to ensure the necessary 'drill' in dealing with a limited component design, and a successful design result is more likely at this (component) order of complexity. There remains the massive problem of stimulating ideas vested in the production process. In so far that a conscious application of Method is not only a stimulus but also a control, and recognising that the developing definitive programme is always short of contemporary data, the most attractive and helpful organisation could be in the form of a Programme Workshop. [2]Within this workshop would assemble, under the guidance of the project controller, all the designers and producers as they are appointed, and the task would be:

(a) to agree the appropriate design method strategies in the examination of inventive and conceptual ideas.

(b) to state the standards and specification of required performance (performance specification)

(c) to establish priorities for expected standard in the light of financial limitations (value analysis)

(d) to prepare alternative spatial diagrams for analysis (feasibility studies) from which.

(e) to finalise the definitive programme (operative) and.

(f) to recommend and adopt a final design (spatial).

The workshop team must include an information officer and a building technologist. The team adopts the identification of the problem, the basic programme statement, the evaluation of the site, and the 'literary' search of past solutions, as constraints on the project—and should proceed to apply methods of analysis in converging upon design solutions. [3]In practice, the first three sequences of divergence, analysis and transformation represent the trial ground for ideas, and the second three, synthesis, convergence and evaluation, begin to solidify into an acceptable design. The flow of ideas in the early stages must not be unduly inhibited, but they will be governed by inputs of varying significance from individual members of the workshop. Inevitably, ideas involve a great number of unsupported value judgements, and single designers—architects in control for example—tend to latch on to particular formal solutions at a very early stage. [4]Idea contributions are usually fragmented, dealing with part of a problem. If they contribute some solution to the priorities set, then an idea can move forward through the filter into the assembled information store. Alexander's diagram (illustrated on Fig. 6—1) shows a possible process of interchange of proposals by members of the workshop, which is accumulatory as information is gradually absorbed into the definitive programme.

Two particular problems emerge in any conscious attempt at design control by applying 'method'. They are the problem of redundancy and incompatibility. The early sequence of analysis will be crowded with data (some redundant and some incompatible) which must be identified and resolved by the time the effort towards convergence is made.

AIDA (Analysis of Interconnected Decision Areas)attempts to identify and evaluate all the compatible sets of sub-solutions to a design problem. In the design and selection of a building element the sets of sub-problems involve decision areas where there may be a number of design options, though some will be found to be incompatible.

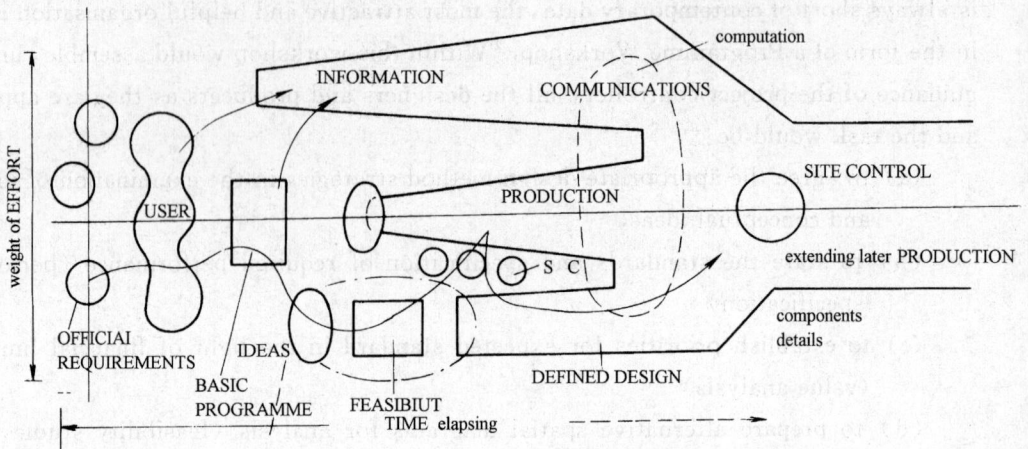

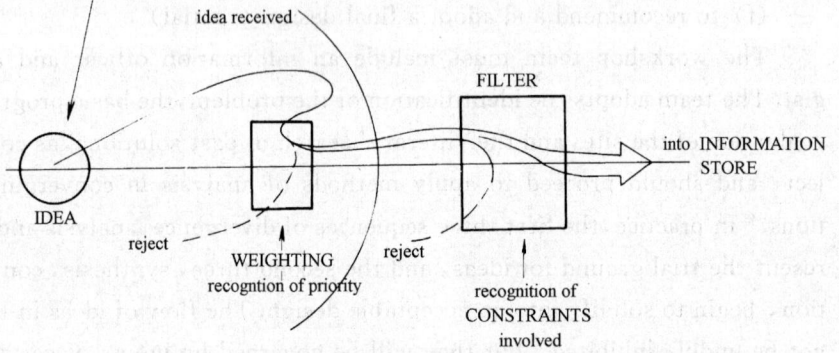

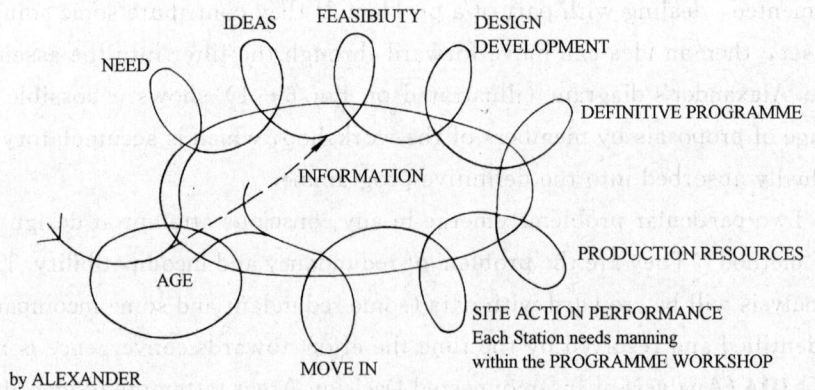

weight of EFFORT

INFORMATION

COMMUNICATIONS

computation

SITE CONTROL

USER

PRODUCTION

extending later PRODUCTION

S C

OFFICIAl
REQUIREMENTS

IDEAS

BASIC
PROGRAMME

FEASIBIUT
TIME elapsing

DEFINED DESIGN

components
details

idea received

FILTER

into INFORMATION
STORE

IDEA

reject

WEIGHTING
recognition of priority

reject

recognition of
CONSTRAINTS
involved

IDEAS

FEASIBIUTY

DESIGN
DEVELOPMENT

NEED

DEFINITIVE PROGRAMME

INFORMATION

PRODUCTION RESOURCES

AGE

SITE ACTION PERFORMANCE
Each Station needs manning
within the PROGRAMME WORKSHOP

MOVE IN

by ALEXANDER

Fig. 6-1

62

Inevitably such methods accept the characteristics of known materials and systems, but future (short term) developments of both, related to their needs or the identification of new constraints, (eg sudden deterioration with time, or a new fire hazard) must receive some consideration. Evolutionary Forecasting must start with the identification of the present situation, recognise its instability, and the likely impact of future events.

In so far as it is possible, future events are projections of present developments. In terms of building, such future projections could be: continuing and alarming rise in costs of fuel; increasing problems of pollution and the introduction of severe controls; payment for water by meter; sanctions to ensure standards of safety and health; compulsory standards of noise and heat insulation, etc. The workshop must take prior decisions as to when such events will become sufficiently significant to require a (present) constituent design change. These activities are figured as a cone expanding with time. Inevitably, in such a technological forecast, there are a lot of assumptions. They may be ill-chosen, and prove to be misconceived, but the reason for the exercise is exploratory, so that the assumptions can be questioned, adjusted, adopted or not adopted, thereby reaching a considered view about the speed and conditions of change. Buildings normally last a long time, and their likely (future) performance requires more care in design than it usually receives.

Notes

①设计方法的扩展对于解决某些设计阶段出现的特定的设计困难有所帮助。由于设计人员不必再参考曾设计过的建筑产品, 理论活动也达到了自身的目的。

②只要有意识地利用设计方法不仅仅是一种刺激因素, 而且还是一种控制手段, 并且认识到建设一个特定的工程项目总是缺乏现成的数据, 那么最有用, 最富吸引力的组织形式可能就是项目组。"in so far that" ＝in so far as, 是一个短语连词, 用来引导表示"范围"或"限度"的状语从句, 意为"就……而论", "在……范围内", 可有不同译法。

③converge upon: 汇集, 集中。

④latch on to (或 onto): 抓住; 缠住不放。

Reading Material B

Architects and Internet

Every few years, high technology spontaneously produces another one of these buzz words that nobody can really define. We've put up with cyberspace and virtual reality and multimedia. ①But now, even the Vice-President of the United States is mouthing the phrase "information highway". ②It almost makes you long for the days of Dan Quayle, for whom a potatoe [sic] was complex and puzzling technology. ③

The information highway will be how most people imagine it: some kind of wire carrying video, graphics, text and stereo sound. Lots and lots of data flood the world. But for most people, the reality of the information highway today is a thing called Internet. [4]

The Internet is based on a network called the ARPAnet that was developed by engineers and computer scientists in the U.S military over two decades ago. [5] They needed a means of sending information so that it always got through no matter what happened——be it bombs, sabotage or mechanical breakdown. They did this by hooking computers together in a web of machines that meant if one link was severed, there was always another route available, and another and another. In what amounts to one of the great ironies of history, according to Ed Krol, in *The whole Internet Catalog ε User's Guide*, the most successful test of the approach came during the Gulf War when the U.S. military had a difficult time destroying Iraqi communications because they too were using an Internet style approach. [6]

But in more peaceful pursuits this computer to computer linkage had an interesting side effect. When universities adopted the protocols of Internet, they found that by sending typed messages via the telephone lines from one university's computer to another they could often avoid long-distance charges. [7] This is still one of the most economical characteristics of the Internet. It can send a message around the world for the price of a local telephone call. (Some have also noted that the mere existence of the Internet confirms that the telephone companies have created a completely artificial pricing structure for long distance charges)

People would type messages on a terminal at one university and they would be sent to the "mailbox" of their correspondent. [8] It was a lot more like letters than a conversation, and hence it was called electronic mail, or e-mail for short. [9] Messages might only be transmitted every hour or more and then you had to wait for a reply until the other person opened their mailbox and typed a response. And those messages were always just text.

The reason that people were only sending data like text across the Internet is because that's all the information you can send with a bandwidth of 14.4k baud (14, 400 bits per second) which is the limit of commercially available modems. To send a video signal, you need a system with a baud rate of between 100 and 200k. In other words, we are still a long way from having interactive movies on our home computers. But you'd never know this from the popular press. They're touting fibre optics as if it were sprouting like crab grass. And fibre optic cables are impressive——they can carry gigabits worth of information. [10] A gigabit is a million bits or 1000k. With this bandwidth you can carry just about anything——movies, music, virtual reality and video-conferencing. [11] It even holds the possibility of interactive, shared environments where an architect and an engineer, both in different cities, may meet in a virtual building to refine its design.

But one of the biggest hurdles is not technological. It's how to get architects to use this stuff. As Sandall says, "One of the real challenges is to convince people that there's something worthwhile in these services. The education process is extremely important. For the technophobes, you even need to show them what a modem is. "②Fortunately, readers of this column will never suffer that crushing humiliation.

In other words, the technologies, the information, and even the public's receptiveness are still sadly lacking. The imagined uses are far from real. Small wonder that it's still only engineers and computer scientists that rave about the Net. But I must admit that I'm fixated on engineers and how they continually seem to be involved with the critical developments of the 20th century, while our profession is relegated to the sidelines. I often wonder what would have happened if architects had taken a broader view of design and had orchestrated the design of networks, such as Internet. While some may see the Net as a purely technical problem, one of its weakest parts is its user interface. Perhaps if architects, with their knowledge of how people behave, had been involved, we would all be using Internet today.

Just like computers in the early days, Interet is someting to be approached with caution. Someday it will be an important part of your practice. Someday, much of your design work will be conducted over the Net. And someday, it will be jam packed with useful information, be easy to use and be dirt cheap to be involved with. That day's not here yet, but keep your ear to the fibre because it's on its way.

Notes

①cyberspace（计算机）网络空间；virtual reality 虚拟现实；multimedia 多媒体。

②information highway 信息高速公路。

③Dan Quayle 丹·奎尔，美布什政府的副总统。

④Internet 互联网络。

⑤ARPAnet＝Advanced Research Projects Agency networks （美）高级研究规划局计算机网络。

⑥Gulf War 海湾战争（指 1991 年美国与伊拉克之间的战争）。

⑦Protocol（计算机）规程。

⑧mailbox 此处指电子邮件信箱。

⑨electronic mail 电子邮件（简称 e-mail）。

⑩fibre optic cable 光学纤维通讯电缆，简称光缆。

⑪video-conference 电视会议。

⑫technophobe 患技术恐惧症者（指害怕技术对社会及环境造成不良影响的人）；modem 调制解调器

UNIT SEVEN

Text   Masonry: Reaching New Heights

[1]   The new structural design standard for masonry, CSA S304. 1 "Masonry Design for Buildings" has gone through the balloting and revision process and is slated to be published next month. ①Increases in basic load carrying capabilities have resulted, generally in the 30% range, but sometimes up to 100%. ②

[2]   In addition to making a much more effective use of the strength of reinforcement and the inherently great compressive strength of masonry, the new design standard sets out provisions which permit significant increases in the slenderness of loadbearing masonry walls. That is, either greater heights can be accommodated with standard wall thicknesses, or thinner walls can be used compared to current practices. ③These changes will of course affect the design of loadbearing masonry, particularly tall walls in single-storey buildings where gravity loads are relatively low.

[3]   Slenderness in loadbearing walls has usually been described using the height-to-thickness ratio, h/t. Traditionally, standards have prescribed a maximum slenderness, and this option continues where a maximum $h/t=20$ is specified for Empirical Design. ④Certain limits on wind pressure and seismic zone must be satisfied, and the permitted slenderness is reduced to account for openings in the wall. ⑤

[4]   The empirical approach is very popular with both architects and engineers. The calculations are very simple and take little time and, in many cases, there is no obvious benefit gained by going through the much more complex and more time-consuming Design Based on Engineering Analysis. ⑥Empirical Design, however, is not applicable to reinforced masonry, and this fact, plus the new design provisions which explicitly permit much more slender walls, make Engineered Design a very attractive option.

Engineering the Tall and Slim

[5]   Another benefit of Engineered Design comes from today's predominantuse of very light roof systems on single-storey masonry buildings. These roofs often require substantial anchorage of the roof to avoid having the roof lift off the wall due to wind uplift forces. Frequently, reinforcing bars must be anchored several metres down into the wall to hold the roof secure. In such cases. the wall is already partially reinforced and it costs very little to continue the reinforcement to the foundation so that the wall is reinforced over its full height. Given this situation, there is an opportunity to use the reinforcement to resist out-of-plane bending in the wall due to wind pressure as well as to hold the roof down.

[6]   In the new design standard, a slenderness limit of $kh/t=30$ applies to all reinforced

or unreinforced walls provided that calculated strengths are sufficient to carry the applied loads. In this equation, the "k" term is an "effective height" factor which varies between 0. 8 and 1. 0 to account for wall support conditions. The new standard can translate into a wall almost twice as high as one calculated using Empirical Design.[7]For example, using a standard 20 cm masonry unit (actual thickness t＝0. 19 m), the maximum wall height ranges between $h=30t\div k=30$ (0. 19) $\div 1=5. 7$m and 30 (0. 19) $\div 0. 80=7. 125$m. This maximum compares to $h=20(0. 19)=3. 8$m for Empirical Design. In most cases, reinforcement at fairly wide spacing can satisfy the strength requirements and, when gravity loads are light (e. g. , weight of roof, services, snow and rain), there is often a sizable reserve capacity.[8]

[7]　　To take advantage of the inherent flexural capacity of reinforced masonry, provisions for the design of Very Slender Walls (with kh/t more than 30) are an entirely new feature of the design standard.[9]To use this design method the axial load must be less than 10% of the axial capacity of the section, and the maximum amount of reinforcement is limited to ensure ductile behaviour. On this basis, slenderness ratios (h/t) well over 40 are often achievable. This would mean, for example, that on a building using 20 cm units, a wall height of 7. 6m or more is possible.

Practical Points and Economies

[8]　　For structural designers, the design provisions to account for slenderness and to calculate capacities closely parallel the provisions for the design of reinforced concrete. Although there will be a learning period, most structural designers have extensive experience in this area and should have little trouble making the transition. For very slender walls, the direct calculations of deflection for both serviceability and strength checks are new but are standard forms of analysis. Although the structural design may cost slightly more than when the rules-of-thumb in Empirical Design are used, the building costs will be substantially less. There is even a saving in floor area.

[9]　　The design of Very Slender Walls requires relatively high masonry compressive strengths. These strengths are achievable within the range of products currently available but, because they are non-standard (i. e. block strength greater than 15 MPa), testing and quality control are more important. Construction details should optimize the economic benefits of, for example, reinforcing a 20 cm masonry wall at 1. 2 m bar spacing compared to using 30 cm units in unreinforced walls or using pilaster construction. Wide bar spacing and using grout only in cells where it is needed to hold the reinforcement in place help reduce costs.

[10]　　The use of reinforced masonry for Slender or Very Slender Walls produces more economical construction, satisfies the requirement to hold roofs down and, because of the reinforcement, provides a tougher structure which is more able to resist unexpected

loads. For the building envelope, there is little effect other than perhaps that the workmanship may be improved due to the structural requirements. Provisions resulting in similar designs have existed in the Uniform Building Code (applicable to most of the western U-nited States)for the past 10 years. ⑩They have resulted in economically and technically successful designs.

Future advances

[11]   Because deflection often controls wall design, an area for improvement is to increase the stiffness of the wall. Experience with prestressed concrete and early results from tests of prestressed masonry suggest that prestressed reinforcement is the next opportunity for design of even more slender walls. The presence of the prestressed reinforcement delays the occurrence of flexural cracks and hence results in very much reduced deflections. Although prestressed masonry is permitted in the new design standard, not much guidance is given. However, with tests showing that slenderness around $h/t = 60$ may be possible, this approach can be considered for special projects. With parallel developments in Australia, Switzerland, the U. K. and the U. S. A. , the option of using prestressed masonry on a regular basis should not be too far down the line. ⑪

New Words and Expressions

ballot ['bælət]	v.	投票
slate [sleit]	vt.	预定
slenderness ['slendənis]	n.	高厚比
option* ['ɔpʃən]	n.	选择，选择权（事物）
empirical* [em'pirikəl]	a.	（根据）经验的，经验主义的
seismic* ['saizmik]	a.	地震的
anchorage ['æŋkəridʒ]	n.	锚固，固定
uplift [ʌp'lift]	n.	上升，浮升力
secure [si'kiuə]	a.	牢固的，稳定的
equation [i'kweiʃən]	n.	等式，方程式
factor ['fæktə]	n.	系数
spacing* ['speisiŋ]	n.	间距，间隔
sizable ['saizəbl]	a.	相当大的，广大的
flexural* [flekʃərəl]	a.	变形的，挠曲的
ductile* ['dʌktail]	a.	可延展的，塑性的
deflection [di'flekʃən]	n.	变形的，偏差
rules-of-thumb	n.	经验做法，较粗糙的方法
non-standard ['nɔn'stændəd]	a.	非标准的

68

pilaster [pi'læstə]	n.	壁柱，半露柱
grout [graut]	n.	灰浆，沙浆
prestressed ['priː'strest]	a.	预应力的
compressive strength		抗压强度
gravity load		静荷载
out-of-plane bending		平面变形
masonry unit		砌块
construction details		施工图
hold…in place		把……固定就位，固定在适当位置

Notes

①revision process 修订过程。

②basic load carrying capabilities 基本承载能力。

③…be accommodated with standard wall thicknesses ……与标准墙厚相适应。意即：按标准墙厚增加高度。

④Empirical Design 经验设计方法。

⑤account for sth 是……的原因，考虑到……。

⑥Design Based on Engineering Analysis 根据工程分析进行设计的方法，工程分析设计。

⑦translate into 转变成。此处意为：可以允许建造。

⑧reinforcement at wide spacing 宽间距配置钢筋；reserve capacity 储备承载能力。

⑨Very Slender Walls 超薄墙体。

⑩Uniform Building Code 通用建筑法规。

⑪on a regular basis 广泛地。…not be too far down the line 不会为期太远。

Exercise

Reading Comprehension

Ⅰ. Say whether the following statements are true (T) or false (F) according to the text.

1. The purpose of this article is to criticise objectively the advantages and disadvantages of the new structural design standard for masonry. （　　）

2. When the new structural design standard for masonry comes into effect, Empirical Design will be no longer useful. （　　）

3. Though the new structural design standard is advantageous, it will take most structural engineers quite a long time to get familiar with it. （　　）

4. The practice in most of the western United States for the past ten years may prove that there will be little effect on the building envelope except some possible improvements on the workmanship. （　　）

5. The author believes that in the near future prestressed masonry will be popularly used.   ( )

II. Read the text carefully and then choose the best answer among the four choices given to complete each statement.

1. Compared to current practices, the new structural design permits _____ .
    A) greater slenderness of loadbearing masonry walls
    B) greater heights of loadbearing masonry walls
    C) greater thickness of loadbearing masonry walls
    D) greater loadbearing capabilities

2. The empirical approach is simpler and takes less time than Engineered design except for _____ .
    A) reinforced masonry   B) masonry units
    C) reinforcement   D) prestressed concrete

3. In the equation $kh/t=30$, k stands for _____ .
    A) gravity loads   B) reserved capacity
    C) effective height factor   D) applied loads

4. To make use of the new design method, _____ must be less than 10% of the axial capacity of the section.
    A) flexural capacity   B) the axial load
    C) ductile behaviour   D) the maximum reinforcement

5. For the achievement of relatively high masonry compressive strengths for the design of Very Slender Walls, _____ if non-standard products are employed.
    A) wide bar spacing is necessary
    B) grout must be used in the cells of reinforcement
    C) testing and quality control are more important
    D) construction details should optimize the economic benefits

6. For Very Slender Walls, _____ may provide tougher structure to resist unexpected loads.
    A) the building envelope   B) reinforcement in the wall
    C) masonry units   D) the use of reinforced masonry

7. To resist _____ , stiffness of the wall must be increased.
    A) unexpected loads   B) wind pressure
    C) the deflection of the wall   D) the uplift forces

8. Making use of prestressed reinforcement may _____ .
    A) delay the occurrency of flexural cracks
    B) lead to the design of higher walls
    C) result in new design standard
    D) speed up parallel development in other countries

70

Vocabulary

I. Match the words in Column A with their corresponding definitions in Column B.

    Column A   Column B

    1. slenderness   a. a rectangular column set into a wall, often as an ornament

    2. empirical   b. the change of shape or position caused by force or pressure

    3. ductile   c. the ratio of the height to the thickness of a wall

    4. deflection   d. a quick but not very exact way of doing something, learnt by

                              practical experience.

    5. rules-of-thumb   e. guided by practical experience rather than by scientific ideas or

                              theory

    6. pilaster   f. with the quality of the shape being ready to be changed easily

II. Complete each of the following statements with one of the four choices given below.

1. The new standards governing the construction of bridges are _____ to come into effect next September.

    A) cascaded   B) balloted   C) slated   D) aligned

2. By the time the engineers will have had two _____ to their hand. One is empirical and the other is by engineered analysis.

    A) alterations   B) options   C) margins   D) correlations

3. When designing a wall, the designer should consider not only the ductility but also the _____ strength.

    A) compressive   B) puncture

    C) tensile   D) adhesive

4. E=Mc2 is called Einstain _____, which is known to many but really understood by a few.

    A) calculation   B) regulation

    C) equation   D) conduction

5. The deep _____ of the roof system into the wall may greatly increase the strength of the wall.

    A) reinforcement   B) pilaster   C) bending   D) anchorage

6. In the design of a structure, there is usually a _____ reserve capacity to account for the unexpected loads.

    A) facile   B) sizable   C) elegant   D) domain

7. The author believes that the new standards will cause greater _____ of masonry walls.

    A) slenderness   B) axial   C) derivation   D) inlet

8. Under such a condition, even a wide _____ of reinforcement   may satisfy the structural requirements.

A) uplift   B) spacing   C) pilaster   D) masonry

Writing   Summary Writing (1)

Summarizing means writing a short version of an article. To write a summary, you must skim the article so as to have a general idea of the material, underline the main points, make a list of all the points to be used and then with this list write the summary in an Introduction-Body-Conclusion structure, with transition words like "but", "and", "however", "also", etc.

Directions: The following is a summary of the text of Unit Seven and there are several words missing. Now fill in the blanks with some of the words given below: (10 words given, 8 blanks to be filled.)

masonry	provisions	structural	reinforced	slenderness
empirical	thickness	behaviour	compressive	stiffness

The new _____ design standard for _____ will be published soon which sets out that permit greater _____ of loadbearing masonry walls. Advantages of the new standard over the _____ method are in the following two aspects: the use of very light roof systems and the construction of taller and thinner masonry walls, _____ or unreinforced. The new standard is easy to learn, requires higher masonry _____ strengths but may produce economically and technically more successful designs. For the increase of the _____, a regular use of prestressed masonry will be realized in the near future.

Reading Material A

Building Code: Checking Out the New Regulations

[1]   Architects occasionally grumble at the regulatory "overhead" in their work. Most, however, will agree that building codes in Canada are very good. Their merits can be very apparent to designers who work outside Canada. The United States, for example, has no common national code, and none of their major agencies that produce codes is directly supported by a national construction research laboratory. Canadians who work in the U. S. also quickly become aware of code differences between states, and the difficulty in using building technologies that are commonplace here.

[2]   Canadian codes are comparatively flexible and clear. There is also a consistent effort to base them on building science, not just opinion or convention. The anchor of the Canadian code system is the National Building Code of Canada (NBC), a model code produced by the Canadian Commission on the Building and Fire Codes, an independent body supported by the National Research Council (NRC)①The code is developed with extensive input from

the construction industry. A five-year review cycle ensures it is easier to use, allows recent proven technologies to be used, and addresses emerging issues in the health and safety aspects and the durability of buildings. ②

[3]　　There are many improvements in the 1995 NBC due out which will help architects design better buildings. ③Three are discussed below. Full details are available in a series of cross Canada seminars which will accompany the Code's release in the fall.

Material Breakdown and Air Barriers

[4]　　Architects will notice immediately that the title of Part 5 in the 1995 NBC has changed from "Wind, Water and Vapour" to "Environmental Separation. " This change is made in recognition that the provisions of Part 5 are intended to deal generically with building elements that separate environmentally dissimilar spaces. ④Such elements can be within a building, or between the building and outside, including between the building and the ground. The objective is to create a more comfortable and healthy indoor environment through the control of condensation and the transfer of heat, air and moisture through building elements that separate the different spaces.

[5]　　The 1995 NBC is more specific than the 1990 Code in describing what environmental loads and deterioration mechanisms must be dealt with. Where the 1990 Code only addressed corrosion, for example, the 1995 NBC addresses all mechanisms of deterioration which might be expected given the materials used and their service environment. Of key importance to architects is that they must now design building components and select materials with some understanding of their ability to resist deterioration. Although the requirements are directed at preventing premature failures that create a health and safety hazard, they will also generally improve the long-term performance of the building envelope. ⑤

[6]　　Another major change in Part 5 is the specification of a material leakage criterion for the principal airtight component of the air barrier system. The previous Code required only that the air barrier be "continuous" and "effective", two terms which did not provide sufficient direction to the designer. Now a maximum air leakage characteristic is specified for the material in the air-barrier system that provides the principal resistance to air leakage.

[7]　　A material characteristic is specified rather than the overall performance of the air barrier systems in recognition of the difficulty in actually testing the airtightness of large buildings. The specified maximum air leakage rate (0.02 L/ (sec • m²) at 75 Pa) was based on that of unpainted interior drywall. ⑥This material is relatively leaky compared to many other commonly used air barrier materials, but has been demonstrated to perform in the field.

73

More Sprinklers, More Freedom

[8]   Another example of change in the 1995 NBC is in Part 3, fire protection. Because of the undeniable effectiveness of sprinklers in protecting life and property, sprinklers will be mandatory in some building types where they were not required before. These include residential buildings of more than three storeys, buildings for large assemblies, prisons, hospitals, nursing homes and the like. ⑦The code committee recognized that there are increased costs associated with the installation of sprinklers. These costs, however, can be balanced by costsaving measures given elsewhere in Part 3.

[9]   The newly permitted trade-offs can be particularly useful in building renovations. Although the 1995 NBC will not impose a sprinkler requirement on existing buildings, the decision to install sprinklers can lead to important cost-saving opportunities. Installing sprinklers can, for example, allow for the construction of a large addition to a building, allow a reduction in the rating of a fire separation between parts of a building, or permit a relaxation in fire-fighting access provisions. ⑧A fully automated sprinkler system will give more flexibility in the choice of load-bearing structural elements and non-bearing partition systems within a floor. In general, sprinklers should allow building officials to accept many conditions that were previously not allowed.

Ventilating Homes

[10]   The ventilation requirements in Part 9 have been made much clearer and more effective. Ventilation requirements for houses were first introduced in the 1985 NBC. These rather unsophisticated provisions were modified in 1990 as the need for mechanical ventilation became more widely accepted.

[11]   Through research conducted at NRC and elsewhere, there is now a much better understanding of residential air quality issues and the performance of combustion appliances. Suitable technologies have been developed to meet system performance needs. The culmination of this work was CSA Standard F326 "Residential Mechanical Ventilation Systems," which is now referenced in the 1995 NBC. CSA F326 allows a great deal of flexibility in how ventilation requirements are to be met. Because the standard is so comprehensive, however, and is written in performance terms, the 1995 NBC also includes alternatively prescriptively described systems that can be used by those less experienced in the design of ventilation systems.

[12]   In the 1995 NBC, houses will require a total installed ventilation capacity based on the number and types of rooms. This works out to about 0.3 air changes per hour. ⑨All ventilation systems will require a central fan capable of meeting half the total ventilation requirement. It must also be capable of continuous and quiet operation. Other fans, in loca-

tions such as kitchens and bathrooms, are required to provide the remaining ventilation capacity.

[13]   Another major change, therefore, is that all new houses will have ducted ventilation systems.⑩These new provisions, and others dealing with combustion appliances, will do much to ensure that the indoor environment will be healthier and more comfortable.

Notes

①anchor 支撑点;

the National Building Code of Canada 加拿大全国建筑法规; the Canadian Commission on the Building and Fire Codes 加拿大建筑与防火法规委员会; National Research Council (of Canada) 加拿大全国科学研究委员会。

②长达五年的试行验证周期确保该法规使用更加便利,允许采用最新成熟技术,考虑到健康和安全方面的新问题以及建筑物的经久耐用。

③due out 待发的。

④作出这一变动是因为认识到第五章各条款的制订是要广泛地涉及将不同环境的空间进行分隔的建筑构件。

⑤尽管有关规定旨在防止出现威胁健康或安全的过早断裂,这些规定也将广泛改善建筑外层的长期性能。premature failure 过早损坏(断裂)。

⑥该法规的最大空气渗透率(气压 75Pa 条件下 $0.02L/s \cdot m^2$)是以未抹涂层的干燥内墙的空气渗透率为基准的。

⑦residential buildings 居住类型建筑; buildings for large assemblies 大型聚会场所。

⑧例如,安装防火喷水设备可以允许原有建筑大幅扩建,允许降低一幢建筑不同部分之间防火隔离等级,或者允许放松防火安全通道的有关要求。

⑨This works out to… 通风能力可以达到……。

⑩ducted ventilation systems 管道通风系统。

Reading Material B

Means of Escape

This Approved Document, which takes effect
on 1 June 1992, deals with the following
requirement from Part B of Schedule 1 to
the Building Regulations 1991:

Requirement

Means of escape

B1. The building shall be designed and constructed so that there
are means of escape in case of fire from the building to a place
of safety outside the building capable of being safely and effectively used at all material times.

Limits on application

Requirement B1 does not apply to any prison provided under section
33 of The Prisons Act 1952 (power to provide prisons etc.)

Guidance
Performance

In the Secretary of State's view the requirement of B1 will be met if:

a. there are routes of sufficient number and capacity, which are suitably located to enable persons to escape to a place of safety in the event of fire;

b. the routes are sufficiently protected from the effects of fire by enclosure where necessary;

c. the routes are adequately lit;

d. the exits are suitably signed; and if

e. there are appropriate facilities to either limit the ingress of smoke to the escape
route (s) or suitable measures are taken to restrict the fire and remove smoke; all to an extent necessary depending on the use of the building, its size and height. [1]

Introduction

These provisions relate to building work and material changes of use which are subject
to the functional requirement B1, and they may therefore affect new or existing buildings. They are concerned with the measures necessary to ensure reasonable facilities for
means of escape in case of fire. They are only concerned with structural fire precautions
where these are necessary to safeguard escape routes.

They assume that in the design of the building, reliance should not be placed on external rescue by the fire service. The document has been prepared on the basis that, in an e-
mergency, the occupants of any part of a building should be able to escape safely without
any external assistance. [2]

Special considerations, however, apply to some institutional buildings in which the principle of evacuation without assistance is not practical. ③

It should also be noted that the guidance for 1 and 2 storey dwellings is limited to the provision of openable windows for emergency egress in certain situations, and to the provision of smoke alarms. ④

Attention is drawn to the fact that there may be other legislation imposing requirements for means of escape in case of fire with which the building must comply, and which operates when the building is brought into use. The main legislation in this area is the Fire Precautions Act 1971, generally enforced by the fire authority, which provides for the designation of certain uses of premises for which a fire certificate is required and, in the case of certain smaller premises, imposes a statutory duty on the occupiers to provide reasonable means of escape in case of fire. ⑤

Although there is no requirement under the building regulations to provide a means of giving warning in case of fire, the provision of an appropriate warning system is an essential element in the overall strategy for fire safety in an occupied building. Most places of work, many public assembly buildings and institutional and residential care buildings, will be subject to a requirement under other legislation, to provide appropriate means of giving warning in case of fire. ⑥British Standard 5839: Part 1 gives guidance on suitable fire warning for various uses of premises.

Interaction with other legislation

Under the Fire Precautions Act, unless there are regulations made under Section 12 of that Act (and it is necessary to make requirements to satisfy those regulations), fire authorities cannot as a condition for issuing a fire certificate, make requirements for structural or other alterations relating to escape, if the plans of the building comply with building regulations. However if the fire authority is satisfied that the means of escape in case of fire are inadequate by reason of matters concerning particulars which were not required to be supplied to the local authority, in connection with the deposit of plans for building regulation purposes, then the fire authority is not barred from making requirements. ⑦

In addition it should be noted that there are some things that may be required under the Fire Precautions Act that are outside the scope of the building regulations. One example is the provision of first aid fire fighting equipment, for use by the occupants.

Notes

①In the secretary of State's view 按照国务大臣的见解；by enclosure where necessary 借助于必要之处的外围屏蔽；suitably signed 有适当标识；ingress 入口；通道。…all to the extent…and height 所有这些的必要程度取决于建筑物用途、大小及高度。

②The document has been prepared on the basis that… 这一文件的制定是基于如下要求：

......。

③然而，对于应用自救疏散原则不实际的一些医院建筑，应该有专门考虑的措施。

④openable windows for emergency egress 可供用作紧急出口的可开启的窗户。

⑤这方面的主要法令是1971年颁布的《防火安全法》。该法一般由消防部门监督实施。该法规定了必须获得消防安全证书的房产的某些指定用途。对于某些较小的房产，该法还强制规定了房产使用者提供合理的防火安全设备的法定义务。

⑥大多数工作场所，许多公众聚集的建筑以及医疗护理建筑等都必须按其他法令的要求，提供火灾报警的适当手段。

⑦然而，如果依据为了检查是否符合建筑法规而存放的平面图中涉及有关条款的材料（这些材料以前不必交给当地消防部门），消防部门确信火灾安全设施不完备，那么消防部门就可不受限制而提出变动要求。

UNIT EIGHT

Text   **Green Buildings**

[1]   Fundamentally, 'Green Design' is not an identifiable objective but an attitude of mind. It means seeking to adapt our way of life to a more sustainable equilibrium with our fragile planet. This may eventually mean radical changes to how we live, but today for us as engineers it means that we must use our wit, our intellect and our innovative ability to develop technical solutions which work in greater harmony with our planet. This approach certainly involves a realistic attitude to problem-solving, addressing all the underlying issues. ①It also demands reappraisal of conventional solutions and standards.

[2]   Consider, for example, a green approach to an appropriate indoor environment. The conventional solution is to 'manufacture' a totally artificial climate out of 'Black boxes', with all the considerable energy and resources that involves. ②But the basic environmental needs of human beings can largely be met without these devices. Nature can be the prime provider, with mechanical systems giving secondary support. Thus most of the lighting can be by sunlight, cooling by ambient air and heating by human bodies and office equipment. These natural sources can be supplemented by other natural means: solar heating, ventilation driven by wind pressures and by solar buoyancy, cooling by water evaporation. ③These are ancient principles; modern computer-based methods of analysis and simulation enable us to understand them better and apply them with confidence. ④

[3]   Comfort criteria are another part of the story. Convention has it that we need 500 lux illumination and temperatures within a degree of 22℃, even though this over-simplified approach does not reflect our full psychological and physiological needs. ⑤Air-conditioning systems may control air temperature but, because they do not recognise the full range of individual needs and expectations, too often they result in dissatisfied occupants. Today, comfort is being redefined to allow room temperatures that reflect daily and seasonal effects and which permit variations based on individual expectations combined with increased control over their local environment.

[4]   The third element in the green approach to the building environment is the building itself: its form, facade and materials. These act together as climate modifier, smoothing and redirecting the fluctuations of nature. Thus the external wall can capture daylight and transmit it to the inside. It can protect against excess glare, provide shading, ventilation air and cooling ability. It contains internal heat in winter and it provides visual contact with the world outside. Within the building, air movement can be directed by roof form, thermal flues, and atria controlled by louvred openings. The buildings that come from this approach tend to be simpler and more integrated. Internal conditions tend to be more stable, remaining moderate even at extremes of outdoor temperature. They have more flexibility. Should

future circumstances demand it, a passively-cooled, naturally-ventilated building can usually have airconditioning added, but the converse is rarely possible. Capital costs can be reduced. Running costs are less, energy consumption and pollution emissions are lower, and the use of nonsustainable resources is reduced. ⑧Occupants have more control; they are less at the mercy of machinery, the environment is more human and—the real objective—they feel more comfortable.

[5]　　Examples of green building philosophies in practice can be seen in the 22-storey Austrian Cultural Centre in New York City. Designed by Atelier Raimund Abraham, this building uses solar panels, heat pumps, high insulation standards and occupancy and daylight sensors to create an energy-efficient environment.

[6]　　The Cable & Wireless training facility in Coventry designed by MacCormac Jamieson Prichard uses the wave form of the teaching room roofs to generate buoyancy-driven cross-ventilation sufficient to remove the high internal heat gains generated by information technology equipment.

[7]　　The Inland Revenue Centre in Nottingham, designed by Michael Hopkins and Partners, provides 40 000m^2 of naturally ventilated office and ancillary accommodation for completion in late 1994. Its highly integrated architectural, structural and environmental form gives excellent delighting, solar shading and thermal flywheel abilities. ⑨Glazed stair towers provide solar and wind assistance to natural ventilation. The project is the first to gain maximum points under the Building Research Establishment Environmental Assessment Method. ⑩

[8]　　The GSW Headquarters building in Berlin designed by Sauerbruch & Hutton is a 23-storey tower block linked to the 1950s building. A double facade on the west elevation creates thermal flues and induces natural ventilation, thereby eliminating any need for air-conditioning.

[9]　　The brief for the new 6 000m^2 Learning Resource Centre for Anglia Polytechnic University currently on site in Essex, called for an environmentally-conscious low-energy building. In a design by the ECD Partnership, the key elements involve an integrated approach using natural ventilation and exposed high thermal capacity structure. Daylighting at the perimeter is maximised by the window design which incorporates twin internal light shelves. Artificial lighting and opening windows are controlled from the central computer.

New Words and Expressions

sustainable [səs'teinəbl]	a.	可持久的，可维持的
equilibrium* [ˌiːkwi'libriəm]	n.	平衡，均衡
fragile ['frædʒail]	a.	脆弱的，易损坏的
intellect ['intilekt]	n.	才智，智力
underlying* [ˌʌndə'laiiŋ]	a.	潜在的，在下的

ambient ['æmbiənt]	*a.*	周围的，大气的
ventilation* [venti'leiʃən]	*n.*	通风（设备）
buoyancy* ['bɔiənsi]	*n.*	浮力，浮性
simulation [simju'leiʃn]	*n.*	模拟，模仿
lux [lʌks]	*n.*	勒克司（照度单位）
physiological [ˌfiziə'lɔdʒikəl]	*a.*	生理学的，生理的
fluctuation* [flʌktju'eiʃən]	*n.*	变化，波动
flue [fluː]	*n.*	暖气管，烟道
atrium ['ɑːtriəm]	*n.*	天井
louver ['luːvə]	*n.*	百叶窗
converse ['kɔnvəːs]	*a.*	相反的，逆的
emission* [i'miʃən]	*n.*	排放，放射，发射
Coventry ['kɔvəntri]	*n.*	考文垂（英国城市）
ancillary [æn'siləri]	*a.*	辅助的，附属的
sensor* ['sensə]	*n.*	传感器，灵敏元件
revenue* ['revinjuː]	*n.*	税收，税务局（署）
Nottingham ['nɔtiŋəm]	*n.*	诺丁汉（英国地名）
flywheel [flaihwiːl]	*n.*	飞轮
elevation [eli'veiən]	*n.*	正面（图），立视（图）
brief [briːf]	*n.*	摘要，短文，简令
polytechnic [pɔli'teknik]	*a.*	工艺的，多种科技的
	n.	工业大学
partnership ['pɑːtnəʃip]	*n.*	合伙公司，合伙关系
maximize* ['mæksimaiz]	*v.*	使达到最大值，使极大
solar panel		太阳能板

Notes

①problem-solving 解决问题的方法。address *vt.* 从事，研究解决。addressing 短语修饰说明 problem-solving。

② "Black boxes" 喻指封闭的空间。

③solar buoyancy 日照产生的空气升力。

④modern computer-based methods of analysis and simulation 现代计算机分析模拟方法。

⑤Convention has it that… 通常以为……。

⑥Should…demand it 相当于 if 虚拟条件句，但主句用的是陈述语气。passively-cooled 被动制冷的；the converse 指相反的情况。

⑦Capital costs 投资成本。

⑧Running costs 管理成本。pollution emissions 引起污染的各种物质和气体的排放；non-sustainable resources 非永久性能源。

⑨flywheel 喻指调节。

⑩Building Research Establishment Environmental Assessment Method 建筑研究中心环境
    评估。

Exercise

Reading Comprehension

Ⅰ. Say whether the following statements are true (T) or false (F) according to the text.

1. "Green Design" should be the purpose of the architecture at the modern times. ( )

2. To an appropriate indoor environment, a conventional solution is to make use of any
    energy and resources available.   ( )

3. The green approach is to do without any mechanical support.   ( )

4. For the purpose of green design, the conventional comfort criteria should be modified.
                                                                                        ( )

5. An appropriate indoor environment can be achieved through selective form, facade and
    materials of the building.   ( )

Ⅱ. Read the text carefully and then choose the best answer among the four choices given
    to complete each statement.

1. The author's attitude toward the green design is _____ .

    A) critical   B) suspicious   C) positive   D) vague

2. In creating an appropriate indoor environment, the basic difference between a conven-
    tional approach and a green approach is _____ .

    A) the degree the needs of human beings are met

    B) the degree the natural sources are made use of

    C) the amount the artificial energy and resources are employed

    D) the way the cooling and heating systems are used

3. The author believes that _____ .

    A) the conventional comfort criteria are satisfactory to our psychological and physio-
        logical needs

    B) comfort criteria may vary according to individual variations

    C) modern technologies are of little significance in green design

    D) the purpose of green design is to reduce human beings' reliance on mechanical
        means

4. In paragraph 2, the expression "Black boxes" may most probably refer to _____ .

    A) the buildings furnished with various technologies.

    B) the computers controlling the buildings

    C) the devices recording the management of the buildings

    D) the mechanical devices installed in the buildings

5. The example buildings mentioned in the passage are to illustrate _____ .

A) the importance of high-technology in green buildings

B) the way natural ventilation is used

C) the way green design is practiced

D) the way natural resource consumption is reduced

6. "The third element in the green approach" refers to _____ .

A) the way building itself is made use of to control indoor environment

B) the structural elements and materials

C) the way the air movement is redirected

D) the natural ventilation in the building

7. When a building is naturally ventilated, there are the following advantages EXCEPT that _____ .

A) both capital and running costs can be reduced

B) the consumption of non-sustainable resources may be reduced

C) occupants may have more control over the building

D) the real objective of construction may be reached

8. Which of the following buildings has the feature of high integration of architecture, structure and environment?

A) Austrian Cultural Center

B) The Cable & Wireless training facility

C) The Inland Revenue Center

D) The GSW Headquarters building

Vocabulary

I. Match the words in Column A with their corresponding definitions in Column B.

Column A	Column B
1. underlying	a. the upward force to remain afloat in a liquid or to rise in air or gas
2. ventilation	b. imitation; study of the possible future events by high-speed calculation of computer
3. buoyancy	c. admitting fresh air in for the replacement of stale air
4. simulation	d. the action of releasing or sending forth, or what is released
5. emission	e. the income that the government receives as taxes
6. revenue	f. to increase to the greatest possible size, num- ber or amount
7. maximize	g. hidden, fundamental

II. Replace each of the following underlined parts with one of the four choices given below.

1. We should adapt our way of life to a more sustainable <u>equilibrium</u> with our fragile

planet.

A) equality   B) balance   C) correspondence   D) equivalent

2. The building environment is the building itself: its form, facade and materials.

A) fabric   B) front   C) facet   D) confrontation

3. These devices have the functions of smoothing and redirecting the fluctuations of nature

A) fractures   B) changes   C) frictions   D) alternatives

4. Toughened glass, which is of much higher strength than the fragile ordinary glass, is widely used in curtain walls and vehicles.

A) bulky   B) subtle   C) breakable   D) transparent

5. Essential to the achievement of a sustainable energy policy is the use of waste material to produce energy and greatly raise the efficiency of energy utilization.

A) maintainable   B) applicable   C) susceptible   D) reversible

6. Its highly integrated architectural, structural and environmental form gives excellent delighting to the inhabitants.

A) interrelated   B) inverted   C) incorporated   D) intersected

7. A double facade on the west elevation creates thermal flues and induce natural ventilation.

A) altitude   B) top point   C) flat upright side   D) the lift installed

8. The brief for the new 6,000m² Learning Resource Centre calls for an environmental design approach.

A) introduction   B) specification

C) instruction   D) summary

Writing   Summary Writing (2)

Directions The following is a summary of the text of Unit Eight. There are several words and/or phrases missing. Please fill in the blanks with words or phrases found from the text.

Green Design is an _____ of mind which seeks a sustainable _____ with Nature. It involves①making use of Nature as the _____ provider to human needs of indoor _____; ②redefining comfort _____ according to daily and seasonal effects and individual _____, and ③making use of the building form, _____ and materials as _____ modifiers. There are already some successful green buildings as good examples.

Reading Material A

Organic Architecture: Subtlety and Power

At a time when planet Earth, despite the 'green revolution', is undergoing seemingly irrevocable ecological breakdown, it is pertinent to consider architecture which makes an attempt to avoid apocalyptical conclusions. ①Some aspects of progress manifested in short-term priorities conceived for the service of the world market are incompatible, impairing the natural balances essential to our survival. ②Trees continue to be felled to make way for cattle herding and forced cultivation. The earth is a time bomb; the only certainty is that it will explode. But there is time to change things, time to redress the balance and to respond positively. 'Organic' architecture which is linked to green and sustainable development demonstrates, quietly and confidently, a way forward. Here a more harmonious art is being created. Whilst monumental architecture from its beginnings is associated with a profligate attitude towards resources, organic architecture utilises available materials, communing with both the economics of the situation and sustainability. ③

No matter how many diverse styles become popular at any one time, building forms which resist imposition of the right angle continue to engender response. Organic architecture achieves its power through subtlety and presence with a sense of flowing space. Frank Lloyd Wright, a key exponent, expanded the spatial frontiers of architecture into curved and warped space. This form of architecture realises a significant empathy and bond with nature: designs which are not a conquest of nature but a symbiotic embrace. ④

Sidney Robinson considers the organic movement in context. ⑤Placing modern day exponents in relation to historical influences, he asserts that organic architecture is a challenge to complacency and insists on renewal, and therefore on the impulse of the individual; its tolerance for pursuit rather than certainty, its delight in argument and its rebirth all contribute to its rhetorical rather than philosophical status. lmre Makovecz has effected considerable impact on architecture. His wonderful structures possess the ability to free the mind and facilitate the fantastical. Associated groups that have developed in Hungary alongside Makovecz have combined to produce an internationally influential regional organic architecture. The latter's forthright and influential views have inspired a generation to join in the creation of a national style.

Ensouling buildings is the preoccupation of Christopher Day who delights in heartfelt curved lines and in the ability of the building to breathe and instil its totality, superseding appreciation through analysis of separate parts. This aspect is pervasive in organic architecture. For one to feel the pulse of a building is important for Day, who consequently produces an organic architecture from within.

The inclusion of Greg Lynn's essay provokes a different train of thought and wards off 'wholesome' organic architecture—buildings, after all, are not organisms but organs, provisional structures which are already multiplicitous. To disentangle the pact between organic bodies and exact geometric language that underlies architecture's spatial types is a monumental task. Architectural proportion achieves the transcendental status of an abstract, holy organic body, adopting the logic of an organism. ⑥Architecture frequently invokes the paradigm of the inviolate interior of a living body. Lynn makes a plea for us not just to accept the superficial, but to analyse the reality of what we see.

Many of these architects tend to move away from mechanical means of illustrating and 'producing' their designs. Buildings are not necessarily drawn before construction begins but rather the forms marked out on site to indicate how they should 'grow'. Many details are developed in situ ensuring full exploitation of the location. ⑦In the case of Nari Ghandi, as with many of the architects featured here, drawings are produced after completion for building regulations' permission. The final form can only be ascertained when construction is complete, a process heavy with trust and expectation.

With the recent surge of interest in chaos theory and natural phenomena there comes a wider variety of 'organic' interpretations: featured projects range from Camouflage by Doug Garofalo to the 'breathing' buildings of James T Hubbell; form Terry Brown's sinuous sculpture to the rock formations of John Lautner. The categorisation is held together by the intent to create a sympathetic environment.

Has progress in the modern world taken a wrong turn? Jean Jacques Rousseau posits that man is happier when working directly on the land and this happiness is inversely proportional to his distance from it. This issue is tackled by the architects here and what emerges is a positive message: that a firm belief in collaboration with the environment exists. Perhaps a valid path for the future is to explore the truth and cultivate the virtue which can be gleaned from organic architecture.

Notes

①在地球这颗星球（即使有了所谓"绿色革命"）正在经历似乎 无可挽回的生态崩溃之时，对力图避免面对和采取措施去解决现存 的环境问题的建筑艺术重新进行考虑实属必要。 pertinent 必要的，适当的。apocalyptical 有启发的，令人深省的。

②以其短期的优势而显示出来，为了服务于世界市场而开发出来的人类进步的某些方面，是与我们的生存所必需的自然平衡不相容的，并且是有危害的。

③历史上的不朽建筑从一开始无不对自然资源采取一种恣意浪费的态度。而有机建筑利用现有材料，既考虑周围环境的经济情况，又考虑发展的可持续性。profligate attitude 恣意浪费的态度；commune with 考虑。

④这种建筑艺术实现了与大自然意义重大的水乳交融，连为一体：设计 的建筑不是要征服大自然，而是与大自然相互依存。

⑤"consider…in context"下一句提供了理解该短语的线索，即"consider the organic movement" by "placing…in relation to historical influences"。

⑥transcendental 超常的，深奥难懂的。

⑦in situ（拉丁）在原来的位置，在自然的位置。

Reading Material B

Is Intelligent the Opposite of Clever

The term intelligent building (IB) has been in common currency for over a decade, yet there is little consensus as to what makes a building intelligent. ① (John Worthington) Research has indicated that knowledge-based systems (KBS) and software techniques employed in expert systems with fault analysing algorithms may be capable of providing integrated building management systems (IBMS) with the true 'intelligence' required to interpret data. ②These could generate advice to enable, for example, the untrained user to perform repairs.

Eric Loe of Northcrofts is the Deputy Chairman of the Intelligent Buildings Group. He argues that one of the main problems is misapplied technology, as in the European Bank for Research and Development building in Broadgate, London where the large floor plate allowed for an open plan office, but when there were only two occupants, all the lights except for those directly above them turned off producing an eerie atmosphere.

As a construction economist Loe believes that intelligent buildings are those that cater for the user. 'Often the architect designs a concept which the user is forced to adapt'. If architects now need an 'engineering training' to understand the appropriate method of incorporating intelligent technology into a building, then collaboration at concept stage would be an advantage. Inflexible buildings, which cannot adapt to changing requirements are not intelligent. Intelligent buildings are those that not only suit user needs but are conducive to work, thereby increasing productivity. One of the main issues against first generation intelligent buildings was that air conditioned air and static produced from increased computer machinery, contributed to Sick Building Syndrome (SBS)③Andrew Jackson of the Electricity Association claims that the spiral scenario: air conditioning causes global warming which creates a need for more air conditioning, is 'a myth' and that the link between air conditioning and SBS is a 'further misconception'. ④Research has shown that the best defence against SBS could be a combination of an internal temperature of around 20 degrees centigrade, a relative humidity exceeding 20 per cent and a minimum fresh air flow of ten litres per person per minute. The most effective way of achieving these conditions would be by some form of air conditioning—natural air conditioning can often be achieved through intelligent design. Nicholas Philips at Lloyds claims that in order to balance the specific needs of each group in the huge 'vertical village', the building needs some sort of air conditioning. ⑤Conditioned air is distributed through a sub-floor plenum into the offices, while stale air is extracted from above through the luminaries. ⑥The extracted air is passed to the perimeter of the building and forced through the triple-layered exterior glazing.

A good example of an intelligent concept to prevent the physical causes of SBS is the Future Systems Green Building which shows excellent use of intelligent rather than clever features in its use of natural ventilation and lighting. Air movement is created by the buoyancy of warm air and rises due to the 'stack 'effect', to achieve comfort conditions for most of the year. ⑦Fresh cool air is drawn into the triple glazed transparent building at the base of the atrium and hot stale air is expelled through louvers at the top of the building. Complex energy consuming lighting systems are replaced by capitalising on natural light through the full height clear glazing and the glazed top of the central atrium space. Mylar sheeting mirrors are used to reflect light into areas of the office furthest from the facade. Young architectural practices such as Pawson Williams and Stanton Williams are producing passive designs that make maximum use of the building and minimum use of technology in achieving their goal.

Since intelligence is closely related to mental health, it seems appropriate to reflect on the psychological aspects of healthy buildings. Alberts and Van Huut Architects' NMB Bank in Amsterdam is an example of this. The design, which was influenced by Pentagram, consists of ten cluster blocks connected together to enable everyone to sit next to a window which opens. The inclined wall surfaces allow the building to obtain maximum benefit from the sun, to reduce the impact of traffic noise and express the buildings essential earth-bound character. Inside, innovative solutions include the use of rainwater which is collected stored and filtered on its journey to feed the many internal plants. The water meanders down a wide flow-form balustrade at the side of the main staircases, slowly evaporating and cooling the air.

Typically, intelligent buildings are considered to be those with the most up-to-date technology and materials. Most of this technology, if it has moved on from concept stage, is very expensive to implement. It is important to remember when reviewing new technology that using it for its own sake is clever rather than intelligent.

Notes

①has been in common currency 已经广为流传。there is little consensus 几乎没有一致意见。

②fault analysing algorithms 错误分析算法。

③static: *n.* 静电干扰。Sick Building Syndrome (SBS) 过分依赖空调等引起的现代楼房综合症。

④spiral scenario 恶性循环。

⑤vertical village 垂直村落。喻指高大的楼房。

⑥subfloor plenum 底层地板压力通风系统。

⑦ "stack" effect 烟囱效应。

UNIT NINE

Text   **The Ornamental Aesthetics**

[1]   Ever since 1966, when American architect Robert Venturi① observed that "less is a bore," the modern attitude toward ornament and decoration has been undergoing a fundamental change. Venturi transformed the familiar maxim of architect Ludwig Mies van der Rohe②to make the point③ that modern architecture had become too simplistic, had lost touch with life. His convictions, though smacking of heresy at the time, were shared by a small group of architects that included Charles Moore④, then chairman of the Yale School of Architecture. Moore initially expressed his own rebellion by using graphics in a room to override and dismiss whatever was there for a functional reason: 'supergraphics' as critic C. Ray Smith labeled them in 1967. Students coming out of Yale under Moore in the late 1960s were painting the surfaces of their de rigeur boxes⑤ with a vengeance: purple diagonal stripes from floor to ceiling, big yellow dots in the corners—anything to loosen the grip of functionalist theory⑥ and its rules of design.

[2]   Probably the earliest use of supergraphics, although they weren't called that then, was in Venturi's 1962 renovation of Grand's Restaurant in Philadelphia. Four-foot-high stencil letters spelling out of the name of the establishment were painted along one wall, then repeated in mirror image on the opposite wall. This superimposition of oversized letters on a small dining area dramatically expanded the apparent volume of that space. Intended more as spatial experiments than as decoration, exercises like this were followed by increasingly ornamental uses of paint and graphics such as artist William Tapley's intricately patterned rooms. ⑦Most of these super- graphics occured in interior projects, but, by 1970, they were appearing on the outsides of buildings too, in the form of huge wall murals painted to achieve "instant" urban renewal.

[3]   From these early adventures with paint, color, and out-of-scale-signs, a real movement has developed in architecture, the essence of which is ornament: ornament sometimes flat, sometimes fully three-dimensional and applied on both the outside and inside of buildings. ⑧Plain white walls are giving way to rich and complex color combinations; or sprouting pilasters, silhouettes, and other frankly tacked-on embellishments. Gigantic flowers or false columns completely out of scale and unrelated to structure are appearing on the outsides of buildings. Major public spaces are being designed almost as stage sets, evoking history or cultural antecedent with ornamental devices that are at once familiar and startling. The traditional columns and pediments are there, but fragmented, distorted, often ironically juxtaposed to other architectural elements: traditional wood and masonry forms surprise us in⑨ blatantly modern materials like stainless steel and neon.

[4]   The decorative crafts, particularly glasswork, wroughtironwork and brushwork—

which have long been excluded from the mainstream of building design—are receiving more significant architectural commissions. Stencil artists, the last traces of whose craft have been fading on the walls of forgotten farmhouses, are once again executing filigree borders or transforming whole rooms into dreamlike experiences. Furniture designers are creating pieces full of wit and allusion: chairs in the shape of butterflies or desks elaborately inlaid in a manner that recalls the eighteenth century. And a group of artists who constitute what is called the Patterning and Decorating Movement are leaving their canvases and covering entire walls with frankly decorative painting; or filling rooms with fanciful sculptured forms. Many of these artists are working in ceramic tile, dyed cloth, beads, sequins, even pheasant feathers—materials more often associated with the decorative crafts than the fine arts. Traditional distinctions between the two fields are further blurred by the fact that many Patterning and Decorating artists are also making screens, chairs, tables, beds, and lamps—pieces that freely evoke potential "usefulness" yet remain, at the same time, objects of contemplation.

[5]　　This movement is changing the appearance of contemporary architecture in a way that is sometimes called postmodern. But the label postmodern, popularized by critic Charles Jencks in 1975 and quickly taken up by American architect Robert A. M. Stern, is a slippery term implying that the whole of the Modern Movement is now being abandoned and something entirely different is taking its place. This is simply not true. As critic Ada Louise Huxtable has so aptly put it, The high period of modernism is over; the Age of the Masters—Frank Lloyd Wright, Mies van der Rohe, Le Corbusier⑩—is finished. We are clearly or I should say, unclearly—moving on toward something else; in fact, we have been doing so for some time. But whatever come next will be the product or inheritor of modernism, not the radical break that postmodernism is advertised to be. It will have at its heart the twentieth-century revolution that we call modern architecture.

[6]　　It is obvious by looking at most of the work that it could not have been designed prior to the Modern Movement and that the simple forms and technical means of Modernism are still there, just under the surface but still quite visible and useful. Ornamentalism is very much a reaction against the more obvious failures of modernism, but it is not a wholesale rejection of Modernism. In response to the attempt to label him a postmodernist, Robert Venturi maintains that his firm is only practicing Modern architecture, and he is right.

New Words and Expressions

simplistic [sim'plistik]	a.	过分简单化的
conviction [kən'vikʃən]	n.	深信，确信，定罪
smack [smæk]	vt.	掴，拍，打，猛击
heresy ['herəsi]	n.	异端，左道邪说

override *	[ˌəuvəˈraid]	v.	超过，不顾
graphics *	[ˈɡræfiks]	n.	制图法
vengeance	[ˈvendʒns]	n.	报仇，报复
stencil	[ˈstensil]	n.	图案，文字
superimposition	[ˌsjuːpəriˌmpəˈziʃən]	n.	重迭，附加物
mural	[ˈmjuərəl]	n.	壁画，壁饰
sprout	[spraut]	vt.	使萌芽，使生长
embellishment	[imˈbeliʃmənt]	n.	装饰品
antecedent	[ˌæntiˈsiːdənt]	a.	先行的，先前的 n. 前例，前事
juxtapose	[ˈdʒʌkstəpəuz]	vt.	把……并列，使并置
masonry	[ˈmeisnri]	n.	砖的建筑
neon	[ˈniːən]	n.	霓虹灯
filigree	[ˈfiligriː]	n.	金丝（银丝或线等）的细工饰品
tile	[tail]	n.	瓷砖，贴砖
blatant	[ˈbleitənt]	a.	炫耀的，显眼的，吵闹的
inlaid	[ˈinˈleid]	a.	镶嵌的，嵌饰的
sequin	[ˈsiːkwin]	n.	装饰衣服用的金属小圆片
pheasant	[ˈfeznt]	n.	雉，野鸡
blur	[bləː]	vt.	把（界线，视线等）弄得模糊不清
contemplation *	[ˌkɔntemˈpleiʃən]	n.	期望，意图，沉思
slippery	[ˈslipəri]	a.	含糊的，难以捉摸的
tack	[tæk]	vt.	钉住 n. 平头钉
fragment *	[ˈfræɡmənt]	vt.	分裂，成碎片
distort	[disˈtɔːt]	vt.	弄歪，歪曲
wrought	[rɔːt]	a.	锻的，用锤敲击成的
wroughtiron			熟铁，锻铁
bead	[biːd]	n.	念珠，（建）凸圆线脚，串珠线脚
evoke	[iˈvəuk]	vt.	引起，唤起
allusion	[əˈljuːʒən]	n.	暗指，引喻
with a vengeance			彻底地，过度地
give way to			让位给

Notes

①Robert Venturi（1922-）美国著名建筑师，1966 年出版《建筑的复杂性与矛盾性》被当作向现代主义的宣言书，故被称作后现代主义之父，主张用混乱代替纯静。

②．Mies van der Rohe（1886—1969）生于德国，后加入美国籍，著名建筑大师，提出"少就是多"这一建筑设计理论。

③to make the point：不定式作结果状语，意为提出这一观点。

④Charles Moore（1925—　　）美国著名建筑师，强调建筑中的社会性和人性，主张建筑应像人的生活一样充满趣味。

⑤de rigeur：（法语）礼节上所需要的。

⑥functionalist theory：主张形式服从用途和材料。

⑦intended more as…decoration：状语，其中 more…than 为与其说……不如……

⑧Ornament sometimes…of building：which 引导的非限定性定语从句，其中省略掉了谓语 is。

Exercises

Reading Comprehension

Ⅰ. Skim the text and match each of the following ideas with its appropriate paragraph number or numbers in the brackets.

1. Examples of ornamentalism （　　）
2. Characteristic of ornamental movement （　　）
3. Change of modern attitude toward ornament and decoration （　　）
4. The decorative crafts used in ornamentalism （　　）
5. The relationship between Ornamentalism and Modernism （　　）

Ⅱ. Read the text carefully and then choose the best answer among the the four choices given to complete each statement.

1. The main idea of the passage is to _____ .

   A) tell the readers the development of ornamental aesthetic

   B) describe the characteristics of ornamentlism

   C) introduce ornamental aesthetic

   D) compare several decoration movements

2. According to the passage we can infer that _____ .

   A) Before 1966 people dismissed ornament

   B) Functionalists emphasize decoration

   C) The students of Moore believed functionalism

   D) Supergraphics is an architectural expression

3. In the fifth paragraph "this movement" refers to _____ .

   A) Postmodern movement

   B) Modernism movement

   C) Functionalism movement

   D) Patterning and Decorating movement

4. If you are an ornamentalist, you will choose _____ .

   A) plain white wall

   B) traditional chair

C) small flower

D) sprouting pilaster

5. What kind of decoration does ornamentalist want to make?

A) Common

B) Traditional

C) Unique

D) Similar

6. Which of the following statements is true?

A) Ornamentalists think Modernism is out of date.

B) Venturi believed that decoration should be complex.

C) Embellishments are most important in decoration.

D) Venturi was a Postmodernist.

7. Why does author say that Venturi is right in maintaining that his firm is only practicing Modern architecture ?

A) Because he did not reject Modernism wholly.

B) Because his words were one thing, but his actions were another.

C) Because he was afraid that his client would not accept his design.

D) Because he purposely did something against the critics.

8. Functionalists think _____ .

A) decoration serves function

B) in interior decoration, beauty is most important

C) modern materials should not be used in decoration

D) embellishments should be realistic

9. The mention of the renovation of Grand's Restaurant is _____ .

A) to tell the readers what ornamentalism is

B) to show the readers the characteristics of ornamentalism

C) an example of decorative design

D) to demonstrate the difference from the other decoration

10. The ornaments used by the Patterning and Decorating Movement is _____ .

A) supergraphics

B) natural materials

C) useful but full of imagination

D) centered on usefulness

Vocabulary

I . Match the words in Column A with their corresponding definitions in Column B.

Column A   Column B

1. mural   a. a square post that usually sticks out only partly beyond the

wall of a building and is usually only decorative

2. tile   b. a painting which is painted on a wall

3. pediment   c. stones from which a building wall etc. is made

4. masonry   d. a three-sided piece of stone or other material placed above the
                    entrance to a building

5. embellishment e. ornaments

6. filigree   f. a shin shaped piece of baked clay used for covering roofs,
                    walls, floors, etc.

                 g. delicate decorative wire work

Ⅱ. Complete each of the following statements with one of the four choices given below.

1. Computer _____ , by which you can display and change pictures on a screen, are used
   in many areas of industrial design.

   A) graphics   B) calibration

   C) geometry   D) cellular

2. We know from the spirit of architecture that their characteristics must be in harmony
   with the spaces that want to be and _____ what spaces can be.

   A) make   B) evoke

   C) align   D) categorize

3. There is an exhibition of _____ and sculpture.

   A) covering   B) ceramics

   C) cylinder   D) brace

4. The tile pattern on Venturi, Rauch and Scott Brown's ISI Building creates a colour
   and rhythm that ignore and try to _____ the window opening and the structural system.

   A) override   B) overcharge

   C) extract   D) embed

5. Ornamentalist forms are made with most sophisticated factory processes and contemporary materials such as stainless steel and _____ .

   A) filament   B) anode

   C) neon   D) wood

6. Michael Graves addition to the Schulman house purposely _____ the size of new
   clapboard siding.

   A) distort   B) lubricate

   C) revolve   D) superimpose

7. Nothing must intrude to _____ the statement of how a space is made.

   A) blur   B) array

   C) block   D) protrude

8. The _____ curtain adds to the beauty of the room.

   A) cement   B) face

94

Writing   Summary Writing (3)

Directions: Read the text again and complete the summary of the text. You need to add
           about 100 words.

     The Ornamental Aesthetic

     Because American architect Robert Venturi found that "Less is a bore", the Modern
attitude toward ornament and decoration has been undergoing a fundamental change….

Reading Material A

The Ornamental Aesthetics (II)

     One of the reasons that Ornamentalism is so clearly a Modern phenomenon is that it
breaks the cardinal rule of ornament characteristic of all historical styles. ①Whereas ornament in the Gothic, Baroque, or Neo- classical styles usually reinforced or complemented
the forms to which it was applied, in Ornamentalism it frequently contradicts or overrides
them. ②Moreover, the embellishments of Ornamentalism are not applied in a manner sub-
servient to structure as dictated by the theories of the eighteenth and nineteenth centuries. ③For example, the tile pattern on Venturi's ISI Building creates a color and rhythm
that ignore and try to override the window openings and the structural system. Michael
Graves's addition to the Schulman house purposely distorts the size of the new clapboard
siding. ④Outside, the fireplace is depicted as a monumental column; inside it becomes a kind
of giant keystone that one would expect to see thirty feet in the air rather than on the
floor. The old two-story exterior is painted in contradiction to both its traditional gable and
its symmetry.

     Richard Fernau's fast food shop "Franks for the Memory" contains "walls" that rise
through two stories and are punched with cutouts in the shape of giant hot dogs. ⑤Though
they define space in the interior, these walls are otherwise ornamental; they do not keep the
weather out and they do not support anything. Most important, they contradict the real
structure, ceiling, mechanical systems, and exterior walls of the space they occupy.

     The new ornamentalism also violates the well-known dictum of the nineteenth century
English architect Owen Jones: "Construction should be decorated. Decoration should never
be purposely constructed". In Ornamentalism decoration is very purposely constructed, and
constructed in a manner to give it its own independent validity as in Hans Hollein's Austrian Travel Bureau, where the palm trees neither imitate nature nor pretend to support the
structure. Clad in polished metal, they stand free, symbolizing faraway places and, though

purely decorative, become one of the most significant architectural elements of the space. ⑥

This purposeful construction of decoration, along with the tendency of Ornamentalism to contradict rather than reinforce essential structure and function, is important because it allows Ornamentalism to keep clear the distinctions between what is merely on the surface of things and what things really are⑦. Thus we are never fooled by faux bois painting in the way that manufacturers of plastis wood—grain laminate would fool us⑧. The two—dimensional columns appliqued to the facade of Robert A. M. Stern's summer cottage do not try to be authentic in the way that the tract developer's "Southern Colonial" model does.

In this sense, Ornamentalism is quite the opposite of what we call kitsch. It is not an imitation or simulation of something that, by pretending to be real, programs a sentimental response. Ornamentalism may recall historical styles or evoke nature, it may refer to folk art or the human body; but it does so in a way that allows the audience to understand and participate in the process, to know what is genuine and what is not. The pleasures of the new Ornamentalism are all its own, not faked or hand-me-down, and they carry with them many of the aesthetic ideals of the last two hundred years. Ornamentalism, Modernism, and the numerous styles of the nineteenth century have in common the fact that all have expressed the aspirations of the societies for which they were created. Since the Industrial Revolution and its seeming mastery of the economic and technical means to transform the human condition, architecture has been required to depict society as it wishes to become, not, necessarily, as it is.

Now, because the depiction of the machine as a "spiritual" force is no longer plausible, contemporary architecture and art are faced with the challenge of discovering new and appropriate imagery for our society. What are the aspirations of the late twentieth century and how should they be depicted? The Ornamental aesthetic springs from a search for answers to these questions, from a search for new imagery to express the admittedly confused and shifting ideas of what our society ought to become. It begins by denying the old reverence for technology while taking full advantage of the light-switch/vacuum cleaner/toaster conveniences that technology has brought us. ⑨Ornamentalist forms are made with the most sophisticated factory processes and contemporary materials such as laminated plastics, anodized aluminum, stainless steel, and neon. ⑩The economic and practical benefits of machine production are enthusiastically embraced, but the awesome "spirit" of the machine is denied, and in its place, other kinds of imagery are projected. (to be continued)

Notes

①为什么说装饰主义明显是一种现代主义建筑其原因之一就是它冲破了一切历史风格的基本装饰原则。

②Gothic：哥特式的；Baroque：巴罗克建筑形式，指过分雕琢和怪诞的；

Neoclassical：新古典主文的。

③subservient to：辅助。

④clapboard siding：楔形护墙板

⑤…are punched with…hor dogs. 排气装置形状象一个巨大的热狗。

⑥包裹上发亮的金属片。

⑦…with the tendency…structure and function，… 这是一个 with 引导的状语，可翻译为：
  因为装饰主义倾向，不是增强建筑物的必须结 构和功能，而是使它彼此不协调，……

⑧faux bois：（法语）假木刻。

⑨它放弃了对技术的古老尊敬，而又充分利用技术带给我们的灯开关，吸尘器或烤面包器。

⑩laminated plastics：层压塑料，anodized aluminum：阳极氧化铝。

Reading Material B

The Ornamental Aesthetics（Ⅱ）

One source of imagery in Ornamentalism is historical style，particularly Classicism. [①] Although images from almost any period may be used（and some-times combined with startling eclecticism，classicizing imagery abounds because the Classical language of architecture is the most universally recog- nized style of the past，touching Greece，Rome，the Renaissance，and nineteenth-century Neoclassicism simultaneously. [②]But it is not Classicism itself that ornamentalism seeks，so much as the connections between contemporary society and its cultural heritage，the linking of our present with our past.

For example，Piazza D'Italia by Charles Moore and August Perez—with its Doric，Ionic，and Corinthian columns，a pilastered arcade，grand arches，and a fountain—is an "almost" accurate evocation of some nineteenth- century Neoclassical building or public monument in Italy. The whole ensemble is vaguely symmetrical placed on a axis. Yet there is no attempt to be truly historical，for these classicizing forms are made from stainless steel and neon，the most contemporary of materials. The plan reveals that the fountain is actually a map of the Italian peninsula，culminating at the center with Sicily，the region from which most of New Orlean's Italian population originated. This pop reference is annoying or fun，take your pick，but it is also an attempt to touch people's memory，to reach for the past and tie it to the present without resorting to false nostalgia. [③]

The abstraction from historical sources is what distinguishes Ornamentalist design from "Colonial" motels，"Edwardian" boardroom，and "Old English" bars. Historical references in Ornamentalism tend to be dramatically out of scale or context，to be made from materials associated with today's technology，or to be presented as fragments from the past （a part of a cornice，one-half of a molding）rather than as wholes. Michael Graves's pediment fragments and moldings are always too large or too small，never in the "right" place， and usually depicted as fragments. The historical allusions are thus truncated, isolated as if in brackets, often with abrupt beginnings and ends. [4]

Some of the most original Ornamentalist work is based on images of nature to which, historically, the primordial origins of all ornament can be traced. Tested, refined, and elaborated over thousands of years in successive styles, the natural origins of ornament continue to touch the subconscious of our species. Even elements of the Classical orders, such as the Corinthian capital with its acanthus leaves, can be seen as direct references to nature. [5] The most full-blown use of nature in recent architecture is obviously Art Nouveau, that short-lived turn-of-the-century style in which an attempt was made to integrate natural form into the whole of building, even its structure and space. [6]

In Ornamentalist architecture there is no such effort at integration. On the contrary, nature is kept clearly on the surface and it is the surface qualities of nature that are depicted: its colors, shapes, and rhythms rather than its organic structure. For example, the porcelain enamel flower panels on Venturi, Rauch and Scott Brown's Best Products Showroom seem to "paint" a giant garden over the entire building, but the building itself remains obviously a warehouse. Michael Graves, on the other hand, is more abstract in his use natural imagery, developing associations with nature through color: browns for earth, blues for sky, greens for landscape. In the Patterning and Decorating Movement in painting and sculpture, the uses of nature may be more explicit. In the crafts, natural imagery has always been explicit—and the recent renaissance in glass, iron, and brushwork reemphasizes that fact. Traditional nature patterns are revived in the work of stenciler like Cile Lord and Adele Bishop, while forms based in nature are being newly invented by people like metalworker Albert Paley. The appeal of nature as a contemporary image for the expression of our best hopes and dreams lies in its diametric opposition to the machine and in its essentially life-affirming power. [7]

Another source of power in Ornamentalism is its humour.

Ornamentalism permits us to laugh at ourselves, an honest and liberating act. It provides a means of dealing in imagination with our culture, of filtering the monsterously contradictory facts of our existence. Ornamentalism contains its own ideas about what things are and what things ought to be, about what is right and wrong with the twentieth century. But it does not insist on any correspondence between those ideas and some ultimate truth. Ornamentalism is, in part, a process of demystification, of retreat from Modernist claims to an exclusive means of salvation in complicated world. [8]

The force of ornamentalism, its strength and originality, lie in its abandonment of machine aesthetic and its simultaneous ability to keep contradictions alive and explicit in the forms created. It is the first serious attempt in fifty years to make Modernism keep its promise of projecting new possibilities of showing us some release from the burdensome realities of the present. It is not the daily usefulness of technology that Ornamentalism questions, but our tendency to let technology tell us what to do, of our allowing technology to become an end in itself. Ornamentalism dances on the surface of technology, using it but denying its aura. Ornamentalism is a sign of life not of compromise, and it promises a future that will look much different from what we have known for the better part of this century.

Notes

①装饰主义的意象源是历史风格尤其是古典主义。

②touching Greece⋯触及到了。

③take your pick：由你自己决定。

④历史痕迹就这样被淡化了，单独放在一处就好像放在一个括号里，忽然开始，忽然结束。

⑤Corinthian capital with its acanthus leaves 带卷叶饰的科林斯柱头。

⑥Art Nouveau：（法语）新艺术。

⑦diametric opposition to：正好相反

⑧从某种程度上讲，装饰主义是一个使之非神秘化的过程，一个从现代主义的主张中解脱出来，在复杂的世界上形成一种独特的拯救方式。

UNIT TEN

Text   **On Garden**

[1]   The best gardens are much more than an assortment of beautiful plants. Successful gardens generally represent a careful integration of diverse elements, ranging from the purely ornamental to the strictly functional. ①Paths, pools, planters, trellises, arbors, fountains, and fences can contribute enormously to the creation of an exciting and harmonious garden. The same attention one brings to decorating a home and making it "livable" can be used to make a garden a pleasant place to find privacy, to meditate, and to escape the pressures of a fast-moving, machine-oriented world.

[2]   It's a fact that man-made garden accents establish the "style" of a garden more definitively than plants alone. Period gardens—Victorian, French, Elizabethan, American Colonial②—all demand the proper placement of structural and design elements to make them recognizable. Indeed, the simple addition of a particular style of gazebo, bench, or arbor can instantly "identify" a garden. Similarly, with "ethnic" gardens-such as an English cottage garden, a Chinese meditation garden, or an Italian water garden-the selection of appropriate fences, bridges, and ornaments brings style and a sense of permanence to the environment.

[3]   The world over, there are structures that "make" a garden's reputation. At Magnolia Gardens, near Charleston, South Carolina, for example, a sleek trellised footbridge called The Long Bridge is a "trademark" of the garden. Its distinctive design, traversing the corner of a cypress lake, is immediately identifiable. Somewhat French in style, painted white to contrast with the dark water and the tall cypress trees draped with Spanish moss, the bridge helps create a romantic atmosphere, which③probably makes it the subject of more photographs and paintings than any other garden structure in the world.

[4]   Though some structures look good unadorned, as part of a garden composition, others are enhanced by some kind of plant decoration. The British are especially fond of training climbing roses, wisteria, honeysuckle, and ivy up walls, fences gazebos, and summerhouses, sometimes so successfully④ that the structure becomes completely covered in vines, flowers, or foliage.

[5]   Then there are accents that rely on plants alone for dramatic impact. At the Ladew Topiary Gardens, near Baltimore, Maryland, a fox-hunting scene of clipped Japanese yew provides such a whimsical highlight that it has made the garden famous. The realistic, life-size composition of a topiary fox being chased by five topiary hounds and a topiary horse and rider across a section of lawn at the entrance to the garden sets the scene for even more surprising and amusing topiary work in other sections of the garden.

[6]   The roles of plantsman and architect in the creation of a beautiful garden are impor-

tant, but their efforts may fall short without a third important influence-the contribution of artist. The best gardens today seem to combine the talents of plantsman, architect, and artist. Sometimes these three skills are embodied in a single person but more frequently they are achieved by a pooling of talents. For example, the beautiful American estate garden of Filoli, near San Francisco, is a result of the collaboration of Isabellaworn, a plantsperson, and Bruce Porter, a landscape painter. Porter did the overall arrangement of spaces and accents; Worn developed the planting schemes and selected the plants.

[7]　　Impressionist painter Claude Monet was an artist who embodied skills as a plantsman and architect in designing his garden at Giverny, in France. Monet created very simple but stunning flower beds for the entrance of his home. To complement his pink stucco house with distinctive green shutters he planted solid blocks of pink geraniums studded with⑤ pink and white rose standards. He bordered these raised flower beds with grey foliaged dainthus. Bold blocks of color, carefully selected to blend with the nearby structure, is the key to success of this particular garden space.

[8]　　Gardens can also be repositories for works of art. These artworks need not be realistic to be an effective embellishment. Garden art began as symbolism in rocks and dead wood, the ancient Chinese bringing into their gardens boulders representing images of mammals. They gave these rock formations names such as "turtle rock", "owl rock," and "dragon rock" for the objects they resembled. From symbolism in rocks and dead wood, garden makers became obsessed with realism. The more anatomically correct a sculpture, the more highly valued it became, reaching its height⑥ in Ancient Greece and Italy with statues of gods and heroes placed on pedestals in garden settings.

[9]　　Today the art world has turned full circle, with an emphasis once again on symbolism and impressionism. Indeed, artist Esteban Vicente put it well when asked to explain an apparent paradox between the modernistic style of his art and his love of gardening as a hobby. "You cannot make art if you are not involved with nature" he said, "Anything to do with nature has to do with art."

[10]　　The best gardens seem to combine the talents of plantsman, architect, and artist. In a way, all three contributors are artists, for there are many examples of plantings and architecture that can be described as artistic.

New Words and Expressions

assortment* [əˌsɔːtmənt]	n.	分类，各种各类的聚合
trellis ['trelis]	n.	（建）格构，格子结构，棚架
arbor ['ɑːbə]	n.	棚架，凉亭
meditate* ['mediteit]	vt.	考虑，企图，沉思
accent ['æksənt]	n.	特征，特点
gazebo [gə'ziːbəu]	n.	眺台，凉亭

magnolia [mæg'nəuljə]	*n.*	木兰花
traverse* ['trævə (:) s]	*vt.*	穿过
cypress ['saipris]	*n.*	柏树，柏树枝
drape [dreip]	*v.*	悬挂，披
moss [mɔs]	*n.*	苔藓，地衣
wisteria [wis'tiəriə]	*n.*	紫藤，紫藤属植物
honeysuckle ['hʌnisʌkl]	*n.*	忍冬属（金银花）
ivy ['aivi]	*n.*	常春藤
foliage ['fəuliidʒ]	*n.*	（总称）叶子，簇叶（建）叶饰
clip* [klip]	*vt.*	修剪
yew [ju:]	*n.*	紫杉属树木（尤指浆果紫杉）
whimsical ['hwimzikəl]	*a.*	古怪的，怪诞的
pooling ['puliŋ]	*n.*	集中
complement ['kɔmplmənt]	*vt.*	补充，补足
stucco ['stʌkəu]	*n.*	拉毛水泥，灰墁，（拉）毛粉
shutter ['ʃʌtə]	*n.*	百叶窗，窗板
geranium [dʒi'reinjəm]	*n.*	天竺葵
stud [stʌd]	*v.*	点缀
dianthus [dai'ænθəs]	*n.*	石竹属植物
repository [ri'pɔzitəri]	*n.*	宝库，陈列室，贮藏所
boulder ['bəuldə]	*n.*	巨砾，圆石
mammal ['mæməl]	*n.*	哺乳动物
anatomical [ænə'tɔmikəl]	*a.*	解剖的，解剖学的
pedestal ['pedistl]	*n.*	（建）柱脚，（雕像等）垫座
hound [haund]	*n.*	猎狗，狗
paradox ['pærədɔks]	*a.*	自相矛盾的
gardening [,gɑ:dniŋ]	*n.*	园艺（学）

Notes

①the purely ornamental to the strictly functional：定冠词＋形容词，表示一类物。

②Victorian. French. Elizabethan. American colonial：指英王维多利亚时代，法式，英王伊丽莎白时代的，美国殖民主义时代的花园。

③which：指代前面的一句话。

④sometimes so successfully that：修饰 training.

⑤with：表示带有。第二个"with"表示用

⑥reaching its height：现在分词表伴随状态。

Exercises

Reading Comprehension

I . Skim the text and complete the following chart.

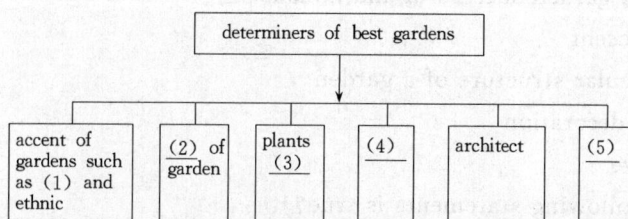

```
              ┌─────────────────────────────────┐
              │  determiners  of  best  gardens │
              └─────────────────────────────────┘
                              │
   ┌──────────┬──────────┬────┴────┬──────────┬──────────┬──────────┐
┌───────────┐ ┌────────┐ ┌───────┐ ┌───────┐ ┌───────────┐ ┌───────┐
│ accent of │ │ (2) of │ │ plants│ │ (4)   │ │ architect │ │ (5)   │
│ gardens   │ │ garden │ │ (3)   │ │ ___   │ │           │ │ ___   │
│ such      │ │        │ │ ___   │ │       │ │           │ │       │
│ as (1) and│ │        │ │       │ │       │ │           │ │       │
│ ethnic    │ │        │ │       │ │       │ │           │ │       │
└───────────┘ └────────┘ └───────┘ └───────┘ └───────────┘ └───────┘
```

II . Read the text carefully and then choose the best answer from the four choices given to complete each statement.

1. Which of the following statements best describes the organization of the text?

A) A general statement is stated and then an example is given.

B) A general concept is defined and then examples are given.

C) A statement is illustrated by an analogy.

D) Parallelism.

2. According to the text we can infer that _____ .

A) successful garden are always functional

B) garden can let people escape the pressure of fast-pace life

C) people once paid no attention to symbolism and impressionism in designing garden

D) Chinese are the first people who used symbolism in designing garden

3. In the sixth paragraph, what does the phrase "fall short" mean?

A) deficit

B) fail to reach a desired result

C) be short

D) destroy the plan

4. What does the author think that best gardens should be?

A) Natural

B) Realistic

C) Symbolistic

D) Artistic

5. Why does the author mention the impressionist painter Claude Monet?

A) Because the author wants to use him as an example to show the relationship of the three contributors.

B) Because he was a famous artist.

C) Because he had a beautiful garden.

D) Because the author wants reader to know his role in designing garden.

6. This passage is mainly about _____ .

   A) classification of gardens

   B) The definition of gardens

   C) The roles of architects, plantsmen and artists

   D) how to make a best garden

7. _____ makes a garden successful and famous.

   A) Garden's accent

   B) Some particular structure of a garden

   C) Man-made decoration

   D) All of above

8. Which of the following statements is true?

   A) The beauty of gardens depends on the work of plantsmen.

   B) The sculpture in Italian gardens are more anatomically. correct than in Chinese gardens.

   C) All gardeners are artist.

   D) The more natural the gardens are the more successful they are.

9. The purpose of garden is _____ .

   A) to beautify the environment

   B) to escape the pressure of a fast-moving, machine-oriented world.

   C) to exhibit the arts

   D) to create a romantic atmosphere

10. In the sentence "reaching its height in Ancient" the word "its" refer to:

    A) symbolism

    B) realism

    C) arts

    D) the exactness of sculputure

Vocabulary

I . Match the words in Column A with their corresponding definitions in Column B

Column A	Column B
1. arbour	a. the base on which a pillar or statue stands
2. gazebo	b. a sheltered place in a garden, usually made by making trees or bushes grow so as to form an arch
3. shutter	c. a covering of plaster on the walls of buildings, often formed into decorative shapes
4. stucco	d. either of a piece of wood or metal covers that can be unfolded in front of the outside of a window to block the view or keep out

the light

5. pedestal   e. a shelter or hut in a garden, where one can sit and look at the view

6. trellis   f. a light upright frame of long narrow pieces of wood, esp. used as support for climbing plants

II. Complete each of following statements with one of the four choices given below.

1. The main road _____ the plain from north to south.

    A) transports   B) traverses

    C) transplants   D) trims

2. Hope's treatise also advocated room settings that were planned down to the minutest detail to _____ the works of art that they contained.

    A) comply   B) compact

    C) complete   D) complement

3. The gardener _____ the shrubbery.

    A) clipped   B) cladded

    C) clamped   D) commenced

4. They are _____ a change in the office arrangement.

    A) manipulating   B) overhauling

    C) meditating   D) overshooting

5. This shop has a good _____ of furniture to choose from.

    A) assortment   B) set

    C) kinds   D) article

6. The Yin-Yang philosophy identified placid water as "Yin" and protruding _____ as "Yang".

    A) waves   B) boulders

    C) bevels   D) surges

7. The walls on each side were _____ in a heavy yellow satin.

    A) decorated   B) draped

    C) deformed   D) detached

8. Many retired people take up _____ as a hobby. They plant trees and flowers in their container.

    A) gardening   B) geology

    C) architecture   D) aeronautics

Writing   **Summary Writing** (4)

Directions: Read the text of Unit Ten and write a summary of the text in about 200 words.

On Garden

Reading Material A

The Oriental Influence

[1]　　At the other end of the world, isolated from European influence until Marco Polo's penetration through the vast mountain ranges and desolate deserts filled with savage tribes, the Chinese developed another art form involving trees. They were the first to use bonsai in their gardens, by transplanting miniature trees found growing in the wild, dwarfed by wind, salt spray, or rock soil①. However, it was the Japanese who then created bonsai artificially, by selective pruning of branches and restricting the roots in shallow container. ②

[2]　　The Oriental garden was the first to become a living, artistic structure—an attempt to humanize nature's wildness. Materials of lasting value (particularly wood, stone, gravel, and sand) were introduced. An early form of Oriental garden was the cup garden. This could be large enough to encompass a lake surrounded by hills-the lake surface forming the bottom of the cup and the slopes of the hills its sides-with walking trails leading to smaller cupgardens in the hillsides. ③Or on the smallest scale, a cup garden could be nothing more than a stone slab with a bonsai in the middle. ④The purpose of a cup garden was introspection and privacy, using definite focal points and symbolism for a close communication with nature. Makers of cup gardens studied the natural order of things-the many ways water can fall into a pool, the contours of hills, the sinuous lines of trees sculpted by a harsh environment-and they sought to symbolize these powerful images in their intimate gardeners. ⑤

[3]　　In particular, the concept of a cup garden includes drawing the viewer's attention to something special-an accent. It might be a plant, a boulder, a pond, or even a building. The ancient Chinese were fond of surrounding themselves with enclosures to shut out the chaos and clutter of civilization. They built earthen mounds, elaborate walls, hedges, and fences to provide isolation, creating within these structures their own small realm of beauty. However, it was not a static environment. The Chinese deliberately designed their gardens for strolling. They liked to walk leisurely along serpentine paths that made maximum use of the terrain, with surprises-or "pictures"-at every turn, something new always coming into view. ⑥Plants were only one element used in creating these pictures. Rocks, waterfalls, viewing platforms, bridges, overlooks and shelters became important components of a garaen, making the stroll an adventure. Indeed, the placement of a structure was more important than the structure itself. The buildings in a classic Chinese garden are first and foremost garden features, just as the hills, rocks, streams, ponds, trees, and flowers are garden features.

[4]   The philosophy of the ancient Chinese was to seek a union between man and nature. They regarded the rivers as arteries⑦, the mountains as the bones of a skeleton, and garden makers searched the natural world for system and order. To help make sense of the nature, the Chinese adopted the principles of yin (female) and yang (male). The yin-yang philosophy identified placid water as "yin" and protruding boulders as "yang", for example.⑧An understanding of this philosophy helped early Chinese garden designers strike a balance in their gardens between strong and subtle features.

[5]   The poet-painter Wang Wei (A. D. 669-759), of the T'ang Dynasty, is believed to have created the first cup garden, in the rugged hills in Shensi, where he built for his mother a garden called Wang Chuan.⑨Our knowledge of this early garden comes from a scroll painting by Wang Wei himself. Though the original has been lost, there are copies of it showing gardens with buildings and pavilions placed in a rugged landscape close to a river. A trail winds among hills and forest clearings from one garden space to another. Many of the gardens are enclosed by a bamboo thicket, a stone wall, or picket fence. Some contain orchard trees, while others appear to be designed as secret places for study and contemplation.

[6]   The early Chinese cup gardens strongly influenced the Japanese, and many examples of these Chinese origins can be seen today in the three imperial gardens in the ancient Japanese capital of Kyoto.

[7]   Perhaps the finest example of a Chinese cup garden outside China can be seen today at the estate called Innisfree, near Millbrook, New York.

Notes

①bonsai：盆栽；…by transplanting…soil. 移栽那些生长在荒野中，由于风，雾，和岩石土壤而变得矮小的树。

②但是，随后日本人才创造了人工盆栽。通过有选择地修剪树林，限制树根在狭小的花盆里生长。

③the slopes of the hills its side：句中省略了 "forming"。

④stone slab：石板。

⑤the contours…environment：山的轮廓，恶劣环境所雕塑出的树的深波状线。

⑥他们喜欢沿着蜿蜒的小路悠闲地漫步，这些小路充分利用了地形。

⑦artery：动脉。

⑧阴阳哲学将静止的水当作阴，将突出的圆石当作阳。其中 Yin，Yang 为汉语 音译。

⑨Shensi：地名：今陕西。

⑩Kyoto：地名：京都（日本）

Reading Material B

Gardens of the VILLA D'ESTE[①]

Appointed Governor of Tivoli following his failure to win the papal elections, Cardinal Ippolito d'Este begin, in 1550, the rebuilding of his seat of government. [②]The former Benedictine cloister was not splendid enough for the son of Lucretia Borgia, and so he commissioned the Renaissance artist Pirro Ligorio with its renovation. [③]The plans, in which the garden was envisaged as a complementary and integral part of the house, were based on an architectural design conforming substantially to the laws of geometry and perspective. [④]

The garden is divided into three parts: one lower, on level ground, and two rising in terraces towards the villa. Its basic form, which is repeated in many of its details, is the square.

The execution of the project caused the architect G. Alberto Galvani more than minor difficulties: one whole district of Tivoli had to be demolished in order to clear enough space for the grounds. In addition, the garden, which for climatic reasons was to be north- facing, had to be underpinned to a quite considerable extent because the mountain range on which it lay ran north-west. [⑤]Originally, in contrast to the present day, the garden was entered not from above, through the villa, but through an entrance gate bordered by two fountains on the lower level. [⑥] From an old engraving one can see that there were originally arbours by the gate and also amphitheatre with statues symbolizing the liberal arts. [⑦]Their exposed position ensured that the visitor was attuned right from the very beginning of his walk up to the villa, to the outlook on life and intellectual stance of its owner, a true Renaissance nobleman.

Pergolas laid out in the form of a cross divided the level region, which one entered first, into four equal squares. There were small pavilions from which the visitor could observe the flower and herb borders. At their intersection, where a wooden summer-house originally stood, there is now a rotunda with what are probably the oldest cypresses in Italy. [⑧] This complex was to have been bordered laterally by two mazes of evergreen hedgerows on each side; in the end, only the south-west ones were completed. [⑨]This lower region was bounded by rows of trees on its outside edges, and by fishponds on the side facing the villa. Four ponds were planned but only three built. On the side overlooking the valley, an exedra-shaped panoramic terrace-only existing in the plans-was to have emphasized this first lateral axis, which separates the lower from the upper garden. [⑩]This design feature is reinforced on the opposite, ascending slope of the garden by the celebrated "water organ". This organ functioned purely mechanically: air, compressed by the cascading waters, caused the pipes of the artfully constructed organ to sound, and set figures in motion.

[5]   Its pendant, also on the hilly side of the garden but somewhat nearer to the villa, was a fountain decorated with owls and other birds. The pathway to the villa continues via three parallel fights of steps on two levels, decorated by cascading waterfalls. On the second level the middle flight of steps divides to embrace the oval basin of the Dragon fountain, which was planned as the iconological centre of the garden. The second main lateral axis is formed by the Avenue of Hundred Fountains, almost 150 metres long, where water pours from stone obelisks, eagles, little boats and lilies into a trough-shaped channel, and then spouts through chimera heads into a second, lower channel.⑪The Ovato fountains-an artificial rock massif of grottoes and allegorical sculptures-and the Rometto fountains-a miniature reproduction of ancient Rome-are two further interesting stopping-points on the way to the villa.⑫

The impressive garden of the Villa d'Este is distinctly different from the villa gardens of Tuscany.⑬

Notes

①埃斯特别墅花园。

②Tivoli：（意大利地名）蒂沃利。

③cloister：修道院；（修道院等）回廊。

④in which the garden…为非限制性定语从句修饰 plan。意为在这个计划中, 花园被设想成
　这座房子的一个补充和整体的一部分。

⑤此外, 由于气候原因, 这座花园应是朝北向, 这就必须极大地加高基础, 因为建花园的
　山脉是西北向的 。

⑥not…but…不是…而是。

⑦amphitheatre with…具有象征自由艺术的雕像的圆形剧场。

⑧rotunda：圆形建筑物圆形大厅。

⑨two mazes…each side：每边都有两个用常绿矮树组成的迷宫。

⑩an exedra—shaped panoramic terrace：四周高全景平台。exedra：高背的椅子。

⑪lateral axis：横轴。

⑫artificial rock…sculpture 有洞穴和寓言雕刻的人造岩石。

⑬Tuscany：地名, 托斯卡拉（意大利）。

UNIT ELEVEN

Text   Aesthetic Plans of Furniture Arrangement

[1]   A room can be both functional and beautiful, although there may be times when one aspect will have to be sacrificed for the other because of specific limitations. When such a problem does arise, creative ability can work out a happy solution. For example, radiators that are not concealed can seriously tax the imagination. One needs them for heating, yet their appearance can mar the beauty of the room. One simple solution is to use bookcases on either side and a metal grille over the front of the radiator. With a shelf over the whole unit, the "problem" may become a very attractive adjunct to a room. Perhaps all problems will not be solved as easily as that, but it is more interesting at least to try some creative approach rather than simply to ignore them. The beauty of a home will depend on how well the principles of design are applied.

[2]   To some extent, natural instincts dictate the placement of furniture in a room. Even people who are not well versed in the fundamentals of art, place the sofa against the long wall in the living room because it seems to "look right " in that position. But a more refined awareness of design establishes the subtle aesthetics that make a room more beautiful.

Harmony

[3]   A room plan blends all the elements so that the whole area expresses a particular theme or mood. The old axiom that the "sum is greater than the total of the parts " can will be applied to the composition of a room. Each object and each element contributes to the whole, but the result must be a unit that has a charm and a personality of its own. The beauty of any room depends upon this interrelationship of all the components. The furnishings must look as though they belong in the room and in the company of one another.

Proportion

[4]   Because proportion is a matter of spatial relationships, the size of the room and the available wall space will determine the types of furniture and the amount of it that canbe used. Furniture should be in scale with the room. A small room will usually appear to best advantage if it has small-scaled pieces and a minimum number of them; a large room can take more massive ones.

[5]   A wall area is broken by the outlines of the furniture and the accessories placed against it. Each wall arrangement must, therefore, be considered in terms of divisions that

110

are pleasing to the eye. Pictures or other accessories that are hung on the wall should accord with both the furniture and the wall area.

[6]   Scale is also important in grouping pieces of furniture. A tiny, delicate table next to a massive chair becomes insignificant, although the table itself may be charming near a more delicate piece.

Balance

[7]   In almost every room there will be some pieces of furniture that are heavier than others. The larger, more important pieces should be distributed around the room in such a way that all areas will be in equilibrium. but the architectural features, such as window or a fireplace, also bear "weight," and frequently must be balanced by heavier pieces on opposite walls.

[8]   Often color can be employed to bring areas into balance. A small area of brilliant color or of a bold pattern takes on an added weight that can often balance a larger area of a more subdued nature. Thus a chair covered in a bright color might balance the more subdued draperies of a large window.

[9]   Balance within groupings of furniture is also important. Most rooms need either formal or informal balance, but in general, modern style and the more casual traditional styles lend themselves to informal balance. Elegance in a stately traditional room may be expressed by groups that are symmetrically arranged. The mood of the room will determine how much of each type of balance one may want to use. Too much asymmetry may lead to confusion and restlessness; too much symmetry may be stiff and forbidding.

Emphasis

[10]   Most rooms are more interesting if there are definite centers of interest that give leadership to their designs. A large room may have more than one dominant center, but in a small room one or perhaps two centers will usually be sufficient.

[11]   One should study each room carefully to determine what or where the center of interest might be. Perhaps a fireplace, a large window, a pair of windows, or some other architectural feature can be used as the area of emphasis. one large wall area can be given importance by furniture, accessories, color, or pattern. For example, wall treated with a mural, painted in a brighter color, or covered with a different texture immediately becomes a dominant onte. A large important piece of furniture, a large picture, or a picture grouping may lend added emphasis to an area.

[12]   Some special activity, hobby, or interest may provide an interesting basis for a dominant area in a room. A musical instrument or a collection of some sort can be emphasized by the manner in which it is placed or displayed. Such a center of interest frequently

gives a room its individuality and may set the theme for the entire plan.

Rhythm

[13] Lines, colors, and textures in the furnishings will cause the eye to move in certain directions. It s usually more pleasing for the eye to move in an easy, graceful manner rather than to move with a jumpy or jerky motion. We have discussed various ways of producing rhythmic sensations, and all of the techniques may be applied in developing a room plan. A pleasing rhythm depends on well- organized. relationships of all the elements of design.

[14] The lines of the more important furnishings are generally more attractive if they follow the structural lines of the room. Rectangular pieces will appear to better advantage when placed with the major line parallel to a wall or at right angles to it. Placing furniture on the diagonal, or catercornered, is often disturbing, except for pull-up chairs or even lounge chairs in some rooms.

[15] Continuity of line helps the eye to travel smoothly. Thus tables that are the same height as the arm of a chair are not only more convenient to use but are usually more attractive in relation to the chair. Pictures and other accessories must be arranged to keep eye movements smooth and easy.

[16] Repetition is an excellent means of providing a feeling of, rhythm, but it must be employed with discretion. Too much may become dull or monotonous; some contrast is necessary for interest.

New Words and Expressions

radiator ['reidieitə]	n.	暖气炉，散热器
tax ['tæks]	vt.	使……耗尽
mar [mɑː]	vt.	损伤，毁损，毁坏
grille [gril]	n.	铁栅
adjunct ['ædʒʌŋkt]	n.	附加物，附属物
subtle * ['sʌtl]	a.	微妙的
axiom ['æksiəm]	n.	公理
furnishings ['fəːniʃiŋz]	n.	家具与陈设品
accessory* [æk'sesəri]	n.	附件，陈设品
massive* ['mæsiv]	a.	巨大的，大而重的
subdue [səb'djuː]	vt.	使比较安静柔和缓和
drapery ['dreipəri]	n.	帐幕，衣饰
accord [ə'kɔːd]	vi.	一致，调和，符合
asymmetry* [æ'simitri]	n.	不对称
jerky ['dʒəːki]	a.	不平稳的，颠簸的

sensation [sen'seiʃən]		n.	感觉，知觉
cater-cornered ['kætəkə:nəd]		a.	对角线的
pull-up		n.	折叠椅
lounge [laundʒ]		n.	躺椅
discretion [dis'kreʃən]		n.	谨慎
be versed in			精通

Exercises

Reading Comprehension

I. Skim the text and fill in the folloing diagram

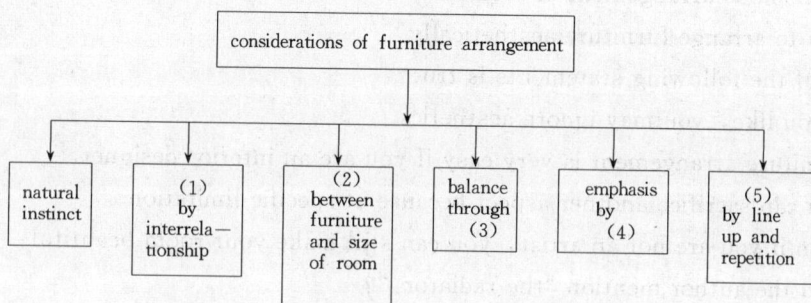

considerations of furniture arrangement

natural instinct	(1) by interrela—tionship	(2) between furniture and size of room	balance through (3)	emphasis by (4)	(5) by line up and repetition

II. Read the text carefully and then choose the best answer among the four choices given to complete each statement.

1. What does the author think is the creative approach to arrange furniture?

   A) Trying to take all elements into consideration.

   B) Arranging furniture by natural instinct.

   C) Ignoring them and keeping them freely.

   D) Keeping furniture in equilibrium.

2. What does the sentence "sum is greater than the total of the parts" mean in the text.

   A) If all pieces of furniture are beautiful, the room must be beautiful.

   B) The overall arrangement of furniture must be harmonious.

   C) The beauty of a room depends on whether the furniture is beautiful or not.

   D) The interior decoration is more important than the furnishings.

3. The author believes _____ is most important in furniture arrangement.

   A) natural instinct

   B) aesthetic plan

   C) scale

   D) balance

4. We can infer from the text that _____ .

A) furniture arrangement can show one's education level

B) furniture represents one's wealth

C) the decoration of a room indicate one's social status

D) furniture arrangement involves one's interest

5. The author writes this article to _____ .

A) furniture designers

B) architects

C) general readers

D) architectural experts

6. The passage is mainly about _____ .

A) exact arrangement of furniture

B) aesthetic plan of decorating rooms

C) harmonious arrangement of furniture

D) how to arrange furniture aesthetically

7. Which of the following statements is true?

A) If you like, you may ignore aesthetics

B) Furniture arrangement is very easy if you are an interior designer.

C) You can sacrifice another aspect because of specific limitation.

D) Even if you are not an artist, you can still make your room beautiful

8. Why did the author mention "the radiator "?

A) Because the author wanted to put forward a solution to furniture arrangement.

B) Because this problem is very common.

C) Because he asked people to fix a radiator in order to make room more comfortable.

D) Because he wanted to tell the readers how to solve the problem if you meet in furniture arrangement.

9. If you are a functionalist, you will arrange your furniture _____ .

A) for the purpose of convenience

B) beautifully

C) symmetrically

D) just as you like

10. The author's attitude towards furniture arrangement is _____ .

A) objective   B) critical

C) preferable   D) innocent

Vocabulary

I . Match the word in Column A with their corresponding definitions in column B.

column A   column B

1. grille   a. apparatus for radiating heat, used for heating building

2. furnishings   b. a frame of upright metal bars filling a space in a door or window

3. radiator   c. articles of furniture or other articles fixed in a room such as bath, curtains

4. lounge   d. cloth arranged in folds

5. drapery   e. comfortable easy-chair

6. adjunct   f. something that is added or joined to something else but is not a necessary part of it

Ⅱ. Complete each of the following statements with one of the four choices given below.

1. The story of paradise told in the Book of Genesis symbolizes mankind's dream of life in mythical _____ with nature.

   A) accord   B) agree

   C) suit   D) fit

2. An understanding of this philosophy helped early Chinese garden designers strike a balance in their gardens between strong and _____ feature.

   A) seemingly   B) subtle

   C) spiral   D) susceptible

3. It is also a part of the system that all _____ furniture with solid surfaces must be avoided because these are also a source of sound reflection.

   A) massive   B) minimal

   C) mobile   D) modal

4. The _____ of a building include the backyard and surrounding pavements.

   A) accessory   B) adjacent

   C) ambient   D) analogue

5. A _____ room is difficult to decorate symmetrically with furniture.

   A) parallel   B) asymmetry

   C) annular   D) planar

6. It is a (n) _____ that a whole is greater than any of its parts.

   A) axiom   B) rule

   C) assumption   D) inference

7. The beauty of the room was _____ by the colour of walls.

   A) decayed   B) preset

   C) marred   D) rugged

8. You are _____ my patience by asking such stupid question.

   A) imposing   B) taxing

   C) retarding   D) reprocessing

Writing   Abstract Writing（1）

Directions: The following is an abstract of the text of Unit Eleven and there are eight words missing. Please fill in the blanks with some of the words given.

（beauty, sacrifice, creative, instinct, balance, harmonious proportion, scale, equilibrium, mood, size, repetition) Aesthetic Plans of Furniture Arrangement

When furniture is arranged, some problems sometimes arise. At that time, the _____ of the room will be _____ for the function and vice versa. But if a creative approach is adopted, the problem will be solved satisfac-torily.

However, to some extent, natural _____ dictate the placement of furniture in a room, so the mentioned problem is unavoidable. But if subtle _____ of furniture arrangement is mastered, the room will be more beautiful.

Firstly, the furniture must be _____. Every piece of furniture should be beautiful but must look belonging in the room and in the company one another.

Secondly, the furniture should be in scale with the room. And _____ is also important in grouping piece of furniture.

Thirdly, all pieces of furniture should be distributed in equilibrium. We can make use of colour to bring areas into balance.

Then, some centers of interest can be established in order to set the theme or mood of the room. But the number of the centers is determined by the _____ of the room.

Finally, pay attention to the rhythm of the room. If you want to attain the aim, you can employ the lines of the furnishing so that they are continued without break and jump. Another way is _____, but carefully used.

Reading Material A

The Ornamental Impulse

The urge to embellish and the love of ornamental effect are basic to human nature. In all ages and cultures the human race has demonstrated a persistent ipmulse to decorate, whether by appeasing the gods with magical signs or by using false shutters and columns to personalize their houses. ①By ornamenting or decorating, people of every society have tried to transform the merely useful into the beauti-ful, giving meaning and ipmortance to an often drab reality. The univer-sal appeal of ornament is precisely its "uselessness" in the strict functionalist sense of that word. Because ornament is not there to hold things up or make things work, it is not bound by all the utilitarian constraints that threaten, at times, to suffocate us. ②Ornament is essentially free: free to move the eye, to intrigue the mind, to rest the soul; free simply to delight us.

Though the essence of ornament is its freedom from function, there are a number of practical necessities that ornament is uniquely able to satisfy. The most obvious is the need for identification: telling people what an object or building is, for what purpose it is intended. Ornament can be a wordless sign like a red-and-white stripped pole signifying "barber shop. " Or it can speak indirectly through socio—historical associations: for example, broad, monumental steps with high colonnaded porch and pediment have come to signify "important public building. " Conversely, because it is stripped of all ornamental clues, a modern bank might easily pass for a dry cleaning establishment or auto parts store, possibly a boon to future recycling but not much help to present users.

In a town-or cityscape, ornament makes places legible, helping people to sort out pathways, districts, and reference points so that, as urbanist Kevin Lynch has explained, "the various parts of a place can be recognized and can be organized into a coherent pattern. " Decorative roof treatments help people to pick out individual buildings at a distance. Ornamental moldings, lintels, cornices, and friezes[3] help to distinguish the tops, midportions, and bases of buildings, giving them clear identity at the ground level. Ornamental surrounds emphasize doors and windows, letting people know where to enter a building and, by the modulation of these elements, what to expect inside. Ornament also helps to orient people, telling them which way is in or out, up or down, toward the center or away from the center. Denied the use of ornament, Modern design has had to rely on the manipulation of space and shape alone to tell people what buildings are for and how to move about in them. Often this is a cumbersome task, requiring the invention of private codes that may communicate to other designers but leave most people baffled. Hence the common complaints about modern buildings: we can't tell what they are, how to get in them, or where to go once we're inside.

Another practical use of ornament in architecture is as a scale device; breaking down the overall mass of a building into smaller pieces that relate comfortably to the human observer.[4] In 1952, at a time when it was not very fashionable to say so, critic Henry Hope Reed argued that "it is only with ornament we can obtain a sense of scale; it is only on ornament that the eye can rest; it is only with ornament that the eye can measure, " One reason that we enjoy older sections of towns and cities is that their scale "feels right " to us. Even the biggest buildings meant to awe us at a distance-like a late-nineteenth-century courthouse or skyscraper—reveal layers of ornament that become more and more intimate the closer we approach. While twentieth century construction technology has permitted buildings to achieve greater height and bulk than the world has ever before seen, Modern design theory has, until recently, failed to acknowledge the serious scale problems that such height and bulk create. The renewed interest in architectural ornament is, in part, an attempt to restore human scale to the built environment, to give people some visual reference against which they can measure themselves and not feel overpowered.

There is also the symbolic force of ornament: the ability of ornament to impart to an object or building some meaning beyond its actual time, place, or purpose. For most people, a house is much more than shelter. It is a statement like clothing or furniture, of self-image; of desired social status, lifestyle, or private fantasy. The roof may keep out the rain, but it is the elaborate lamppost at the front of the drive, the eagle over the door, or the intricate carving on the heirloom table with which people seem to identify. ⑤

Yet this simple impulse——the urge to embellish—has been subjected to some amazingly complicated theories over the last two hundred years. Since the Industrial Revolution, the use of ornament has been considered not only a matter of aesthetics and taste, but of moral propriety. ⑥Such moral theorizing helped to pave the way for the Modern Movement and, in turn, for the reaction to that movement which is now occurring. To put this in perspective we must go back, if not to our ancestors' cave paintings, at least to the Renaissance.

Notes

①用魔术般的标志安抚神或者用假的百叶窗和柱显示出住房的特征。
②Ti is not bound dy all the utilitarian constraints 它不受功利主义的限制。
③ornamental moldings, lintel, cornices, and friezes：装饰性线脚，过梁，嵌线和壁缘。
④scale device：刻度标志。
⑤heirloom：传家宝。
⑥装饰的运用被认为不但是一个美学和趣味问题，而且是一个道德礼貌问题。

Reading Material B

The Rise of Interior Decoration

It cannot be simply coincidence that the term 'interior decoration' was coined by Thomas Hope, the celebrated collector and scholar of the antique, at the very beginning of the century. ①Emulating the publication Recueil de decorations interieures⋯of 1801 by the architects Percier and Fontaine who enjoyed the patronage of Napoleon I, and with whom Hope was acquainted, he produced a book of designs for furniture and 'interior decoration' in 1807. ② This gave a title and a framework to one of the most widely pervasive artistic achievements of the nineteenth century. But more important by far than the mere coining of a phrase was the circulation of these 'designer' ideas that publication afforded. The accessibility of these schemes for decoration was to inspire the growing middle-class population with hitherto undreamed-of aspirations for their personal surroundings. ③The importance of the development, at this same date, of practical colour reproduction for publications on interior design and decoration cannot be over-stressed.

In 1822 Walter Scott wrote to his friend, Danieel Terry, the architect turned actor: 'Pray is there not a tolerable book on upholstery-I mean plans for tables chairs, commodes, and such like. ④If so I would be much obliged to you to get me a copy.' Terry replied some six weeks later: 'I have hunted London for a book on furniture and have ascertained that there is none of any character, hope's is merely his own house which is entirely Grecian and there is a French one of Bonaparte's Palaces but not one of a style appertaining to your castle….'⑤

Scott would have found Henry Shaw's specimens of Ancient Furniture to be exactly the publication he was seeking. This handsome volume with its seventy-four plates appeared in 1836. and contained examples of mainly Gothic and Elizabethan furniture and metalwork. It was dedicated to the collector and antiquary Thomas Lister Parker, and indeed included illustrations of pieces belonging to him. Plates from this book were copied in a later French publication, Asselineau's *objets bu Moyen Age et de la Renaissance* (1844), and it was recommended by John Claudius Loudon in the later editions of his own immensely influential Encyclopaedia of Cottage, Farm and Villa Architecture, which first appeared in 1833. Shaw's 1847 Encyclopaedia of Ornament was to be the inspiration for the many pattern books of historical ornament that were produced in the nineteenth century. ⑥

Thomas Lister Parker was one of the very first to experiment with the Elizabethan style: his alterations to his house, Browsholme, date from before 1810. Parker was responsible for starting the architect Anthony Salvin on his Elizabethan enthusiasms, and thus for inspiring some of the finest nineteenth-century neo-Elizabethan schemes, for example at Harlaxton; but the focal point of antiquarian inspiration remains Walter Scott. To quote Clive Wainwright, "The influence of the interior decoration and furnishings at Abbotsford was, I am convinced, widespread and international. Any serious study of the Gothic, Elizabethan or Tudor revivals and the antiquarian movement in the nineteenth century must start at Abbotsford. "

Proliferating publications set the seal of approval on a concern with the decoration of the home, which became increasingly widespread as the industrial middle classes became more prosperous. But the choices that so much information offered were almost overwhelming, and interior decoration came to be perceived as a complex operation only to be carried out with the help and advice of professionals. Such advice was to be forthcoming in bewildering profusion, much of it proffered with a high-handed disregard for the sensibility and the preferences of the patron, but much also of sensible and practical application. ⑦

Thomas Hope was a perfectionist and his counsel certainly verged on the high—handed. He believed that the Classical style was the only possible mode of decoration and would not even consider the claims of the Gothic taste. His attack, in 1804, on James Wyatt's neo-Gothic plans for Downing College, Cambridge, caused Wyatt's plans to be dropped, thus earning Hope an enemy for life. By no means everyone shared his rigorous design princi-ples; after the publication of Household Furniture and Interior Decoration in 1807, Sydney Smith wrote in the Edinburgh Review:

Everything is to be adorned according to Mr Hope, with emblems and symbols connected with the uses to which it is applied, and all these emblems are to be derived from classical mythology, He has made a perfect hieroglyphic or enigma of most of his apartments by this means, and produced something so childishly complicated and fantastic as to be impenetra-ble without a paraphrase and ridiculous when it is interpreted. Hope's treatise also advocat-ed room settings that were planned down to the minutest detail to complement the works of art that they contained. The design of the furniture was meticulously researched and ap-propriate forms and ornament used to set off the extensive and important collections of Greek and Egyptian antiquities housed in his London house in Duchess Street and at The Deepdene in Surrey.

Nevertheless, Hope's ideas were influential; and although there is little evidence of di-rect copying of specific examples from his designs, his ideas appear transformed but still quite recognizable in the work of some of his successors.

Notes

①it cannot be simply coincidence：不是简单的巧合。

②Recueil de Decorations interieures（法语）《室内装饰集》。

③hitherto：到目前为止。

④upholstery：室内装潢。

⑤Bonaparte's Palace（法国）波拿巴宫。

⑥Objets du Moyen Age et de la Renaissance（法语）《中世纪和文艺复兴时斯的物品》。

⑦proffer：提供。

UNIT TWELVE

Text   A Theory of Landscape Architecture

[1]   Landscape Architecture involves the five major components: natural process, social processes, methodology, technology, and values. Whatever the scale or emphasis of operation, these five components are consistently relevant. Social and natural factors must permeate every facet of a profession that is concerned with people and land. Problem solving. planning, and design methods apply at all scales. Good judgment is consistently required.

[2]   Consider how natural factors data are relevant to both planning and design. At the regional scale, the impact of development or change in use on a landscape must clearly be known and evaluated before a policy to allow such action is set. An inventory of the natural factors, including geology, soils, hydrology, topography, climate, vegetation, and wildlife and the ecological relationships between them is fundamental to an understanding of the ecosystem to which change is contemplated. Equally important is an analysis of visual quality. Land use policy can thus be made on the basis of the known vulnerability or resistance of the landscape. In other circumstances the natural processes which add up to a given landscape at a given moment in its evolution may, as at Grand Canyon and elsewhere, constitute a resource to be preserved and managed as a public trust. ①On a smaller scale, soil and geological conditions may be critical in the determination of the cost and form of building foundations: where it is most suitable to build and where it is not. The sun, wind, and rain are important
factors of design where the development of comfort zones for human activity
or the growth of plants is a primary objective. Thus in many ways the natural factors of site or region interact in the process of landscape planning and design.

[3]   The social factors apply equally at various scales. In site planning and landscape design, cultural variation in the use and appreciation of open space and parks and the physical and social needs of the young and old are some of the many variables to be considered in a design process that aims to be responsive to social values and human needs. ②In decisions related to appropriation of landscape for recreation and aesthetic value people's perception of the environment and the behavioral patterns and tendencies of people in the out-of-doors are clearly relevant. It is important that designers understand the impact of environment on behavior and also appreciate the basic human need to manipulate and control the environment.

[4]   Technology is the means by which a design is implemented or on which a policy depends. Some of it changes year by year as new materials and machinery and techniques are developed. Its role in the three types of landscape architecture is clear. Specific areas of

technology include plants, planting and ecological succession, soil science, hydrology and sewage treatment, microclimate control, surface drainage, erosion control, hard surfaces, and maintenance.

[5] Design methodology involves systems whereby conflicts can be identified and landscape problems defined. ③It is a process in which all relevant factors and variables can be given values and brought to bear on the development of a solution to the problem. Computer graphics, analytical techniques, and notation systems aid in this process. In addition, there is much to commend an investigation of the creative process as proposed by Halprin. ④He suggests scoring techniques, as in music or choreography, as a device to open up and make visible the design process. This, according to Halprin, allows more people to participate in design and decision making and facilitates the generation of new ways to plan and design large scale complex environments and regions leading to more humanistic solutions.

[6]   The objective of combining these components is the development of a basis from which landscape planning and detailed design can be made responsive to human behavioral patterns (people) and specific situation characteristics (the setting). ⑤Since both will vary in terms of culture, region and neighborhood there can be no panaceas and no preconceived solutions. Thus analysis of social and natural factors is critical in comprehensive problem definition leading to unique and appropriate design form and plan relationships.

[7]   The process of design, the aim of which is the evolution of forms and relationships suited to the needs of people, may be compared to the fundamental form-giving processes which have created the geomorphology of the great natural landscapes of the world. Here the visual form of the land's surface-valleys and ridges, water-filled basins, and jagged peaks-represents an evolutionary stage in the interaction between the geological structure and the agents of erosion. The forms we see result from the response of inorganic material to a set of imposed conditions of weathering. The variations in vegetative cover from north to south slopes, from meadow to subarctic plateau, from river valley to rocky talus constitute exact responses to the range of environmental conditions created by the physiographic differentiation of the landscape. In turn, the wildlife distribution is dictated by the type and extent of the vegetation. No one aspect of the pattern is without cause or consequence. All merge irrevocably into a self- sustaining and evolving ecological system, representing the resolution of the natural forces and processes up to a specific moment in time. The parallel is perhaps limited, but it is this sense of ultimate resolution of form- giving forces with a built-in potential for change that should be the goal of the landscape planner and designer.

New Words and Expressions

methodology* [meθə'dɔlədʒi]   n.   方法论、方法学
facet ['fæsit]   n.   某方面、（建）柱槽筋凸线

geology [dʒiˈɔlədʒi]	n.	地质学
hydrology* [haiˈdrɔlədʒi]	n.	水文学、水理学
topography [təˈpɔgrəfi]	n.	地形，地形学，地形测量学
wildlife [ˈwaildlaif]	n.	野生物
ecological [ekəˈlɔdʒikəl]	a.	生态，生态学的
ecosystem [ikəˈsistəm]	n.	生态系统
comtemplate [ˈkɔmtempleit]	vt.	沉思，期待
responsive [risˈpɔnsiv]	a.	响应的，易起反应的
appropriation [əprəupriˈeiʃən]	n.	拔给，占用，挪用
succession [səkˈseʃən]	n.	连续，接续，（生物）演替
sewage [ˈsju (:) idʒ]	n.	（阴沟处的）污水，污物
erosion* [iˈrəuʒən]	n.	腐蚀，侵蚀
choreography [kɔːriˈɔgrəfi]	n.	舞蹈，舞蹈设计
humanistic [hjuːməˈnistik]	a.	人道主义的，人文主义的
panacea [pænəˈsiə]	n.	治百病的灵药，万应药
preconceive [ˈpriːkənˈsiːv]	vt.	预想，事先想好
geomorphology [ˈdʒiəmɔːˈfɔlədʒi]	n.	地貌学
jagged [ˈdʒægid]	a.	锯齿状的，凹凸不平的
inorganic [inɔːˈgænik]	a.	无生物的，无机的
vegetative [ˈvedʒitətiv]	a.	植物的，蔬菜的
meadow [ˈmedəu]	n.	草地，牧草地
subarctic [ˈsʌbˈɑːktik]	a.	近北极的，亚北极的
talus [ˈteiləs]	n.	斜面，山麓堆积，塌磊
physiographic [fiziəˈgræfik]	a.	地文学的，自然地理学的
irrevocable [iˈrevəkəbl]	a.	不可改变的，不能挽回的

Notes

①Grand Canyon：科罗拉多大峡谷（美国）。

②此句中 that 引导的从句修饰 a design process. 其主语为 cultural variation in use, appreciation of open space and parks，the physical and social needs of the young and old.

③whereby：凭那个，由是，引导一个状语从句。

④there is much：有理由；

⑤Halprin：（1916—）生于纽约，美国著名景园建筑大师。

⑥此句是一个复杂句，which 指代 basis。

Exercises

Reading Comprehension

I . Complete the following incomplete sentences

1. Landscape architecture includes the five major components: natural process _____, methodology, _____ and _____.

2. Natural factors are _____, soil, hydrology, _____, climate, vegetation, and wildlife, and _____ relationships between them.

3. Social factors include _____ in the use and appreciation of open space and parks and the _____ and social needs of the young and old.

4. Design methodology include computer graphics, _____ technique and _____ _____ systems. _____ technique is also a useful method.

5. Specific areas of technology include plants _____ and ecological succession, _____ science, hydrology and _____ treatment, microclimate control, surface drainage, erosion control, hard surfaces, and maintenance.

II . Read the text carefully and then choose the best answer among the four choices given to complete each statement.

1. In the text the author mainly tells us _____.
    A) what the five major components are
    B) the five major components and their roles
    C) how to design a landscape
    D) how natural factors affect the landscape design

2. What is the relationship of the five components?
    A) relevant
    B) irrelevant
    C) contridictory
    D) interaction

3. If you combine these components you can _____.
    A) have a good landscape planning and design
    B) only obtain a basis of design
    C) ignore other factors in the design
    D) draw the sketch immediately

4. From the text, we can infer _____.
    A) in the landscape design the analysis of social and natural factors is critical
    B) the analysis is basis; the process of design is result
    C) social factors are more important than natural factors
    D) design methodology can be ignored

5. In the process of design, as regards natural factors we should _____.

    A) obey the natural principle of ecosystem

    B) alter the natural conditions

    C) consider the built-in potential for change

    D) pay more attention to environmental conditions

6. Which of the following statements is true?

    A) Environment is the most important factor in designing landscape.

    B) Designers should make use of environment.

    C) The relationship between people and setting can be ignored.

    D) The aim of design process is to change the environment.

7. In paragraph 6, line 4, the word "both" refers to _____.

    A) people and setting

    B) design analysis and design process

    C) landscape planning and detailed design

    D) culture and region

8. As an architect of landscape architecture, you should take _____ into account first.

    A) policy of land use

    B) social and natural factors

    C) good judgment

    D) design methodology

9. The process of design may be compared to _____.

    A) choreography

    B) formation of base

    C) evolution of forms

    D) geomorphology

10. Among the five factors, "value" means _____.

    A) judgment of architects

    B) appreciation of people

    C) assessment

    D) cost of building a landscape

Vocabulary

I. Match the words in column A with their corresponding definitions in column B

    column A   column B

    1. topography   a. aspect

    2. facet   b. the character of an area esp. as regards shape and height of
                            land

    3. geomorphology   c. a field of wild grass and flowers

4. meadow   d. sloping mass of fragments at the foot of a cliff

5. ecosystem   e. the science of studying the surface of the earth

6. talus   f. all the plants, animals and people in an area together with
                      their surroundings, considered from the view of their rela-
                      tionship to each other

II. Complete each of the following statements with one of the four choices given below.

1. All the potential constraints must be _____ and adapted before a final decision is
   made.

   A) preconceived   B) retracted

   C) prepared   D) ruptured

2. Despite the fact that pollution is increasingly endangering the existence of all beings
   on the earth, industries are continuously discharging _____ into rivers, lakes, or the
   sea.

   A) surge   B) slab

   C) sewage   D) seam

3. Before the pipes are buried in the ground, treatment against _____ must be conducted
   to prolong their life span.

   A) corruption   B) erosion

   C) desposition   D) torsion

4. The new consciousness of _____ problems will help generate a universally understood language of design criteria as the basic principles of natural water management.

   A) geological   B) economical

   C) geometrical   D) ecological

5. In particular, designers usually design not just because they enjoy doing it but also
   because they tend to be _____ to the things they want to create.

   A) responsive   B) repetitive

   C) responsible   D) respective

6. There is no universal solution to all the problems in design just as there is no _____
   for all diseases in the world.

   A) ingredient   B) constituent

   C) recovery   D) panacea

7. Rooms can make sound poetic. But it can not be added to the space after- ward and
   therefore must be _____ during the initial conception of a space.

   A) contempted   B) complemented

   C) contemplated   D) condensed

8. The resistors are connected in series, and the current in the circuit flows through each
   resistor in _____ .

   A) essence   B) succession

   C) contour   D) equilibrium

Writing   **Abstract Writing**（2）

Directions: The following is an abstract of Unit Twelve, and there are 8 words missing. Please fill in the blanks with the words found from the text or with your own words.

A Theory of Landscape Architecture

Landscape architecture involves five major components: natural process, social processes, methodology, techonology and values. The five components are consistently _____ .

_____ factors include geology, soils, hydrology topography, climate, vegetation and wildlife and ecological relationships between them. They affect the choice of _____ and plants, the cost and form of landscape.

The social factors involve cultural variation, the physical and social need of the young and old. Thus the landscape must _____ social values and human needs.

If the previous _____ are taken into consideration, then how to realize the idea or thoughts, we turn to technology and design _____ . _____ is a means which a design is implemented or on which a policy depends. It will solve the detailed problem such as planting, erosion control, sewage treatment, microclimate, etc. Design methodology helps us find the conflicts among the factors and put forward a solution to the landscape problem. It includes computer graphics, analytical techniques and notation systems.

During the process of design, a good _____ is consistently required.

Reading Material A

Elements of Landscape Architectural Design

As with all art forms and design disciplines, there is a distinct set of media characteristic of the profession of landscape architecture. ①Landform, plant materials, buildings, pavement, site structures, and water are, in numerous combinations, the primary physical components comprising most works of landscape architecture. ②They are the media that landscape architects utilize to formulate space and establish experiences that delight the eye as well as the emotions. In a purely artistic sense, the physical design elements of landscape architecture are analogous to the words of a poem or notes of a piece of music. ③Collectively, they constitute a composition affecting the human physical and emotional senses.

Individually the physical design elements of landscape architecture each have their own unique qualities and roles to fulfill in the outdoor environment. Landform is the base or floor plane of the landscape. It is the one element that supports and unites all the other components of the environment. Landform's configuration affects such diverse factors as the structure of the outdoor environment, land use location, views, drainage, and microclimate in addition to spatial definition and character. [4] Furthermore, landform is a plastic medium in its own right that can be molded to create solids and voids on the ground plane in many possible ways. [5]

Plant materials provide the aspect of life in the landscape. They are living, breathing elements that grow and change with time. Their relatively soft, sometimes irregular shape along with their living green appearance provide a habitable feeling in the outdoor environment. In addition, plant materials fulfill a number of more practical functions such as defining space in all three planes of enclosure, modifying microclimate, cleansing the air, stabilizing soil, and acting as important visual elements based on their size, form, color, and texture.

Buildings, the locus of numerous human activities, are solid volumes in the outdoor environment. Compared with either landform or plant materials, buildings are a relatively hard, firm medium in the landscape. As compositional elements, buildings may be treated as either single objects of individual significance in the environment or located in clusters that define spaces and spatial sequences of numerous possible temperaments. Building masses usually establish fixed, nonpliable spatial limits in the organization of outdoor functions and activities. [7]

Pavement is one of the materials that can be employed on the ground plane. Pavement, in contrast to landform, plant materials, and buildings, is a flat, planar element that can be used as a durable, fixed support of human and vehicular functions of intense or repeated use. Furthermore, pavement may function as both a directional and nondirectional element, accentuate different uses on the ground plane, influence perceived scale, provide unity, and impress spatial character.

Site structures are constructed three- dimensional elements of the outdoor environment directly relating to the ability of people to use the outdoor environment conveniently. Steps, ramps, walls, fences, and seating contribute to the comfort and safety of outdoor spaces as well as to the delineation of humanly scaled outdoor rooms. [8] As a group, site structures are hard elements of an architectural quality used in the landscape to reinforce the spatial and functional organization provided by landform, buildings, and plant material.

Finally, water is a specialty element of the landscape with a strongly compelling quality. Water, similar to plant materials, is a life- giving element that helps to provide a feeling of vitality and animation. As a fluid element, water is a highly varied and flexible medium. It may be utilized as a static element in the outdoor environment to calm the senses of sight and sound or it may be employed as a dynamic element of motion, exciting the eye in addition to providing a sound stimulus. However it is used, water is a unique feature easily attracting people to it.

128

Besides the individual qualities of the major landscape architectural design media, they possess other distinguishing characteristics when considered collectively. Perhaps one of the most notable aspects of landscape architectural design elements is that they are components of the exterior environment where they are directly subjected to the forces of nature. Unlike the media of certain other design disciplines that must be protected or delicately treated, landform, plant material, buildings, pavement, site structures, and water are all exposed to such factors as sun, wind, precipitation, temperature variations, and erosion. In some circumstances, these forces are mild and insignificant in their influence on the physical design elements of the landscape. In other situations, the natural forces of the exterior environment are so harsh as to be destructive.

The consequence of natural forces is that all the design media of the landscape weather and change over time, if only subtly. A pavement may become worn, a slope may erode slightly, plant materials may grow and die, the coloration of a wall may either fade or darken with age, or the water in a pond may vary in level and quality. The landscape architect must accept these changes and allow them to occur and recognize that nature provides the final touch to a design located in the exterior environment. The challenge for the landscape architect is to be able to properly anticipate and understand the influence of the natural forces so that they enrich the quality of a landscape architectural design with time, not the opposite.

Notes

①就艺术形式和设计原理而言，景观建筑这一职业有一系列明显的手段特征
②Landform，plant…and water：地貌，植被，建筑物，道路，地质结构和水；
③in numerous combinations：在无数由这些成分构成的景观中。
④analogous to：类似于。
⑤landform's configuration：地形的轮廓
⑥plastic medium：可变媒介物；
⑦建筑群常常确定固定的、不能改变的室外功能和活动的空间限制。
⑧the delineation of humanly scaled outdoor rooms：描绘人为标出的室外空间。

Reading Material B

Office Landscape

A new and very special type of interior is the "office landscape". The curious term, a literal translation of the German Buro-landschaft, describes a system of office planning developed during the last few years in Europe which is attracting considerable attention at the present time. ①An "office landscape" interior tends to be quite shocking to most designers on first exposure, particularly when seen in plan, because it seems to violate all the generally accepted principles of good design. In plan it appears that furniture and portable screens have been thrown into a space at random with a chaotic absence of pattern. On closer examination, however, it becomes clear that the originators of office landscape have some very specific and reason-able ideas which lead to these unusual results.

The developers of this method, the Quickborner Team of Hamburg, are, in fact, office management consultants rather than designers. ②Their study of office operation has led them to the belief that office planning should be based on patterns of communication, with all other values (such as appearance, status recognition, and tradition) either ignored or given a very minor status. ③Placement of work stations is determined by the flow of communication, which is the vital part of daily office functioning.

It is also basic to the "landscape" idea that partitioning be avoided. Even so-called movable partitions that take time and money to move are considered barriers to communication and flexibility. Without partitioning, change to accommodate changing work patterns becomes both quick and inexpensive. Communication is always easy in an office space without subdivision, there is a saving in space resulting from the sharing of circulation space that would otherwise have to be duplicated in each private space, and the reduction in emphasis on the symbolic values of status turn out to be helpful to office morale and work efficiency. ④

Without partitions, loss of privacy becomes most bothersome in terms of noise. ⑤For this reason, an office landscape requires complete carpeting of floors and elaborate acoustical treatment of all ceilings. It is also a part of the system that all massive furniture with solid surfaces must be avoided because these are also a source of sundreflection. Noisy office machines are removed from the general office space to special isolated locations. Permanent files are also placed in remote locations so that only small open file baskets are used in the regular office space.

The office landscape planning method begins with a survey of all communication in the office organization-whether by conversation, written memo, or telephone. Every staff member keeps a log of communications conducted for a period of two weeks. These data are then analyzed, in the case of large organizations with the help of a data-processing computer. This leads to a plan placing each work station so as to minimize the length of the most active lines of communication. People who must be in frequent contact are placed close together, those who have little need for contact end up far apart. Departmental organization and official "lines of command" are ignored in order to arrive at an arrangement that will reflect the real needs for proximity. Detailed layout is not geometric (since this would restrict the ease of following the guidance of the communications-dictated plan), but follows certain rules about details so as to avoid, for example, seating any two workers in a face-to-face position.

Once the basic plan has been arrived at, a scale model is built with movable furniture and portable screen elements placed according to the proposed plan. This model is made available to representatives of the working staff who will occupy the office so that criticisms and changes can be considered. In practice. it has been found that few changes result from this step, but that it is very helpful in securing the understanding and cooperation of those who will finally use the office There is also aroutine continuing study of needed changes, with a general rearrangement taking place approximately every six months to deal with all the accumulated needs for revision that have developed during that time. Since there are no fixed, architectural elements, such change is quick and inexpensive.

Notes

①Buro-Landschaft：［德］办公室景园。

②office management consultants：办公室管理顾问。

③···. with other values···either ignored or given a very minor status：忽略 其他方面或不太重视其他方面。

④office morale：办公室人员的士气。

⑤没有隔板，噪声也就成了令人烦恼的问题。

UNIT THIRTEEN

Text   **Urban Sense**

[1]   Half a century of planning activity has transformed the built environment, but has failed to capture the public's sympathies. The disillusionment with modernist town proposals has been particularly evident in the last two decades. Projects once hailed as manifestations of a brave new global vision have shown themselves to be inadequate as long-term settlements. ①Most conspicuous in post-war developments has been the absence of a sense of place. By zoning towns into distinct and unrelated sectors, modernist planning divided and polarised community life.

[2]   The growing public disaffection has helped to bring about alternative views in the architectural and planning professions, views which embrace traditional towns as models for new developments. ②These older models have been carefully studied by a new generation of professionals who introduce into urban design the idea of neighbourhoods with a diversity of communal, commercial and residential functions. The use of traditional urban models has resuscitated age-old questions about continuity and change in the relationship between architecture and the city, the setting of new towns and villages in the natural landscape, and the dialogue between built form and communal open spaces. ③

[3]   Despite the growing public support that new traditional towns have enjoyed, some critics have claimed that these models cannot work today, as they fail to address contemporary social and technological issues. What critics have failed to appreciate, however, is that the most viable contemporary urban centres are in fact historical enclaves that evolved not out of tabula-rasa attitudes like those expounded by the Modern Movement, but a wholesome investment in the notion of 'res publica', or public realm. ④The question of technology is not posed by the new traditionalists in awe of science, but in practical terms: how it can be harnessed to a common-sensical urbanism, rather than the other way around. Science then, needs to be used correctly—to warm our houses, aid us in our daily endeavours, expedite our business, if this remains within the bounds of a healthy urban life.

[4]   The new attitudes regarding technology are perhaps most evident in the way the problem of the car is being handled. The new traditionalists seek to limit its use to peripheral areas, creating pedestrian neighbourhoods and quarters that will ultimately reduce the reliance on automobiles. More central to the argument, though, is the appreciation of communal or public space as a generator of civic environments. At Belvedere Village in Ascot, Demetri Porphyrios sets up what he calls a 'nucleus of a settlement' : a pattern of buildings and spaces intended not merely for long-term use but for gradual transformation and adaptaion into a larger regional urban centre. At Windsor in Florida, Andres Duany and Eliza-

132

beth Plater-Zyberk have codified the elements of urban growth, setting up a building programme that limits idiosyncrasy in favour of an appreciable pattern of streets, squares, greens and street elevations.

[5]   The same attitudes are in evidence in better-known masterplan for Poundbury by Leon Krier, which dispays the entire range of civic amenities necessary for a balanced urban environment. The public spaces are bounded by communal buildings, residential blocks look onto central greens, commercial districts are located always at walking distance within the neighbourhoods.

[6]   Not least of the new practices in urban design is the respectful provision of a 'hard edge' along the boundaries of new towns, one which no longer seeks to expand haphazardly into the natural landscape but to treat it as a separate, sovereign entity. For the new traditionalists, delineation is paramount; whether one delineates the edges of a square, a green, a park, or the urban periphery, the act derives from the same appreciation of the integrity of every element that constitutes our environment. The Modern Movement purposefully blurred the differences in the city. Potsdamer-Platz in Berlin is a point in case, the area having since the war been diluted with the most diverse, eccentric structures—buildings clamouring for attention in a desolate, unaccommodating area that has been reduced to a loosely-knit, confused cluster of interstitial spaces. In their masterplan for the region, Hilmer and Sattler have ventured to reaffirm the historic pattern of streets and squares, setting up the right mix of uses and a system of public spaces that they deem indispensable in any urban proposal.

[7]   Absent from this group of professionals is the view of the architect as procurer of high-tech panaceas—the new traditionalists choose the more realistic path of collective experience and common sense, refusing to be seduced by industrial iconography or be lured into the guilt-ridden culture of anti-traditional rhetoric. They argue that if there is to be a brighter vision for the city, humanity must learn to make use of the good that is engrained in traditional urban models.

New Words and Expressions

disillusionment [ˌdisiˈluːʒənmənt]	n.	幻想破灭
hail [heil]	vi.	欢呼
conspicuous [kɔnˈspikjuəs]	a.	明显的，引人注目的
sector* [sektə]	n.	区，段，部门
polarise* [ˈpəuləraiz]	v.	（使）极化，两极分化
resuscitate [riˈsʌsiteit]	vt.	（使）苏醒，（使）复活；（使）复兴
continuity* [kɔntiˈnju (ː) əti]	n.	连续，连续性
enclave [ˈenkleiv]	n.	飞地
tabula-rasa [ˈtæbjulə-ˈreisə]	n.	［拉］擦去了文字的书板；白板

expound [ik'spaund]	vt.	详细解释；阐述
wholesome ['həulsəm]	a.	健康的，审慎的，安全的
res publica ['reis'pʌblikə]	n.	〔拉〕国家
pose* [pəuz]	v.	提出；（使）摆好姿势
awe [ɔ:]	n.	畏惧，敬畏
expedite ['ekspidait]	vt.	加快；促进
codify ['kɔdifai]	vt.	编纂；整理
idiosyncrasy [ˌidiə'sinkrəsi]	n.	特有的风格
greens [gri:nz]	n.	植物，绿色草本
masterplan ['mɑ:stəplæn]	n.	总体规划
amenity [ə'mi:niti]	n.	（建筑的）配套设施
sovereign ['sɔvrin]	a.	具有独立主权的
delineate [di'linieit]	vt.	描绘，描写，描画
periphery* [pə'rifəri]	n.	周边，边缘
integrity* [in'tegriti]	n.	完整，完全；正直
eccentric [ik'sentrik]	a.	古怪的，不同圆心的
clamor ['klæmə]	vi.	吵闹，喧嚷
desolate ['desəlit]	a.	荒芜的，荒凉的
unaccommodating [ˌʌnə'kɔmədeitiŋ]	a.	不与人方便的，不随和的
loosely-knit ['lu:sli'nit]	a.	松散的
interstitial [ˌintə(:)'stiʃəl]	a.	空隙的
reaffirm [ri:ə'fə:m]	vt.	重申，再肯定
deem* [di:m]	vt.	认为，相信
procurer [prə'kjuərə]	n.	获取者
high-tech ['hai-'tek]	n.	高技术
panacea [pænə'siə]	n.	治百病的灵药，万应药
seduce [si'dju:s]	vt.	诱惑；诱使……堕落（犯罪）
iconography [ˌaikɔ'nɔgrəfi]	n.	象征（手法）；传统形象
guilt-ridden ['gilt'ridn]	a.	充满内疚的
engrained [in'greind]	a.	根深蒂固的

Notes

①句中 once hailed as manifestations of a brave new global vision 为过去分词短修饰主语 Projects。manifestations of a brave new global vision：一个大胆、新颖的整体设计观念 的体现。

②…views which embrace…new developments. views 作前一行 alternative views 的同位 语，which 引导 views 的定语从句。

③The use of traditional models…continuity and change in… 本句后面 in 引导的三个介词

134

短语均作 continuity and change 的定语；the setting 及 the dialogue 前面均省掉了介词 in。

④What critics have…or public realm. what critics have failed to appreciate 是主语从句，that the most viable contemporary urban centres…至句末为表语从句。表语从句中，that evolved…至句末为 enclaves 的定语从句。not（out of ）…but… 不是……而是……。

Exercises

Reading comprehension

Ⅰ. Skim the text and match each of the following ideas with their appropriate paragraph number or numbers in the brackets.

1. Criticism of new traditional towns and the author's defence of it.   （   ）

2. Alternative views to replace modernist proposals by new traditionalists.   （   ）

3. Providing a "hard edge" to achieve integrity of the city.   （   ）

4. Public disaffection with modernist planning.   （   ）

5. Examples to show how the car problem is being dealt with and how public space is used as a generator of civic environments.   （   ）

Ⅱ. Read the text carefully and then choose the best answer among the four choices given to complete each statement.

1. Which of the following about the first paragraph is not true?

   A）The planning activity in the past half century has not gained nice remarks from people.

   B）Pople are not satisfied with modernist town proposals and the related projects.

   C）Most post-war developments have failed to benefit community life.

   D）There have been no sufficient long-term settlements.

2. According to paragraph two, the use of traditional models _____ .

   A）intended to have embraced traditional towns as models for new developments

   B）has been carefully studied

   C）has introduced into urban design the idea of neighbourhoods with a diversity of communal, commercial and residential functions

   D）has revived age-old questions about continuity and change in urban planning

3. In paragraph two, "a new generation of professionals" refers to _____ .

   A）modernists

   B）new traditionalists

   C）administrative officials

   D）people who combine the views of both the modernists and the new traditionalists

4. According to the author, some critics believe that the most viable contemporary urban centres _____ .

135

A) evolved from tabula-rasa attitudes

B) didn't evolve from tabula-rasa attitudes

C) developed from a wholesome investment in the notion of a public realm

D) originated from neither tabula-rasa attitudes nor a wholesome investment

5. The word "address" (para. 3 line3) can best be replaced by _____.

A) make a speech   B) direct a remark

C) tackle   D) speak or write to

6. Paragraphs four to six deal with _____.

A) attitudes towards technology

B) new practices resulting from the new attitudes regarding technology

C) how the problem of the car should be handled

D) the idea that city planners should provide public space as a generator of civic environments and hard edge along the boundaries of new towns

7. The new town of Windsor, Florida and the Belvedere Village in Ascot are used as examples _____.

A) to manifest new traditionalists' views

B) to prove that new traditionalists failed to address contemporary social and technological issues

C) to show that the architect can be a procurer of high-tech panaceas

D) to illustrate that the new traditionalists have successfully reduced the reliance on automobiles

8. The author's purpose in writing this article is _____.

A) to make a comparison between modernist planning and that of the new traditionalists

B) to teach readers how to be procurers of high-tech panaceas

C) to analyse why modernists have failed to capture the public's sympathies

D) to articulate the new traditionalist views and practices

9. Judging from the way the author talks about the new traditionalist views and practices, we may say that this article is most probably _____.

A) a book review   B) a research report

C) an editorial of a magazine   D) an introduction to a book

Vocabulary

I. Match the words in Column A with their corresponding definitions in Column B.

Column A   Column B

1. sector   a. uninhabited or deserted

2. interstitial   b. personal mannerism

3. desolate   c. part of an area or of society

4. periphery   d. symbolism or traditional image

5. idiosyncrasy   e. of narrow space between things or parts

6. iconography   f. surrounding space or area

II. Complete each of the following statements with one of the four choices given below.

1. In reality, there is no universal _____ for all problems just as there is no universal cure for all diseases.

   A) panacea   B) boundary

   C) enclave   D) consistency

2. _____ include shops, restaurants, libraries, theatres, parks, or anything else that appeals to the prospective homeowner.

   A) appliances   B) amenities

   C) appendix   D) accessories

3. Public attitudes towards a building are _____ into what may be called "left and right wings": high density to promote community and low density to protect privacy.

   A) multiplied   B) impinged

   C) traversed   D) polarized

4. All the details, such as construction methods, building materials, machines and tools, quality control, and safety ensurance, must be _____ in a bid proposal.

   A) evaculated   B) impeded

   C) expounded   D) precluded

5. A study of feasibility may _____ practical solutions to the basic programme but the final adoption of them depends largely on the decision-makers.

   A) augment   B) pose

   C) ascribe   D) weave

6. The Design and Construction Regulations _____ by the Ministry of Construction must be applied to large and small projects.

   A) allocated   B) denoted

   C) codified   D) facilitated

7. Mixed-use projects are _____ to be a feasible solution to the shortage of retail and commercial space in large cities.

   A) deemed   B) confounded

   C) postulated   D) conferred

8. With the development of science and technology, many are _____ by the assertion that "we will no longer be surrounded by doubts and uncertainties". The truth is, however, that we are and shall be accompanied by all of them forever.

   A) worshipped   B) suspended

   C) seduced   D) suspected

Directions: Read the text of Unit Thirteen again and write an abstract of the text using the words and phrases given below

Urban Senses

modernist planning fail to a new generation of introduce … into criticism harness rather than new traditionalists seek a number of results conclusion

Reading Material A

Urban Design and the Physical Environment
——Conventional Concerns in Urban Design

What, then, are the major concerns of urban design? The primary focus is on the design of place. There is a clear shift away from the individual building, for example, towards a more integrated streetscape, with an emphasis on usable public places and human scale, heritage retention, traffic calming and landscape, so that the place has a sense of identity. [1] This focus also includes the concept of free and equal open access for the pedestrian, unencumbered by barriers, with a rejection of the privatisation of public areas, typified by enclosed shopping malls and walled residential enclaves.

A second theme in urban design is that of contextualism. This often abused idea revolves around the concept that no one element of a city should be too different from the texture of the city as a whole, that change of the fabric of a city should directly reflect its inheritance. The morphology of the city becomes a starting point for design objectives. The essential concept is that what is worthwhile about the character of a city as a whole has a public value, is a shared resource and as such should not be abrogated by sectionalist interests. [2] This is one concept where there is considerable disputation, particularly by those parties which have an ideological or financial position in favour of elitist (non-democratic) processes. Contextualism is also seen as operating at the scale of the individual building, although the present author would argue that this can, and often does, lead to pastiche. It also raises the point that the future form of a city may not necessarily be an extension of the past, but clearly the underlying form and function of a city is one starting point.

In contrast, urban designers often emphasise the need for a stimulating mix of form and land use. The point is often made that modernist urban form lacks the casual intermix of multiple use and informal opportunities for social intercourse, and there is a secondary concern that too often one place is all too much like many others, particularly in the suburbs, and this leads to a lack of identity and indeed can confuse occasional visitor.

Also, in a general sense, a change in thinking is occurring as to what urban design needs to achieve. While there has been strong concern with matters of architectionics, appearance, townscape and decorative effect, there is increasing concern with the ways in which pressing contemporary issues can be addressed, such as supply of low-price housing, urban renewal, environmental protection, equity and accessibility. There is also a shift away from central city design to matters that affect the suburbs, with initiatives such as the Model Residential Code that aim at redirecting the pattern of suburban development.

Within this refocusing it is recognised that even the most carefully devised setting may be less than ideal as a place to live in. Indeed, most urban areas seem to have informal gathering places, not planned for in any real sense, that capture the very essence of what it is that makes for a vital and interesting urban experience. [3] And the converse also appears often to be the case: planned public places that are dreary, ugly and deserted. Indeed, Peter Rowe has argued that there is a new morphology in the contemporary (American) city, unrelated to European precedents, in the form of a proliferation of isolated objects, with ubiquitous public spaces filled with freeways and carparks, having no specific cultural value relating to locale or historical circumstances. He includes much of suburbia in this genre.

It is beyond dispute that the livability of any specific city has a lot to do with the cultural norms existing among the residents, and urban design therefore needs deeply to reflect these norms. Indeed, one pertinent argument is that the design professionals——architects and planners——have too readily imported and imposed irrelevant and spurious design ideologies that conflict with local cultural norms and the environmental context. There is every indication that, in matters of urban design, an insistence on parochialism is often the best option, notwithstanding the intimidatory position adopted by head office in London or Tokyo.

Urban design, therefore, has a clear materialist perspective, both in terms of goals and outcomes. It is also very clearly a political process, if only because there is a claim being made for public values. It also has an econmic agenda, for the same reason. And in a practical sense, urban design is seen as needing to be deeply rooted in the social and environmental context.

Notes

①城市规划关心的焦点有明显的变化。例如：以前人们关注的是单个的建筑物，而现在则更注重街道的整体景观，强调可利用的公共场所与人口比例，保留传统，静化交通，美化风景，以使该地区具有自己的特色。

②一个基本的观念是城市总体特点中有价值的部分具有公用价值，是一种公有资源，因而不能因为地方主义者的利益而废除。that 至句末为表语从句。表语从句中，what is worthwhile about the character of a city as a whole 为主语从句, has a public value, is a shared resource, should not be abrogated by sectionalist interests 为三个并列谓语。as such＝therefore

③这个句子可分解为：Indeed, most urban areas seem to have informal gathering places. 和 These places were not planned for gathering in any real sense, but they capture the very essence of what makes for a vital and interesting urban experience. make for＝help to make sth. posible，contribute to sth. 有利于……，对……有益。

Reading Material B

The Practice and Problems of Town Planning

In practice, the town planner is expected to be able to operate to secure adequately related activity in the various parts of the framework of a comprehensive town and country planning system involving the local, urban, metropolitan, regional, rural and natural resource fields. Furthermore, this traditional role of controlling and allocating the use of land among competing activities has been substantially enlarged to take account of social and economic factors. In addition, he is expected to assist in the selection of overall goals for the welfare of the community at the policy-making level of local government, and in the organization and management of local government itself.

These wide terms of reference call for peculiar skills and present many problems. First, on the one hand the professional town planner attempts to direct, guide and influence the formulation of a plan and exert pressure to gain its acceptance and implementaion. He theorizes on bigger and better ways of planning. He seeks to establish policy, coordinate departments, set goals, outline objectives and control development. On the other he is charged with discovering, examining and acting upon the wishes of the local community, and translating their dictates into a feasible plan through the application of professional skills, techniques and judgement. ①He is thus faced with a situation where he is both master and servant.

Second, he is expected to undertake a comprehensive appraisal and detailed analysis of all problems related to the physical environments. He must grapple at the same time with transport, housing, education, commerce and recreation, and consider them in their economic, social and physical contexts, bearing in mind their national and regional as well as local connotations. With each component, in each context, and at every level he is attributed with exceptional proficiency. Thus the planner is made both generalist and specialist.

Third, he is repeatedly confronted with the problems of poverty, deprivation, loneliness, old age, discrimination and unemployment. Yet all too often he is forced to reconcile these contentious and controversial long-term aspects of town planning with short-term financial and political expediency. ②He is thus asked to provide both social and economic planning expertise.

Fourth, the town planner is presumed to possess taste and judgement in aesthetic and environmental matters. Being vested with powers of conservation and protection, he is taken to be the guardian of heritage and the arbiter of architectural and historic interest. Increasingly, however, he is placed in situations which require a methodical and scientific approach, based upon a thorough training in numerate disciplines. In this way he is asked to bridge the gulf between the arts and the sciences.

Fifth, one of the planner's principal accredited skills is that of communication—communication between the planner and the planned, the professional and the politician, one department and another, and from one scale of operation to another. Despite this, there is a marked tendency towards the excessive use of 'jargon' which inclines to confuse what is otherwise clear and over-sophisticate what might well be straightforward. ③The theories and expressions involved are not only often 'lifted' from other disciplines, but also used inaccurately and out of context. He is therefore portrayed as both articulate and esoteric. ④

Last, there are a number of other areas of practice where the town planner is placed in a difficult position, frequently full of conflicts. He is assumed, for example, to reconcile the impact of private and public costs and benefits; at the same time it is often necessary, in order to secure the proper performance of the plan, to stimulate in the short run the degree of private investmet and therefore entrepreneurial reward, sometimes at a long run loss to the community. ⑤These days he is also charged with ensuring that full consultation and liaison with the public take place at all stages of the planning process even though this very participation and discusion of alternative strategies can spread blight like a great plague over the face of the land⑥.

From the all-embracing nature of the complex task relating to the organization and management of the physical environment, it can be seen that it is impossible for the town planner to tackle all aspects, cater for all attitudes, and deal with all dimensions involved. He must be appreciative and selective; where he specializes he must consider the wider repercussions of his decisions; where he acts on behalf of one group, sector of agency he must be aware of the interests of others; and all the time he must direct himself towards the study of uncertainty and the consequences of change——the very essence of planing.

Notes

①另一方面，专业规划人员还要负责发现和研究当地居民的愿望，按照他们的愿望行事，并且利用专业技能和鉴赏能力把他们的心愿变为切实可行的规划方案。句中 with 后 discovering, examining, acting upon, translating 都是 "with" 的宾语。

②reconcile sth. with sth. 使和谐，使一致，使符合。如 reconcile the evidence with the facts

使证据符合事实。reconcile 后也可用 and，如 reconcile work and rest：劳逸结合

③…and oversophisticate what might well be straightforwrd. to confuse what is otherwise clear：把本来清楚明白的事搞得混淆不清。

④involved 作"the theories and expressions"的定语，放在被修饰词的后面，类似用法的词有；present（出席），else，concerned（涉及到的），等。

⑤例如，规划人员要负责协调私人成本和利益与公共成本和利益之间的相互影响；同时为了使规划活动得以顺利开展，常常不得不考虑眼前利益，刺激私人投资，有时甚至是以牺牲社区长远利益为代价。

⑥近来，规划者还要负责保证在规划过程的每一个阶段都与公众充分磋商，以谋求所谓"替换方案"，尽管这种"替换方案"的讨论和参与本身会象瘟疫一样疯狂地蔓延。

UNIT FOURTEEN

Text   Evaluation Methods in Urban and Regional Planning

[1]   Ever since evaluation research began to appear on the agenda of the social and behavioural sciences, techniques have been sought to deal with the changing goals of decision-makers in both the private and public sectors. Urban and regional planners depend heavily on this interaction between objectives and evaluation methods in their analysis, planning and implementation processes. Fifteen years ago, decision makers and analysts from a variety of backgrounds crticised many of the existing methods for their high cost, the large amounts of time they required, their lack of attention to the needs both of officials and programme recipients, as well as their difficulty in implementation. More recent developments in evaluation have shifted the emphasis away from dry 'rational' *ex-ante* approaches, and emphasised instead the implementation and monitoring stages of planning and development.

[2]   Before the analysis is made of the respective methods, it will be useful to consider the notions of efficiency and equity, which have been traditional objectives in plan evaluation and policy analysis. ①Miller called them the 'oil and water of economics', and noted that, in the past, studies have tended to emphasise efficiency effects, whether defined narrowly within the confines of project criteria or more broadly in referring to externalities or spillovers. ②More recently still, equity considerations have become increasingly important. Planners have become more aware that public decisions redistribute costs and benefits among the population of the location in question.

[3]   Miller outlined three main methods of dealing with equity and efficiency in theory and in actual studies. These methods have tended to (i) focus entirely on single objectives; or (ii) set one objective at a particular level as a constraint; or (iii) formulate a multi-objective utility function to address trade-offs among the objectives. Cost-benefit analyses and the Planning Balance Sheet are found in the first two examples, respectively, whereas multi-variable analysis, such as the Goals-Achievement Matrix or Concordance Analysis, is an example of the latter.

[4]   Financial appraisal techniques, which originated in the private sector, merged elements of welfare economics to account for the increasing social implications of investment decisions. Cost-effectiveness and cost-benefit (also known as social cost-benefit) analyses have emerged as the most common manifestations of quantitative evaluation, although cost-benefit analysis (CBA) is more prevalent.

[5]   Two basic processes characterise CBA; these present the decision-maker with the information needed to make a selection and the selection itself, which represents the best

investment of capital and operating cost over the next best alternative. Cost-effectiveness analysis, more limited in scope, helps to choose between mutually exclusive alternatives in order to reach a clearly defined benefit by showing that a set of cost specifications can yield results. CBA has been criticised on technical grounds as well as on more fundamental issues concerning its theoretical underpinnings.

[6] Technical criticims of CBA may be summarised under five major headings: quantification, discount rates, risk and uncertainty, intangibles and externalities, and distributional equity. Quantification asks whether costs and benefits are enumerated accurately; Self took issue over the use of monetary values for goods that lack exchange markets, and Mishan questioned the quantification of such intangibles as noise and well-being. The use of market versus shadow prices has also been disputed; in some circumstances, market processes may not provide adequate indicators of social values and shadow prices such as labour. The choice of method for calculating discount rates focuses on disputes over assumptions concerning future profits and losses, public versus private sector projects, and the effects of large-scale projects on national and international cash flows and investment capital. Accounting for risk and uncertainty is also the subject of debate over which method to adopt, thus forcing analysts either to take a calculated risk or to ignore its effects altogether. Intangibles and externalities raise questions regarding the transferability of monetary quantification and the utility of CBA in environmental and other development issues. Furthermore, Hill argued that CBA does not deal adequately with allocational and political issues (if at all) —yet often these are pivotal issues in a project's ultimate success! Finally, researchers are divided over the attention given to distributional equity in CBA, with criticism coming both from economists, who support the technique, and social scientists, who dispute the assumptions of welfare economics.

[7] Charges of more fundamental shortcomings in the theoretical basis of CBA were levelled by Hill, who asserted that this method was devised for the private sector and is at best only analogous to the needs of the public sector. The difficulties in expressing dynamic effects by using CBA have been cited. Self charged that the entire school of economic efficiency uses rationality and objectivity without any firm basis for doing so. In his view, e-conocrats place a veil over what are essentially arbitrary decisions articulated through abstract mathematical expressions. [9] This paternalistic attitude is evidenced by a lack of respect for public officials, which can lead to inattention to political considerations——a hazardous omission.

[8] In spite of these shortcomings, CBA remains a viable method for more limited issues; however, it does not resolve trade-offs between equity and efficiency, between quantifiable and intangible outcomes and between rational theories and irrational actors.

New Words

agenda [ə'dʒendə]	n.	议事日程
ex-ante ['eks'ænt]	a.	预期的，事先的
analyst ['ænəlist]	n.	分析者
recipient [ri'sipiənt]	n.	接受者，接受器
externality [ˌekstə'næliti]	n.	外差因素，外部效应；外在性
spillover ['spilˌəuvə]	n.	外溢因素；过剩；溢出（量）
formulate* ['fɔːmjuleit]	vt.	用公式表示；明确地表达
multi-objective ['mʌlti-ɔb'dʒektiv]	a.	多目标的
multi-variable ['mʌlti-və'raiəbl]	a.	多变量的，多元的
concordance [kən'kɔːdəns]	n.	和谐，一致，协调
originate* [ə'ridʒineit]	v.	起源，发生
underpinning [ˌʌndə'piniŋ]	n.	[pl.]（学说、理论等的）基础
quantification [ˌkwɔntifi'keiʃən]	n.	数量，量化
discount ['diskaunt]	n.	折扣；贴现率
intangible [in'tændʒəbl]	n.	难以确定的东西；无形资产
enumerate [i'njuːməreit]	vt.	数；点；列举
well-being ['wel'biːiŋ]	n.	福利；幸福
versus ['vəːsəs]	prep.	对；与……相对 (abbr. vs)
indicator ['indikeitə]	n.	指标；指示器
transferability [trænsˌfəːrə'biliti]	n.	可转移性
allocational [ˌælə'keiʃənəl]	a.	分配的，分派的
pivotal ['pivətl]	a.	中枢的，关键性的
analogous* [ən'æləgəs]	a.	类似的，相似的
cite* [sait]	v.	引用，引证
objectivity [ˌɔbdʒek'tiviti]	n.	客观（性）；客观现实
rationality [ræʃə'næləti]	n.	合理性；理性观点
veil [veil]	n.	面纱
econocrat [ikɔnə'kræt]	n.	经济效益论者
paternalistic [pəˌtəːnə'listik]	a.	家长式统治的；家长作风的
inattention [inə'tenʃən]	n.	疏忽，不注意
hazardous* ['hæzədəs]	a.	危险的，冒险的
omission [əu'miʃən]	n.	忽略，遗漏
irrational [i'ræʃənəl]	a.	荒谬的，无理性的
take issue（with sb）over（about, on）sth.		不同意，与……争论
place a veil over		把某事掩盖起来，避而不谈某事

Notes

①efficiency and equity：效率和公平，是西方福利经济学的基本内容。一些福利经济学家主张把效率和公平结合起来，因为发展商品经济必然会产生甚至扩大财产和收入分配的不均等，如果不适当地通过再分配加以社会调节，势必会导致贫富过份悬殊，影响经济发展和社会稳定。发展商品经济总要寻找效率和公平之间的适度替代关系。

②externalities：外差因素，也称外部效应或外溢因素（spillover），经济学术语，是市场经济缺陷的主要内容之一。由于经济活动是相互影响，相互依存的，无论生产者还是消费者，他们最大限度地追逐私利时，都会使其他生产者和消费者享受额外的利益或承担额外的成本，从而产生社会利益和私人利益，社会成本和私人成本之间的差额，而且带有偶然性和附随性。

③econocrats：经济主义者。-crat：名词后缀，意为：（某种政府或统治的）成员，拥护者、支持者。如：democrat 民主主义者，bureaucrat 官僚主义者。

Exercises

Reading Comprehension

I. Skim the text and match each of the following ideas with its appropriate paragraph number or numbers in the brackets.

1. Shortcomings in the theoretical basis of CBA.   （　　）
2. The notions of eff iciency and equity   （　　）
3. The shifting of emphasis in evaluation methods.   （　　）
4. CBA remains a viable method for all its shortcomings.   （　　）
5. Advantages and disadvantages of CEA and CBA.   （　　）
6. Technical criticism of CBA   （　　）

II. Read the text carefully and then choose the best answer among the four choices given to complete each statement.

1. Recent developments in evaluation _____ .
   A) have discarded the old evaluation techniques altogether
   B) are easier to implement and monitor
   C) are better in that they originated from social and behavioural sciences
   D) do not depend on the interaction between objectives and evaluation methods

2. By calling efficiency and equity the "oil and water of economics", Miller is _____ .
   A) contrasting the differences of the two groups of notions
   B) emphasizing the importance of the concepts of efficiency and equity
   C) stressing the importance of oil and water to economics
   D) demonstrating that efficiency and equity are traditional objectives in plan evalua-

146

tion and policy analysis

3. According to paragraphs 4 and 5, which of the following statements is Not true?

   A) CBA is more popular than CEA)

   B) CEA is more limited in scope than CBA.

   C) CBA is ineffective in terms of its theoretical underpinings.

   D) CBA is quantitative whereas CEA is qualitative.

4. The word "level" (Para. 7, Line 2) can best be replaced by _____ .

   A) put off   B) equal with

   C) bring forward   D) pull down

5. Morris Hill's attitude towards CBA was _____ .

   A) negative   B) positive

   C) objective   D) optimistic

6. The author's opinion towards CBA is that _____

   A) it is still useful in some issues despite its defects

   B) it is of little value since it has so many shortcomings

   C) it will remain the most viable method

   D) it should be prohibited for all its failures

7. In the following paragraphs, the author is most probably going to _____ .

   A) demonstrate the shortcomings of CBA

   B) exemplify the long points of CBA

   C) analyse other evaluation methods

   D) give more examples to show the limitations of CBA

Vocabulary

I. Match the words in Column A with their corresponding definitions in Column B.

   Column A   Column B

   1. formulate   a. a list of things to be dealt with

   2. originate   b. agreement or state of being in harmony

   3. analogous   c. quote or mention as an example or proof

   4. cite   d. similar or parallel to

   5. concordance   e. have as a cause or beginning

   6. agenda   f. express (a theory, a plan) in a systematic way

II. Complete each of the following statements with one of the four choices given below.

1. In any planning, _____ caused by the spillover of the population must be taken into account.

   A) internality   B) rationality

   C) externality   D) liability

2. According to the real estate agent, a buyer can enjoy 10 percent _____ once he pays

up all the cost of a flat in cash.

   A) discount   B) advantage

   C) detraction   D) interest

3. Before a sound judgment is formed, all the different aspects of a project must be carefully studied, reviewed, and assessed, and no _____ is permissible.

   A) justification   B) option

   C) repulsion   D) omission

4. Investing in a project without overall analysis of the total cost is considered _____ .

   A) malfunctional   B) irrational

   C) appreciable   D) subjective

5. Pollution produced by arbitrarily located factories is now _____ to the existence of ecosystem.

   A) haphazard   B) harmonic

   C) hazardous   D) discrete

6. In some cases, the uncertainty in evaluation may be eliminated by _____ the constraints.

   A) substituting   B) enumerating

   C) superimposing   D) presetting

7. Continuity and contrast are not _____ . They can be seen everywhere in our daily life.

   A) complex   B) interchangeable

   C) hybrid   D) intangible

8. We can not ignore the fact that political objectives often play a _____ part in the implementation of a proposal.

   A) pivotal   B) minimal

   C) finite   D) consecutive

Writing Abstract Writing (4)

Directions: Read the text of Unit Fourteen and write an abstract of the text using the words and phrases given below.

Evaluation Methods in Urban and Regional Planning

Various evaluation techniques deal with changqing goals of decision makers cost-effectiveness analysis (CEA)

cost-benefit analysis (CBA) technical criticisms of CBA in conclusion.

Reading Material A

Underlying Issues in Evaluation

Academicians and practitioners need to confront as well as work with each other in e-valuating planning methods. Their relationship has a symbiotic quality, in that they require mutual feedback, support and criticism in order to refine techniques and gain insight into the impact of their respective work. ①This section, therefore, has set for itself the task of identifying issues in the literature.

The preceding section revealed several unresolved questions inherent in evaluation processes. In particular, there seems to be a link between general planning theories and subsequent evaluation techniques. Two basic types of method can be identified: linear planning and cyclical planning. In linear progression, the planner/analyst may be viewed as technician, augmenting a policy advocated by the sponsoring client or agency. The style is a comprehensive, often optimising approach, usually adopted in large-scale projects. The linear method has been the dominant trend in planning over the years, but it has been criticised for its shortcomings in the implementation and monitoring stages, as it remains largely 'idea' - 'rather than operation' -oriented. ②The cyclical approach may be linked with, but is not necessarily exclusive to, incremental planning. Here, the planner assumes a more active role and may negotiate among factions; planning is shortterm and periodically revised. Evaluation processes that reflect this approach emphasise compromise and successful implementation.

The nature of the relationship between analysts and decision-maker will also have an impact on the choice of approach as well as on its subsequent structure. At this point, one must consider the overall purpose of the evaluation, i.e. whether it is merely to clarify the issues for decision makers or whether it is supposed to produce the decision. One's response to this question will influence the structure of an evaluation study, both in terms of how data are gathered and recommendations given, and in relation to the roles designated for analyst and decision maker.

This aspect of planning analysis and design concerns itself with the perception and boundaries of the decision maker by the analyst, and vice versa. ③Should officials be thought of as active partners in evaluations and allowed input during the various stages? Alternatively, should the decision-makers remain a client to be consulted at the outset and then given the finished product at the end? The role that one partner assumes as being appropriate may not be accepted by the other parties involved, and should be clarified as early as possible to avoid later inconsistencies.

In addition, the need to strike a balance between theoretical purity and feasibility leads to a trade-off, by which practitioners must choose between fidelity to a model and grappling with practical problems in the field. Abstract, methodologically focused works stress the intrinsic importance of models that try to resolve how best to measure risk, externalities and equity effects. By contrast, case studies and analysts report major difficulties in the field, where the lack of recent data, time constraints, research problems and political or institutional biases interfere with the progress of a study. Often, this trade-off surfaces when analysts and clients must decide whether to employ complex techniques that may be methodologically sound but may alienate a decision maker, who then could easily turn to someone else for advice in 'translating' the study into specific policy action. ④

Although no model can fully approximate actual problems and remain current forever, approaches are often labelled 'static' (based on a one-time 'snapshot' of data) or dynamic (process-oriented) Either type, however, may not provide adequate means of resolving conflicts among goals and/or factions. In many cases, a neat set of complementary objectives is produced so that the analysis will run smoothly, although the goals included may not reflect the entire picture. Thus conflicts in operational goals and political or power issues may not be identified or dealt with at this stage, often leaving them for someone else to resolve (if at all) Finally, more radical critiques argue that current methods are biased in favour of the status quo. ⑤Incremental, conservative changes seem to be preferred to large-scale reforms, whereby uncertainty, risk and opportunity cost have a greater tendency to affect assumptions and, hence, possibly outcomes, as well.

Notes

①他们之间有一种共生关系，彼此都需要来自对方的反馈、支持和批评，方能使各自的技能更臻完美，也才能深入了解各自工作的重要性。symbiotic [simbai'ɔtik] a. 共生的。gain insight into: 洞察、看透。

②在规划活动中，线性方法多年来一直处于统治地位，但其实施和监控阶段的缺陷也一直受到批评，因为这一方法偏重理论而不着重操作。oriented ['ɔːrientid] 同 orientated，定向的。常加在名词后面构成复合形容词。如：a sports-oriented course 一门偏重体育的课程。

③规划评估和设计中存在的这种情况涉及到双方的认识问题以及决策者与评估专家互相划定的职权范围问题。vice versa: 反过来也一样，此处表示评估专家给决策者划定职权范围，决策者也给评估专家划定职权范围。

④当评估专家和其委托人必须决定是否采用某些虽然在理论上可靠却会疏远决策者的复杂的方法时，权衡利弊的重要性就会显露出来。决策者很可能去找别人咨询如何把理论研究转变为具体的政策行动。

⑤status quo 现状。

Reading Material B

Variables for Application of Techniques

This section, drawing almost exclusively upon the later work of Morris Hill, presents a group of variables that highlight various aspects of evaluation technique that enable planners to select a method addressing pertinent issues.

Perception of the Public Interest

Economics-based methods like CBA assume the public interest to be unidimensional. Multi-variate methods, holding that the public interest is a function of many, sometimes conflicting, parts, broaden this approach. With some projects, like defence, public interest may be fairly united; with others, like environmental issues or urban redevelopment, there will be a more complex range of views.

Treatment of Uncertainty

Of the major methods, only CBA explicitly incorporates risk and uncertainty into the analytical process. Dutch researchers have used a variety of mathematical and statistical models in their applications, notably the work of Nijkamp and Voogd. Others have used decision and game theory in attempting to take into account possible future outcomes. It should be noted, however, that the treatment of uncertainty remains a difficult issue, and much debate still exists regarding the validity and accuracy of these various methods.

Treatment of Time Preference

The importance of the 'lifetime' of a project is particularly evident in CBA and other financial-appraisal methods concerned with capital budgeting and the opportunity cost of an investment. This indicator is less common in multi-variate methods.

Ex-ante, Ex-post and Continuous Evaluation

Nearly all of the most common evaluation methods were formulated for *ex-ante* studies, although some may be used in *ex-post* evaluations. [1]Only more recently have specifically designed *ex-post* studies taken place, often on economic or social programmes. Also, researchers are currently interested in developing continuous evaluation tools to meet both short-and long-term needs.

Externalities

External effects often play a significant part—in many ways far greater than one might anticipate—particularly in the later stages of a study. In choosing what method to adopt, it is important first to identify potential and latent sources of externalities and then to estimate roughly their significance to the proposal at hand. Do they have the potential seriously to hamper successful implementation? As has been stressed earlier, methods that rely heavily on the quantification of all the effects of a scheme often do not adequately address the issue of externalities, thus placing the entire evaluation in doubt.

Clarification of Boundaries Regarding Possible Trade-Offs

Defining appropriate boundaries in terms of the trade-offs mentioned earlier will assist not only in the selection of a method, but also in forming the basic structure of the evaluation scheme. One type of trade-off that shoud be considered concerns deciding on the appropriate level of technical models to be employed in the study versus the ability to communicate effectively to the targeted audience. ②Another trade-off involves the need to balance the opposing forces of thoroughness (i. e. data level) and cost. In the real world, information is not free.

Finally, one must consider the need to be aware, if not openly solicitous, of solid support and political commitment for a scheme while avoiding formulating an evaluation that will reflect only the opinions of those who must ultimately decide its fate. ③The analyst needs to find a way to pay careful attention to political objectives without becoming a pawn in the chess game. This can be accomplished either by setting explicit requirements or drawing inferences from the client and from those ultimately responsible for the effects of decisions.

The indicators discussed above do not by any measure constitute a final list, nor may they all be equally relevant in every case. They do, however, pinpoint necessary areas for consideration that seem to be in the interest of any evaluator to address while formulating a strategy for any evaluation study.

Notes

①ex-post evaluation 追踪评估（过期评估）

②一种必须加以考虑的选择就是如何选定将用于分析的技术模式，其等级要与同交流对象进行有效沟通的能力相适应。

③最后，我们还必须考虑这种必要：即使不公开表示强烈愿望，也得有意识地坚决支持某一方案，及其在政治上要承担的义务，同时避免作出只反映那些对这一方案的命运有最终决定权的人的意见的评估。

UNIT FIFTEEN

Text   **Fatal Remedies**
——**The Sources of Ineffectiveness in Planning**

[1]   That we learn by our mistakes is an axiom of the rational model of urban and regional planning. Feedback procedures should, in theory, result in the prompt amendment
or abandonment of policies that prove to be ineffective. In the longer term, at the national
level, widespread and rigorous appraisal should permit the codification of sources of planning failure and generate a more sensitive and informed understanding, by professionals,
governments and the community at large, of the possibilities of planning and the limits of
government. Both individual plans and planning systems can be subject to this kind of monitoring. In neither case does practice live up to theory.

[2]   As far as individual plans are concerned, the review process is usually more casual
than formal, if it occurs at all. Planning agencies tend to review and revise their work irreg-
ularly, in accordance with political priorities, or in response to a cacophony of complaints
by vested interests including other government instrumentalities. The latter occasions often
represent a kind of planning epilogue which has the merit of resolving politically contentious questions avoided earlier in plan preparation. Few planning organisations have the
resources, time, or inclination for systematic or continuous performance evaluation. Whether by intention or by default, planning is typically carried on as a 'disjointed incremental' process. Third party appraisal, often comprising academic analyses of policy effectiveness, is sometimes more wide ranging, thorough, and impartial. However, few local
plans are subject to detailed independent appraisal. Even where policy appraisal is conducted with considerable analytical rigour, as was the case with ' Moore and Rhodes' 1977 e-
valuation of British regional policy, the outcome is more ingenious than convincing. ①In the
case cited, difficulties in defining policy, policy conflicts and shifts, the openness of the economic system, questionable indicators, heroic assumptions, and doubtful statistical techniques all tend to vitiate the findings.

[3]   Performance evaluation, then, is a difficult task. To start with, it is not often easy
to identify what is being evaluated. Policy, strategy and individual measures may be covert,
implied or specific and there is the problem of null policy. ② Moreover, if particular objectives are the subject of overlapping measures implemented by several agencies, it may be
difficult to isolate the set of policies concerned with a given problem. For that matter, even
within a single planning document, a single objective may be addressed by several policies. Secondly, the necessary data are rarely available and, at best, unsatisfactory surrogate
indicators must be used. Finally, the measurement of cause and effect can pose insurmountable difficulties in open and complex societies—especially where various policy measures

are mutually reinforcing or antithetical, or where lagged responses are marked.

[4]   Performance monitoring of planning systems, or of planning as such, appears to have attracted more consistent attention. Business, community groups, governments, bureaucracies and academics all have an abiding interest in criticising the procedures by which plans are prepared and planning decisions are made, and in making suggestions for improvement. A modest, and reasonably practical approach to system evaluation is commonly adopted by governments. The emphasis is on collecting data about such matters as the time taken to approve development applications, and the aim is to make gradual improvements to existing mechanisms. Occasionally, a more dramatic overhaul is attempted.

[5]   At a deeper level, there are many serious thinkers who doubt whether planning systems can ever achieve what they are purportedly designed to achieve—not that this has discouraged planners from plugging bravely on. It has been argued that 'urban policy is fundamentally too complicated to be successful'. Analysts have not been slow to identify factors which fundamentally preclude successful planning in capitalist societies. Written in a so-called critical idiom, much of this literature starts from an *idee fixe* of the just society and its correlates in urban form, but offers little practical assistance towards the improvement of planning systems in liberal democratic mixed economies. David Harvey concludes that 'the planner seems doomed to a life of perpetual frustration', while Michael Dear and Allen Scott comment: 'the reactive and palliative nature of urban planning is not simply the result of some technical, analytical or human failure. It is, instead, the inevitable concomitant of a social logic that sets definite barriers around the range and effectiveness of all political action.'

[6]   Part of the problem with any assessment of planning systems is that urban and regional planning is concerned with only one of the many sets of concerns which fall within the jurisdiction of sovereign governments. Other desiderata may include increasing the production of goods and services and national income, the maximisation of comparative advantage in international trade, ensuring a high level of social and economic adaptability or the protection of individual freedom of choice and responsibility. These ends may conflict, and, to the extent that they do, trade-offs are necessary. Any evaluation which does not confront these trade-offs tells only part of the story and is unlikely to be much of a guide to system improvement. [3] Moreover, a thoroughly rational critique of a planning system should also encompass the behavioural, analytical and information limitations of the community being planned, those doing the planning and the politicians taking the final decisions.

[7]   In reality, narrower forms of analysis are likely to be the only practical option, and may well offer sharper insights than studies designed to grasp the complete picture. A variety of evaluative approaches, individually incomplete as they may be, but originating in a range of disciplines and contributing in their own way to a greater understanding, is thus to be welcomed. [4] Planners can learn much, for example, from the literature on such mat-

154

ters as conflict management, bureaucratic and political decision-making, or the imperatives of private property development.

New Words

amendment [ə'mendmənt]	n.	改正，修正；修正案
rigorous* ['rigərəs]	a.	严格的；严密的；精确的
codification [ˌkɔdifi'keiʃən]	n.	编纂；整理
at large		大多数，整个；不受约束的
cacophony [kæ'kɔfəni]	n.	不和谐音；刺耳的声音
vested ['vestid]	a.	既定的，既得的
instrumentality [ˌinstrumen'tæliti]	n.	机构；工具，手段
epilogue ['epilɔg]	n.	尾声；收场戏
contentious [kən'tenʃəs]	a.	引起争论的
inclination* [inkli'neiʃən]	n.	倾向；趋势
disjointed [dis'dʒɔintid]	a.	不连贯的；没有条理的
effectiveness* [i'fektivnis]	n.	有效性；效率
impartial [im'pɑːʃəl]	a.	公正的，不偏袒的；无偏见的
rigour ['rigə]	n.	严密，精确；严格
ingenious* [in'dʒiːnjəs]	a.	机灵的；有独创性的；精制的
vitiate ['viʃieit]	vt.	使（契约等）无效；使有缺陷
covert ['kʌvət]	a.	隐藏的
null* [nʌl]	a.	零（位）的，空的
	n.	零（位），空
overlap* [ˌəuvə'læp]	v.	与……部分相同，与……重迭
surrogate ['sʌrəgit]	a.；n.	代用品（的），替代（的）
insurmountable [insə(ː)'mauntəbl]	a.	难以超越的；不可克服的
mutually ['mjuːtʃuəli]	ad.	相互地，彼此地
antithetical [ˌænti'θetikəl]	a.	对立的
lagged ['lægid]	a.	落后的；迟缓的
bureaucracy [bjuə'rɔkrəsi]	n.	官僚主义；官僚
abiding [ə'baidiŋ]	a.	持久的，永久的
overhaul* ['əuvəhɔːl]	n.；vt.	大修；仔细检查
purportedly [pə(ː)'pɔːtidli]	ad.	有意识地
plug [plʌg]	vi.	苦干
id'ee-fixe [iː'dei'fiːks]	n.	［法］固定观念；成见
capitalist ['kæpitəlist]	n.；a.	资本主义的；资本家（的）
doom [duːm]	v.	注定，命定
perpetual [pə'petjuəl]	a.	永远的，永恒的

frustration [frʌsˈtreiʃən]	n.	受挫，挫折
palliative [ˈpæliətiv]	a.	姑息的；掩饰的
concomitant [kənˈkɔmitənt]	n.	伴随物；伴随情况
jurisdiction [ˌdʒuərisˈdikʃən]	n.	权限；管辖范围；司法（权）
desiderata [diˌzidəˈreitə]	n.	（复）迫切需要的东西
maximisation [ˌmæksimaiˈzeiʃən]	n.	最大值，最高限度
confront* [kənˈfrʌnt]	vt.	使面临，使遭遇（危险等）
bureaucratic [ˌbjuərəuˈkrætik]	a.	官僚政治的；官僚主义的

Notes

①as was the case with···, the outcome is more ingenious than convincing. as 引导非限制性定语从句，修饰前面整个句子。the case：actual state of affairs，situation，事实。more ···than··· 与其说，不如说。

②to start with 首先；开始时

③story：内情，真相。如：These figures gave only part of the story. 这些数字只能说明部分问题/情况。much of a＋名词："了不起的，""称得上······的"，常用于否定句和凝问句。

④individually incomplete as they may be＝though（although）they may be individually incomplete 这一句型用部分倒装，as 可用 though 换，引导的是让步状语从句，但不能用although 代替as.

Exercises

Reading Comprehension

Ⅰ. Skim the text and find out the topic sentence of each paragraph if there is.

Para. 1 _____

Para. 2 _____

Para. 3 _____

Para. 4 _____

Para. 5 _____

Para. 6 _____

Para. 7 _____

Ⅱ. Read the text carefully and then choose the best answer among the four choices given to complete each statement.

1. According to the author, the role of feedback is to _____ .

   A) help people revise or give up invalid policies

   B) lower the cost of evaluation process

   C) enable people to draw lessons from the failures gathered and get a deeper insight into the nature of planning

D) both A and C

2. From the 2nd paragraph, it is implied that _____ .

A) evaluation process is casual and irregular

B) planning agencies only respond to the claims of some interest groups

C) many plans have not been assessed before put into implementation

D) evaluation by the third party is rarely more efficient and feasible

3. The main idea of the 3rd paragraph is that _____ .

A) it is impossible to establish a policy that satisfies all parties

B) different variables are entangled with each other, which makes performance evaluation difficult

C) people have different perceptions of what is being evaluated

D) performance evaluation is such a complex task that few achievements have been made

4. Which of the following may be the positive result the performance evaluation has achieved?

A) The issue has aroused increasing concerns and proposals are raised to improve the current mechanisms.

B) Individuals and government agencies are more liable to accept criticisms.

C) People tend to adopt more prudent approaches in planning.

D) Interest groups are prepared to provide more cooperations any evaluation requires.

5. Many serious thinkers doubt whether planning systems can achieve what they are purportedly designed to achieve because _____ .

A) planners are discouraged from plugging bravely on

B) urban policy is too complex

C) analysts have been too quick to identify sources of planning failure

D) literature in this field offers little practical assistance

6. If any evaluation is to be a practical guide to planning activities, it must, most importantly, _____ .

A) confront necessary trade-offs

B) avoid facing any conflict

C) preclude the behavioural limitations of the community being planned

D) promote economic development and increase the national income

7. The author seems to favor _____ .

A) the kind of evaluation method designed to grasp the complete picture

B) a combination of all evaluative approaches available

C) narrower forms of planning assessment

D) none of the above

8. The word "literature" (para. 5, Line 6) means _____ .

A) any printed material

B) novels and stories

C) works of art

D) writings on planning failure

9. Which sentence best sums up the main idea of the passage?

A) Narrower forms of analysis are likely to be the only practical option.

B) Performance evaluation is a difficult task.

C) That we learn by our mistakes is an axiom of the rational model of urban and regional planning.

D) Many serious thinkers doubt whether planning systems can ever achieve what they are designed to achieve.

Vocabulary

I. Match the words in Column A with their corresponding definitions in Column B

Column A	Column B
1. inclination	a. range of authority or power
2. ingenious	b. clever or having great mental ability
3. null	c. tendency or sloping
4. overhaul	d. being invalid or zero
5. indicator	e. person or thing that points out or gives information
6. jurisdiction	f. thorough examination for repairing

II. Complete each of the following statements with one of the four choices given below.

1. The most difficult task in land planning then is the management of the _____ interests of all parties concerned.

A) antithetical   B) Complementary

C) prevalent   D) incremental

2. A large number of constraints (and inhibitions) must be recognized and adapted, without which any program is _____ to fail.

A) dominated   B) discreted

C) doomed   D) deteriorated

3. The zoning regimes (方法) tend to be associated with a constant flow of _____, and the perception grows in the public mind that the zoning can be, and is, changed rather frequently and easily.

A) codification   B) amendments

C) configuration   D) continuity

4. Without public support, all the efforts made by the planners will end in _____

A) obstruction   B) impetus

C) discrepancy   D) frustration

158

5. Urban and regional planners _____ complex issues which are characterised by an extraordinary plurality of goals and multiplicity of relevant agencies.

    A) encompass   B) preclude

    C) vitiate   D) confront

6. Everything is in change, but man's endeavour in search of _____ truth is never changed.

    A) perpendicular   B) stationary

    C) perpetual   D) temporal

7. It is not what you want, but what you sense in the order of things which tells you what to design. In this sense man and nature are _____ influential.

    A) mutually   B) ambiently

    C) respectively   D) arbitrarily

8. In the process of construction _____ safety precautions must be taken to prevent possible work accidents.

    A) helical   B) rigorous

    C) macroscopic   D) analogous

Writing Abstract Writing (5)

Directions: Read the text of Unit Fifteen again and write an abstract of the text in about 120 words.

Reading Material A

Sieber's Mechanisms for Planning Failure
——Functional Disruption

Sieber's sociological analysis, begins with the observation that 'few institutions, programs or leaders are immune to the vexatious experience of worsening the condition that they set out so nobly to alleviate. ' The question he raises is: how and why do the effects of policy initiatives so often end up being the reverse of what was intended? He suggests seven mechanisms, which he refers to as *conversion mechanisms* because they convert the hoped-for effects of a policy intervention into different effects.

Sieber's mechanisms for planning failure

---

   1. FUNCTIONAL DISRUPTION

     1.1 Functional imbalance: emphasis on a particular requirement at the expense of another.

1. 2　Perverse diagnosis: misunderstanding a situation.

1. 3　Overload: attempting to achieve too much

1. 4　Functional shift: retention of outmoded programmes.

2. EXPLOITATION

2. 1　By non-target communities/groups.

2. 2　By implementers/deliverers: (may be licit, semilicit, or illicit)

3. GOAL DISPLACEMENT: Means become ends in their own right.

4. PROVOCATION: Plan preparation or implementation galvanises community action against policy.

5. CLASSIFICATION: OR, RATHER, MISCLASSIFICATION

5. 1　Derogatory: vicious circle effect of stigmatisation.

5. 2　Deferential: preferential treatment accorded some participants.

5. 3　Exemptive.

6. OVER-COMMITMENT: Over-ambitious goals; exhaustion/withholding of resources.

7. PLACATION: Symbolic action for worried communities with two main adverse outcomes:

(i) a lulling effect (e. g. false sense of security)

(ii) exasperation

The first such mechanism involves a failure to recognise, or respect, the dynamics of social or physical systems. Sieber calls this *functional disruption*. He goes on to nominate several varieties of that basic syndrome. The first involves questions of *imbalance*. For example, administrators looking for instant solutions to pressing problems may be tempted to focus in an unbalanced way on one element of a system, with the result that the system readjusts in unexpected directions. Problems of imbalance may also arise where a system has needs that conflict: the satisfaction of one need or goal works against the satisfaction of another. In the planning context one thinks, for example, of the way in which planning authorities may seek to extract so much from developers, to cover the cost of providing utility services, public open space, social facilities and so on, that the development industy withdraws from the field and invests its capital elsewhere. Alternatively, development may take place, but the developer's costs are passed on and the land and houses are marketed at a price beyond the reach of young first-home buyers.

The objective of a well-serviced residential area is achieved, but the objective of creating affordable housing is negated. To some extent these planning-imposed cost pressures can be mitigated by constructing smaller lot sizes. This also has the virtue of reducing the volume of raw land consumed by urban expansion, although, paradoxically, it may be at the expense of residents' perceived quality of life, should they value highly private open space.[②]

In a slightly different sense, public action is driven by sets of antithetical needs of a

160

methodological kind. For example, community participation is seen as a path to consensus and a source of new ideas, but tends to conflict with the need for strong leadership. A successful mix of these qualities is difficult to achieve, and Sieber sees over-reliance on one mechanism or pendulum-like swings between extremes as setting the stage for self-defeating action.

Another kind of problem occurs when policy-makers simply misunderstand a problem or misread a situation, and thus select an inappropriate response. Sieber refers to this as *perverse diagnosis*. [3]In New South Wales in the early 1970s, for example, a perception grew that prime agricultural land needed to be preserved in efficient full-time agricultural use. As a holding measure, the then State Planning Authority introduced a general 40 ha minimum subdivision size in rural zones, on the assumption that this would discourage the creation of hobby farms[4]. In some areas, however, the 40 ha minimum was insufficient to stop the tide of demand for rural residential property. The result, one might argue, was that land was swallowed up in giant 40 ha bites rather than in the small pieces that many rural residential buyers would probably have preferred. Is it possible that the 40 ha minimum has actually caused more land to be lost to full-time agriculture than would have been lost if no minimum had applied? Hard evidence on this is unfortunately lacking. (In some respects the distinction Sieber draws between 'perverse diagnosis' and other forms of 'functional disruption' is artificial. The saga of 40 ha minimum subdivision could be interpreted as another example of one over-simple policy initiative being adopted as a universal panacea. It seems that all forms of functional disruption contain some element of perverse diagnosis.)

In some cases, a policy may impose on its target system some requirement which the system is unable to cope with; the results, again, are contrary to the objective of the policy. Sieber calls this *overload*. Consider the case of land-use zoning. The justification for zoning, as planners use it in Australia, is partly that it provides a degree of certainty to landowners and developers. But the more that planners pursue this goal of certainty, by drafting rigid and inflexible ordinances which specify in considerable detail the uses which may be made of particular parcels of land, the more pressure grows for special exceptions and rezonings. [5]The urban system is complex amd dynamic; in practical political terms it cannot be put in a strait-jacket[6]. Inflexible zoning regimes therefore tend to be associated with a constant flow of amendments, and the perception grows in the public mind that the zoning can be, and is, changed rather frequently and easily. The general feeling of uncertainty may even be stronger, in that situation, where rezonings are endemic, than in a situation where rigid zoning is not even attempted.

Sieber draws attention to another process which may perpetuate an inappro-priate intervention. Even though the intended objective of a policy is not being achieved, the policy may survive because some other, unanticipated, objective is being satisfied. He describes that as a *functional shift*. One might again look to zoning for examples. In the United

States it is clear that zoning is popular in some communities not simply as a mechanism for separating incompatible land-users, which was its original rationale, but because it can be used as a tool for social segregation.

Notes

①西伯尔的社会学分析以其观察结果开始：人们一心想缓解规划失败的局面，结果却搞得更糟。任何社会机构、计划或领导人很少有不为这种经历所烦恼的。"the condition"指上文和下文都提到的"the effects of policy initiatives so often end up being the reverse of what was intended（'a strong definition of failure'）"，即规划政策往往取得与意图相反的效果，事与愿违。

②这样可减少城市发展所消耗的土地量，虽然从另一角度来说如果居民特别看重私有空地，这也许牺牲了他们的生活质量。should they value highly private open space 为表示虚拟的条件从句，省去了 if 引起主谓倒装。

③perverse diagnosis 误诊

④as a holding measure 作为土地（量度）单位；ha＝hectare 公顷。

⑤然而，规划者越是追求"明确"这个目标，便会受到越多的压力要求特殊处理或重新规划，因为规划者制定的僵硬条款详细规定了每一块土地的用途。

⑥城市体系错综复杂，不断发生变化，不可能受通常政治意义上的束缚。put…in strait-jacket 使……受约束，束缚。

Reading Material B

Commentary on Sieber's Mechanisms

This brief Sieberian (should it be Siberian?) analysis of planning leaves several questions unanswered. Have we in fact identified the major sources of bureaucratic failure? Are there other better ways of categorising the mechanisms of failure? Is planning inherently more prone to failure than other forms of public intervention? There are grounds for arguing that it might be. Urban and regional planners confront complex issues which are characterised by an extraordinary plurality of goals and multiplicity of relevant agencies. This leads to the paradox that planners are at once faced with too much and too little information.①

Let us take the latter first. planning is ostensibly a future-oriented activity, but reliable information is difficult to obtain even for the short term. The quality and quantity of information tends to decline exponentially the further we look into the future. We know, too, that the description of present conditions is often incomplete and that explanation of why these events have occurred is open to ideological or scientific dispute. The shortage of data and reliable analysis is further confounded by the planner's proclivity for the false god of comprehensiveness. The target system for intervention often appears as nothing less than the local or regional system in its totality: physical, social and economic. Whereas water authorities, for example, concentrate successfully on supplying water, road authorities build roads, social security departments pay out pensions, egg marketing boards market eggs, and so on, town planners take it upon themselves to worry about almost everything. [2]One would therefore expect, on *a priori* grounds, planning to be strongly prone to functional imbalance, perverse diagnosis, overload, provocation, over-commitment and classification rather than the more venal Sieberian sources of failure. Perhaps Patrick Geddes was to blame; he who preached the need, back in 1915, for a full understanding of the city or region: 'All our activities—industrial and commercial, hygienic and educational, legal and political, cultural, and what not—become seen in relation to one another, as so many aspects and analyses of the city's life.' [3]Of course, they are all linked. But to understand an urban or regional system in its entirety is a task which is beyond the powers of any single organisation.

This leads us to the second problem, which is information surfeit. Many planning-related agencies are faced with an abundance of information on some issues, to the extent that its thorough sorting and analysis is infeasible. Never mind that this 'abundant' information is simultaneously of doubtful reliability and incomplete. Even greater difficulties stem from the need to marry the incompatible sets of information held by different agencies and private interest groups. [4]The task may be unmanageable even with the widespread availability of high-powered geographic information systems. This has something to do with what, in systems theory, is called the Law of Requisite Variety, which states, in effect, that the capacity of a regulator to maintain a system in a given state is only as great as its capacity to match the variety of disturbances acting on that system; or, to put it another way, that the capacity of a regulator cannot exceed its capacity as channel of communication. In communications jargon, if 'noise' appears in a message, the amount of noise that can be removed by a correction channel is limited to the amount of information that can be carried by that channel. Information problems may provide the seed-bed for many of the kinds of processes Sieber describes. These pathologies arise because various actors in the planning game—the planners themselves, politicians, bureaucratic empire builders and private interest groups—are able to exploit lack of information and confused analysis for their own ends.

Sieber's framework is useful in two respects. It suggests the kind of problems which need to be investigated and provides a system by which various studies can be integrated. It is only when we more fully understand the sources of error or failure that we can think effectively about potential remedies.

Notes

①This leads to the paradox…这种情况造成了这样一种似是而非的局面：规划人员得到的信息既太多又太少。at once…and…＝both…and

②take it on/upon oneself to do sth：未经许可擅自决定做某事。

③and what not：等等；诸如此类

④有必要把不同机构及不同私人利益集团所掌握的相互矛盾的信息结合起来，而这种需要会产生更大的困难。to marry sth. and sth（or：with sth）＝to combine sth. successfully with sth. else，使成功地结合。

UNIT SIXTEEN

Text   The Two Paradigms of Zoning

[1]   There are two competing paradigms of zoning, understood as a kind of government regulatory measure, in terms of economic theorisation: the Pigovian paradigm, developed on the basis of Professor Arthur C. Pigou's book *The Economics of Welfare*, on the one hand, and the Coasian paradigm developed mainly on the basis of Ronald Coase's Nobel Prize paper 'The Problem of Social Cost' of 1960 on the other. ①The Pigovian paradigm refers to the articulation of the concept of 'external effects' ('neighbourhood effects' or 'externalities') In modern welfare economics, an externality is a kind of market failure. It arises where the cost suffered by a party due to the activities of another is uncompensated (such as a factory producing smoke which impinges upon neighbouring houses) or, conversely, where the benefits produced by one party are captured by another without compensation (such as a rose garden which is freely looked at by passers-by) The former is called a negative externality and the latter a positive one. The Pigovian tradition typically describes pollution as a kind of negative externality. Such uncompensated costs and benefits would create economic inefficiency. The reason held by Pigovian economists is that as the market only responds to private costs and benefits, it would fail to equate marginal value and marginal social costs, which is required as a condition for Pareto economic efficiency. ② They therefore argue that the state or government should intervene in the market to correct the inefficiency. The Pigovian paradigm is said to be interventionist, perceiving a positive role for government or state regulation of the land market, whereas the Coasian paradigm constantly casts doubts about the cost of such regulation. In Coasian economic texts about the contrasts between the two approaches, it has been said that the Pigovians assume zero transaction costs for policy formulation and implementation and treat policies as if they are 'exogenous' or 'autonomous'. What the Coasians are trying to assert is that one should not jump to policy prescriptions when problems are identified in the operation of the unregulated market. Some scholars go a step further to assert that market solutions are superior in terms of economic efficiency. In the planning arena, the Pigovian paradigm is one for zoning whereas the Coasian paradigm is against zoning.

[2]   The above dichotomy in the economic interpretation of zoning is generally found in American literature. Although British literature does not discuss zoning as such, a fundamental aspect of this debate emerges under the broader theoretical discussion of 'planning' ('town planning', 'town and country planning', or 'urban planning') In the United Kingdom, most traditional texts on the economics of planning, exemplified by William Lean's *Aspects of Land Economics* and *Economics of Land Use Planning*, adopt the Pigovian justification for planning. The equivalent of the Pigovian *vs* Coasian debate in the

British literature is the discussion within the planning profession about the conventional dichotomy of 'plan' versus 'market' 'planning' versus 'price mechanism', 'libertarian planning' as informed by Hayek or 'property rights' as *policy* alternatives to the status quo of planning regulation and various non-economic 'arguments against planning'[3]. In the British literature on planning, Friedrich von Hayek's influence, or reaction against such influence, is more strongly felt, probably due to his polemic literature attacking the 'drastic provisions' of the British Town and Country Planning Act of 1947. The key feature of the British articulation of 'property rights' is treating, unnecessarily, 'property rights' as categorically distinct from 'development control' or other regulatory measures instead of regarding 'market' and 'plan' as alternative modes of property rights, or rules of competition.

[3]   It is perhaps odd from the economist's point of view that in Sorensen and Day's discussion of externalities, Hayek's works, which challenge the concept of externalities, are extensively used but, strikingly, no reference is made to Coase's 1960 seminal paper on the concept. Similarly, B. J. Pearce's citation of Pigou's work on externalities is not followed by any reference to Coase, although the following works on property rights inspired by and ensuing from Coase's 1960 paper, those of Harold Demsetz and Steven N. S. Cheung, are utilised. Indeed, Klosterman's exposition of the economic arguments for planning adopts the standard Pigovian concept without mentioning their stereotype Coasian antithesis. Graham Hallett's *Urban Land Economics*, as a text book, refers to Coase's analysis of externalities very briefly and does not relate the matter to zoning. Philip Cooke's *Theories of Planning and Spatial Development*, a leading work on planning theories, makes no mention of Coase and, as such, is illustrative of the proposition that Coase's writings have had little influence in British academic circles. K. G. Willis'book *The Economics of Town and Country Planning* is probably unique in bringing home in much greater detail the messages of the emigrant prophet. Even in the discussion of M. E. Avrin's empirical test on zoning, little indication is made of the intellectual influence of Coase. It seems, therefore, that the lengthy epilogue of John Burton in Steven Cheung's *The Myth of Social Cost*, cited in Pearce's treatises, remains the clearest exposition of Coase's economic concept in the British academic realm. There are probably two reasons for Coase's lack of attention in the British planning literature: namely the absence in the British planning system of an explicit zoning system such as prevails in the United States; and the entrenchment of welfare statism in the country. In the planning schools of the United States, the impact of or reaction to the Coasian approach is more strongly felt. In part, this is due to their adoption of Williams Fischel's text *The Economics of Zoning Laws* as general reading and the influence of Robert Ellickson's articles, notably 'Suburban Growth Controls'. This is, of course, also due to the fact that explicit statutory zoning systems have been widely adopted in the United States.

New Words

regulatory*	['regjulətəri]	a.	调节的，调整的
theorisation	[ˌθiərai'zeiʃən]	n.	建立理论
uncompensated	[ʌn'kɔmpenseitid]	a.	未得补偿的
inefficiency	[ˌini'fiʃənsi]	n.	无效，效能差
impinge*	[im'pindʒ]	v.	碰撞，冲击，对……有影响 (on/upon/against)
compensation	[ˌkɔmpen'seiʃən]	n.	补偿，赔偿
equate	[i'kweit]	vt.	使相等；同等对待
marginal	['mɑːdʒinl]	a.	边际的；少量的
intervene*	[ˌintə'viːn]	vi.	干涉，干预；介入 (in)
transaction	[træn'zækʃən]	n.	处理；业务，交易
exogenous	[ek'sɔdʒinəs]	a.	外源的；外因的
autonomous	[ɔːtɔnəməs]	a.	自发的；独立存在的
prescription	[pris'kripʃən]	n.	规定；惯例
unregulated	[ʌn'regjuleitid]	a.	不规范的；未受控制
arena	[ə'riːnə]	n.	（活动，竞争）场所
exemplify*	[ig'zemplifai]	vt.	举例，说明
libertarian	[ˌlibə'tɛəriən]	n.；a.	自由意志论者（的）
polemic	[pɔ'lemik]	a.	引起激烈争论的
provision	[prə'viʒən]	n.	条款，规定
categorically	[ˌkæti'gɔrikli]	ad.	绝对地，明确地
seminal	['seminl]	a.	有重大影响的；开创性的
citation	[sai'teiʃən]	n.	引述；表扬
ensue	[in'sjuː]	vi.	接着发生
exposition	[ekspəu'ziʃən]	n.	阐述；展示
antithesis	[æn'tiθəsis]	n.	对立，正相反
illustrative	['iləstrətiv]	a.	说明的，作为例证的 (of)
emigrant	['emigrənt]	n.	移民
prophet	['prɔfit]	n.	预言家；倡导者
myth	[miθ]	n.	神话
treatise	[ˌtriːtiz]	n.	论文
entrenchment	[in'trentʃmənt]	n.	（对权利等的）保证；防御工事
statism	['steitizəm]	n.	中央集权制
statutory	['stætʃutəri]	a.	法定的，依照法规的
bring (sth.) home (to sb.)			使明了，使认清

Notes

①Arthor C Pigou 亚瑟·皮古（1877－1959）英国经济学家，剑桥大学教授，福利经济学剑桥学派的主要代表之一。依据功利主义和边际效用原理，提出了福利经济学学说，是福利经济学的创始人。主要著作有《福利经济学》、《失业理论》、《就业与均衡》。

②"external effect"西方经济学术语，"外部效应"亦称"外差因素"（externalities），或"相邻效应"（neighbourhood effects）"外溢因素"（spillovers）。指当一个经济主体的消费行为或生产活动给社会提供了好处而取得相应的报偿，就提供了"外部经济"（external economies），如他的消费行为或生产活动给社会带来了损失而并未给受损者赔偿，则造成"外部不经济"（external diseconomies）。前者为积极因素，后者为消极因素。（参见第13单元课文注②）。

③Pareto economic efficiency 帕雷托经济效率。帕雷托（1848-1923）意大利经济学家，洛桑学派的主要代表之一。提出在收入分配为既定的条件下，资源配置达到最佳状态，经济达到最优效率，就实现了最大福利（即"帕雷托最适度"）。

④status quo 现状

Exercises

Reading Comprehension

Read the text carefully and then choose the best answer among the four choices given to complete each statement.

1. Paragraph one is mainly concerned with _____ .
    A）different thorizations of zoning
    B）origin of the two paradigms of zoning
    C）defining the concept of market efficiency
    D）advantages and disadvantages of zoning

2. The pigovian paradigm maintains that _____ .
    A）great cost should be paid for zoning
    B）no compensation should be made for the costs produced by zoning
    C）private costs and benefits should not be taken into consideration
    D）market is not versatile therefore government should take and active part in the regulation of market mechanism

3. The Coasian paradigm asserts that _____ .
    A）no policy is necessary to be made
    B）market can regulate itself well by its own law
    C）the uncompensated cost will not bring about economic inefficiency
    D）private interests are the only drive to push everything forward

4. Paragraph two deals with _____ .

   A) the problems raised in zoning

   B) the debate between the Pigovian versus Coasian scholars in British literature

   C) British Town and Country Planning Act

   D) the significance of property rights

5. The British Planning realm _____ .

   A) has a strong prejudice against the Coasian paradigm

   B) does not think much of a explicit zoning system

   C) seems to be in favour of the Pigovian paradigm

   D) challenges the concept of externalities

6. In paragraph three, the author _____ .

   A) describes the fact that the Coasians have little influence in Britain

   B) analyses the reasons for Coase's influence in America and his lack of being noticed in Britain

   C) discusses the concept of externalities in detail

   D) both A and B

7. "The emigrant prophet" (Para. 3 Line) refers to _____ .

   A) Philip Cook   B) Arthor Pigou

   C) Ronald Coase   D) John Burton

8. The author's attitude toward the Coasian paradigm is _____ .

   A) objective   B) critical

   C) subjective   D) negative

9. The author's purpose in writing this article is _____ .

   A) to examine the paradigm of zoning and conclude which is a better one

   B) to analyse the influence of the two prevailing paradigms by reviewing the literature on zoning

   C) to recommend the Pigovian paradigm

   D) to point out the present situation in zoning

10. Which of the following readers is this article written for ?

    A) The general readers.

    B) Government policy-makers.

    C) students at large.

    D) Planning Specialists.

11. This article is probably _____ .

    A) a literature review

    B) an epilogue of a book on architecture

    C) an introduction to a test book

    D) a defence of the Coasion paradigm

12. Immediately following this part, the author is probably going to talk out _____ .

A) America's zoning system

B) Coase's influence in the U.S.

C) influence of William Fischel and Robert Ellickson

D) both A and C

Vocabulary

I. Match the words in Column A with their corresponding definitions in Column B.

Column A   Column B

1. polemic   a. show by example

2. arena   b. ordered or required by regulation

3. exemplify   c. place or scene of activity or conflict

4. provision   d. a fixed or conventional notion or conception by a number of people

5. treatise   e. controversial

6. regulatory   f. a piece of written work dealing systematically with one subject

7. stereotype   g. a clause or condition in a legal document designating or requiring specific things

II. Complete each of the following statements with one of the four choices given below.

1. Le Corbusier's concrete walls serve to shield his building's interior spaces from the world of the university. In this respect, it is the very _____ of an academic building.

A) stereotype   B) antithesis

C) regulation   D) analogue

2. In the process of zoning, interest groups may well _____ with requirements of their own.

A) intervene   B) intersect

C) intercept   D) interlock

3. _____ costs refer to all costs other than the costs of physical production, and include costs of information, searching, negotiation, contract enforcement, etc.

A) Transaction   B) Justification

C) Statutory   D) Compensation

4. A visit to the slum areas of the town has _____ to me what poverty really means.

A) brought home   B) brought off

C) brought through   D) brought about

5. A proposal of building an _____ city, one that is highly self-sustainable, is under consideration.

A) emigrant   B) automatic

C) exogenous   D) autonomous

6. City's appearance and form _____ from the planning, on which a focus is placed that

everything responds to the human demand for work, inhabitation, culture, and recreation.

    A) ensures   B) inherits

    C) ensues   D) incurs

7. The extension of the human sphere and the means of its determination go far beyond any built _____ . We, architects and engineers, have to redefine them by means of building.

    A) instrumentation   B) exposition

    C) optimization   D) manipulation

8. Growing concerns are raised that skyscrapers have been irremediably _____ on the dynamic order of the nature and the quality of life.

    A) compensating   B) embedding

    C) fabricating   D) impinging

Writing Abstract Writing (6)

Directions: Read the text of Unit sixteen again and write an abstract of the text in about 120 words.

Reading Material A

Visions of the City of the Future

Given that the urban designer is concerned with the development of the city not only in the present but 15 to 20 or more years into the future, it is important to have some concept of what cities in the future might be like. ①The literature of architecture, planning, and urban design is fortunate to have many references as to how the cities of the future might or should look. Ideas range from Frank Lloyd Wright's Broad Acre City to R. Buckminster Fuller's mile-wide geodesic dome for Manhattan to Le Corbusier's Ville Radieuse. Behind each of these concepts was an idea about how city dwellers should respond to social and technological change. For example, in the Ville Radieuse (Radiant City), Le Corbusier envisioned high-rise residential towers which would be placed in a park-like setting. Major roadways would link together sectors of the city.

The organization of buildings and patterns of land ownership conceived for La Ville Radieuse are in sharp contrast to Wright's concepts for Broad Acre City. In La Ville Radieuse the land would be owned in common, whereas Wright would have each individual or family own a one-acre lot. Homes and industry would be connected by major roadways. Wright felt that ownership of land by broad segments of the population was important in preserving a democratic society. His political and social philosophy were translated into the design proposals contained in the plans for Broad Acre City.

Other visionaries have suggested more radical approaches to structuring the future city. The architect Paulo Soleri is constructing a small new community called Arcosanti in the desert north of Phoenix, Arizona. The purpose of building the community is to demonstrate new ways of organizing urban functions while enabling inhabitants to remain in close contact with nature. [2]

Drawings and models by Soleri depict megastructures with heights as great as the tallest skyscrapers but covering as much as several hundred acres of ground. The structures contain both housing and employment for a population of 100,000 or more. Soleri has labeled this general set of studies "arcology". Like ecology, which is the study of animals in their natural homes, arcology is the study of how best to build urban structures which can accommodate homes, manufacturing, and public facilities in a fashion which is compatible with nature. [3] In addition to suggesting new ways of organizing living space, Soleri's proposals contain predictions of completely automated manufacturing facilities which might be placed underground.

Have such visions of the future city been a useful guide? None of these proposals offers a plan in its entirety. Instead they tend to focus on one or two factors which their authors consider to be of primary importance. However there is an underlying assumption in each of the proposals that the design of the physical environment affects human behavior.

One task for the urban designer is to combine aesthetic considerations with what we have learned about the relationship of physical design and human behaviour to obtain a result which actually improves the quality of people's lives. [4] we have learned through experiences with programs such as Urban Renewal and federally assisted housing that although physical design does affect human behavior, it is not the single most powerful determinant. Rather, it is one aspect of a complex array of physical, social, economic, cultural, and psychological factors which are present in our everyday lives.

For example, public housing experience has taught us that high-rise construction does not necessarily work out well for all populations. It is hard for a mother living on twelfth floor to keep an eye on her children as they play outdoors. The relative anonymity of a high-rise seems to make high-rise public housing prone to crime and may also make it more difficult to build up a feeling of community and mutual help. On the other hand high rise development may work very well for a young affluent population, as many a successful condominium developer could testify. The negative sociological effects that we now know to be associated with some high-rise, high-density housing were not anticipated by Le Corbusier. Rather than take his proposals literally as ideas to be applied to all urban areas and all urban populations, it is best to consider them as suggesting options to be explored and evaluated. The modern city needs a coherent vision of the future to guide its development, yet it must accommodate a wide diversity of values, hopes, and perspectives [5]. Concepts of the future must address how urban people should live, how neighborhoods should be organized, and how we can preserve natural beauty and the quality of the environment as increasing numbers of people inhabit the globe.

Notes

①如果城市设计者关心的不只是目前，还关心未来15～20年的城市发展的话，就很有必要了解未来城市的发展方向。given：如果。相当于 provided (that)。

②修建该社区的目的是为了展示组织城市功能的新途径而又能使居民同大自然继续保持密切联系。

③正如生态学是研究自然环境中的动物一样，"建筑生态学"研究如何建造能融合家园、生产及公用设施使之与大自然协调的城市建筑。arcology＝architecture＋ecology

④城市设计者的一个任务是如何既注重美学考虑，又照顾城市设计与人类行为的关系，以获得能真正提高人民生活质量的结果。

⑤现代城市需要前后一致的未来观念指导其发展，还必须对各种各样的价值观念、愿望和看法进行协调。

Reading Material B

Reflections on the Future Residential Landscape
——Low-rise/High-density as a Planning Ideal

The typical way in which sustainable development is conceived in the urban design literature is through what might be called the historicist approach. This is the approach that is represented by such influential authors as the County Council of Essex, Krier and Cusmano, and that argues for a renaissance of the European city through the creation of higher density, pre-modern urban forms that are said to possess a richer and more attractive visual environment than has developed in the modern era, the nineteenth and twentieth centuries.① The proposal for the imaginary urban village of Greenville, by Reid and Lyons on behalf of the Urban Villages Group, provides an example. The proposal is for quite a different type of development compared with the typical English landscape. This latter comprises, as everybody knows, a combination of two-storey terraces, semi's and detached dwellings, with low-rise and high-rise flats in local authority estates. In contrast, Greenville consists almost entirely of four-storey tenement flats, organised around a series of broad avenues and squares, with grouped car-parking on the village periphery.

The historicist approach can generate commercially successful schemes, if used selectively. The use of long established models of urban design appeals to consumer desires for continuity and permanence in housing. The underlying theory is backward looking, however, and rests heavily on a *priori* aesthetic judgements made independently of users. The historicist preference for pre-modern cities is, in any case, open to dispute. The legacy of the nineteenth century city has, in particular, experienced a re-evaluation as a result of the renewal programmes of the 1970s and 1980s.

The historicist preference for higher densities has generated a reaction in calls for dispersed living patterns. Clark et al have argued that sustainable development implies a 'self-support economy' and requires 'more land for outbuildings and outdoor activities···and a general reduction in net residential densities.'[2] Likewise, Robertson has argued in favour of a decentralised future based upon a return to the countryside and a revival of rural values. Such formulae for low-density living are, of course, just as much based on *a priori* assumptions as their historicist opponents. Personal attitudes towards work and life-style will change, it is assumed, in a way that promotes self-reliance and small-scale economic activities.

In addition, the opposition between the historicists and their critics has led Breheny and Rookwood to argue in favour of a compromise between extremes. The high-density solutions favoured by the European Commission ignore consumer preferences. The low-density/dispersed solutions overstate the capacity of the countryside to absorb large numbers of people without destroying the quality of life in these areas.

The question is how a compromise might be conceptualised and elaborated. Marcus and Sarkissian provide a possible way forward, based on the residents' experience. Marcus and Sarkissian share the concern of the historicists that the modern residential environment is often unsatisfactory. Equally, they share, with the historicists, a rejection of low-density solutions on the grounds that these isolate their occupants away from urban services. The difference is a rejection of aesthetic solutions, such as those promoted in the Essex Design Guide, on the grounds that these ignore popular notions of social acceptability and local conceptions of the home.

Marcus and Sarkissian conceptualise their proposal as medium-density, to be more precise, low rise/high density 'clustered housing'. This provides a compact alternative to the typically dispersed American suburb. At the same time, it applies the lessons of numerous consumer surveys that an overwhelming preference exists in the English speaking world for the typical visual and environmental features of a suburban estate—features such as a private entrance at the ground level, private open space, convenient car parking generally within the householder's private garden and a pleasant open aspect from the windows.[3]

In the inner city, clustered housing allows 'people to enjoy a green and quiet environment within easy access to city jobs'. On the city fringes, clustered housing would, 'if repeated often enough', increase overall densities and render public transport more economic. In addition, clustered housing offers the advantages of high rise flats (privacy, efficient domestic maintenance, the possibility of communal facilities without their disadvantages (distance from ground, feelings of anonymity) High-density/low-rise, as conceived by Marcus and Sarkissian, would be limited to three, or occasionally four, storeys.

Though the authors are silent on the point, the low-rise/high-density architectural form of clustered housing has other advantages. Low-rise, high-density reduces the cost of land acquisition and site infrastructure for the developer, while avoiding the additional costs of lifts and other services in high rise. It is also well adapted to terraces and low-rise flats that are the most cost-effective building forms in housing and are also energy-efficient in comparison with semi-and detached housing in terms of the relation between internal floorspace and exposed wall-area. [④] Low-rise/high-density is therefore largely consistent with the objective of providing affordable housing. Moreover, low-rise/high-density, as presented by Marcus and Sarkissian, is based on conventional house types and is, therefore, likely to escape the building cost penalties of unusual design. In contrast, the proposals for Greenville and of the Urban Villages Group use complex architectural forms and details. For example, Georgian door and window surrounds and specific types of building materials, such as stone, in a way that would almost certainly increase building costs.

High-density/low-rise or clustered' housing is no panacea, though.

Notes

①这种方法的代表是一些有影响的倡议者，比如：埃塞克斯县议会，克里亚和卡斯曼罗。它主张通过创建高密度的近代城市形式来复兴欧洲城市，这种城市形式据认为比现代（19世纪和 20 世纪）城市拥有更丰富诱人的视觉环境。

②Clark et al=Clark and others 克拉克及其他人

③同时，他们的建议还吸取了从许许多多消费者调查中得出的教训，那就是：在英语国家，人们普遍喜欢郊区房屋的典型视觉环境特征——底层有私用出入口，私有空地，方便的停车库，私人花园，以及赏心悦目的窗景。it 指上文的 proposal；that 引导 lessons 的同位语从句；features such as…为前面一个 features 的同位语。

④密集型住宅同低矮平房也很协调，而平房是最省费用的建筑形式；同半密集型和分散型住宅相比也很节能（就室内地面空间与暴露的墙面关系而言）。主语 it 指本段第一句中的 low-rise/high-density architectural form of clustered housing，即，低高度、高密度的密集型住宅。

Appendix I   Vocabulary

A

aberration   *n.* 偏离常轨；离开正道   (03)

abiding   *a.* 持久的，永久的   (15)

abound   *vi.* 大量存在   (02)

accent   *n.* 特征，特点   (10)

accessory*   *n.* 附件，陈设品   (11)

accommodation   *n.* 调和；迁就；住处
    (06)

accomplishment   *n.* 成就；成绩   (04)

accord   *vi.* 一致，调和，符合   (11)

acknowledge*   *vt.* 承认；感谢   (04)

adaptable   *a.* 适应性强的   (06)

adhere   *vt.* 坚持；粘附（常跟 to）   (02)

adjunct   *n.* 附加物，附属物   (11)

adversity   *n.* 逆境；不幸   (03)

aesthetic   *a.* 美学的，审美的   (01)

agenda   *n.* 议事日程   (13)

akin   *a.* 类似的，同样的（常跟 to）   (05)

allocational   *a.* 分配的，分派的   (14)

allowance*   *a.* 流量；容差；补助   (05)

allusion   *n.* 暗指，引喻   (09)

ambient   *a.* 周围的，大气的   (08)

amenable*   *a.* 经得起检验的   (02)

amendment   *n.* 改正，修正；修正案   (15)

amenity   *n.* （建筑的）配套设施   (13)

analogous*   *a.* 类似的，相似的   (14)

analyst   *n.* 分析者   (14)

analytical   *a.* 分析的，解析的   (05)

anatomical   *a.* 解剖的，解剖学的   (10)

anchorage   *n.* 锚固，固定   (07)

ancillary   *a.* 辅助的，附属的   (08)

anonymous   *a.* 无特色的   (06)

antecedent   *a.* 先行的，先前的
    前列，前事   (09)

antiquity   *n.* 古代；古风   (03)

antithesis   *n.* 对立，正相反   (16)

antithetical   *a.* 对立的   (15)

appropriation   *n.* 拨给，占用，挪用   (12)

arbor   *n.* 棚架，凉亭   (10)

arena   *n.*   （活动，竞争）场所   (16)

arguable   *a.* 可争辩的；可论证的   (05)

articulate   *vt.* 表现（思想）；明确表达
    (02)

artifact   *n.* 人工制品，低劣艺术品   (06)

assessment   *n.* 估计；评价   (05)

assortment*   *n.* 分类，各种各类的聚合
    (10)

asymmetry*   *n.* 不对称   (11)

at large   大多数，整个；不受约束的   (15)

at one stretch   一口气，连续的   (01)

atrium   *n.* 天井   (08)

authenticity   *n.* 可靠性，真实性   (06)

autonomous   *a.* 自发的；独立存在的   (16)

autonomy   *n.* 自主权，人身自由；自治
    (06)

avant-garde   *n.* 前卫派；先驱   (03)

awe   *n.* 畏惧，敬畏   (13)

axiom   *n.* 公理   (11)

axonometric   *a.* 三向投影的   (01)

axonometric plan   三向投影图   (01)

B

ballot   *v.* 投票   (07)

banality   *n.* 平庸；陈腐   (04)

Baroque   *n.* 巴罗克式建筑   (01)

cross section　剖面图　　　　　　　（01）

crudity　*n.* 简陋，粗糙　　　　　　（06）

crusading　*a.* 改革的；讨伐的　　　（03）

culminate　*vi.* 达到顶点　　　　　（04）

cult　*n.* 信仰，崇拜　　　　　　　（01）

cypress　*n.* 柏树，柏树枝　　　　　（10）

D

deadweight　*n.* 重负，自重　　　　（03）

deem*　*vt.* 认为，相信　　　　　　（13）

deflection　*n.* 变形的，偏差　　　　（07）

delineate　*vt.* 描绘，描写，描画　　（13）

demolish　*v.* 拆毁，推翻　　　　　（01）

descendant　*n.；a.* 弟子；后代；祖（遗）传
　　　　　　的　　　　　　　　　　（04）

desiderata　*n.* （复）迫切需要的东西（15）

desolate　*a.* 荒芜的，荒凉的　　　（13）

detract*　*vt.* 减损；降低　　　　　（02）

detractor　*n.* 毁损者　　　　　　（03）

devolve　*v.* 转移，退化　　　　　（02）

dianthus　*n.* 石竹属植物　　　　　（10）

dichotomy　*n.* 一分成二；二分法　（06）

differentiate*　*v.* 区别，区分　　（01）

dignity　*n.* 真正价值；尊严　　　　（06）

dilemma　*n.* 困境；进退两难　　　（02）

directive　*n.；a.* 指示（的），指导（的）
　　　　　　　　　　　　　　　　　（06）

disconcert　*vt.* 挫败；使窘迫　　　（04）

discourse　*n.；v.* 论说；谈论　　　（02）

discretion　*n.* 谨慎　　　　　　　（11）

disillusionment　*n.* 幻想破灭　　（13）

disjointed　*a.* 不连贯的；没有条理的（15）

disparity*　*n.* 差异；悬殊　　　　（06）

distort　*vt.* 弄歪，歪曲　　　　　（09）

doom　*vt.* 注定，命定　　　　　　（15）

draftsmen　*n.* 绘图员　　　　　　（06）

drama　*n.* 戏剧性；戏剧效果　　　（04）

drape　*v.* 悬挂，披　　　　　　　（10）

drapery　*n.* 帐幕，衣饰　　　　　（11）

drastic*　*a.* 激烈的；严厉的　　　（06）

drawback*　*n.* 欠缺；障碍　　　　（02）

ductile*　*a.* 可延展的，塑性的　　（07）

E

eccentric　*a.* 奇怪的；不同圆心的　（13）

eclecticism　*n.* 折衷主义　　　　（04）

ecological　*a.* 生态，生态学的　　（12）

econocrat　*n.* 经济效益论者　　　（14）

ecosystem　*n.* 生态系统　　　　　（12）

effectiveness*　*n.* 有效性；效率　（15）

elevation　*n.* 正视图　　　　　　（01）

elevation　*n.* 正面（图），立视（图）
　　　　　　　　　　　　　　　　　（08）

embellishment　*n.* 装饰品　　　　（09）

emigrant　*n.* 移民　　　　　　　（16）

emission*　*n.* 排放，放射，发射　（08）

emotion-laden　*a.* 带情绪的　　　（02）

empirical*　*a.* （根据）经验的，经验主
　　　　　　义的　　　　　　　　　（07）

enclave　*n.* 飞地　　　　　　　　（13）

engrained　*a.* 根深蒂固的　　　　（13）

ensue　*vi.* 接着发生　　　　　　（16）

entrenchment　*n.* （对权利等的）保证；
　　　　　　　　防御工事　　　　　（16）

enumerate　*vt.* 数；点；列举　　　（14）

epilogue　*n.* 尾声；收场戏　　　　（15）

equate　*vt.* 使相等；同等对待　　　（16）

equation　*n.* 等式，方程式　　　　（07）

equilibrium*　*n.* 平衡，均衡　　　（08）

erosion*　*n.* 腐蚀，侵蚀　　　　　（12）

evade　*vt.* 逃避；避开　　　　　　（02）

evoke　*vt.* 引起，唤起　　　　　　（09）

ex-ante　*a.* 预期的，事先的　　　（14）

exemplify*　*vt.* 举例，说明　　　（16）

exhibitionist　*n.；a.* 表现狂（的）　（06）

exogenous　*a.* 外源的；外因的　　（16）

idiom　n. 风格；惯用法；习语　　　（06）

idiosyncrasy　n. 特有的风格　　　（13）

ignorance　n. 不知；无知　　　　（05）

ill—digested　a. 消化不良的　　（03）

illustrative　a. 说明的，作为例证的（of）
　　　　　　　　　　　　　　　（16）

immature　a. 未成熟的；未臻完美的（06）

impartial　a. 公正的，不偏袒的；无偏见的
　　　　　　　　　　　　　　　（15）

impinge*　v. 碰撞，冲击，对…有影响
　　　　　　（on/upon/against）（16）

inappropriate　a. 不恰当的，不合适的
　　　　　　　　　　　　　　　（06）

inattention　n. 疏忽，不注意　　（14）

inclination*　n. 倾向；趋势　　（15）

incoherently　ad. 前后矛盾的，支离破碎
　　　　　　　　的　　　　　　（02）

incomprehensible　a. 不可理解的，不易
　　　　　　　　　领会的　　　（01）

indicator　n. 指示；指示器　　（14）

indulge　v. 满足，沉溺　　　　（01）

inefficiency　n. 无效，效能差　（16）

ingenious*　a. 机灵的；有独创性的；精致
　　　　　　　的　　　　　　　（15）

inlaid　a. 镶嵌的，嵌饰的　　（09）

inorganic　a. 无生物的，无机的（12）

instrumentality　n. 机构；工具，手段
　　　　　　　　　　　　　　　（15）

insurmountable　a. 难以超越的；不可
　　　　　　　　克服的　　　　（15）

intact*　a. 完整的，未受损的　（01）

intangible　n. 难以确定的东西；无形资产
　　　　　　　　　　　　　　　（14）

integrity*　n. 完整，完全；正直　（13）

intellect　n. 才智，智力　　　（08）

interstitial　a. 空隙的　　　　（13）

intervene*　vi. 干涉，干预；介入（in）
　　　　　　　　　　　　　　　（16）

intricacy*　n. 错综复杂；难以理解（06）

intrinsic*　a. 内在的；固有的　（04）

intuitively*　n. 直觉上，直观上（05）

ipso—facto［L.］　照那个事实；根据事
　　　　　　　　实本身　　　　（05）

irrational　a. 荒谬的，无理性的（14）

irrevocable　a. 不可改变的，不能挽回的
　　　　　　　　　　　　　　　（12）

Italian Renaissance　意大利复兴运动（时
　　　　　　　　期）　　　　　（04）

ivy　n. 常春藤　　　　　　　（10）

J

jagged　a. 锯齿状的；凹凸不平的（12）

jerky　a. 不平稳的，颠簸的　（11）

juggernaut　n. 不可抗拒的力量（03）

jurisdiction　n. 权限；管辖范围；
　　　　　　　　司法（权）　　（15）

jury　n. 评审员；陪审团　　　（02）

justification*　n. 正当理由；认为正当
　　　　　　　　　　　　　　　（05）

juxtapose　vt. 把并列；便并置　（09）

L

lagged　a. 落后的；迟缓的　　（15）

landmark　n. 里程碑；界标　　（04）

libertarian　n.；a. 自由意志论者（的）
　　　　　　　　　　　　　　　（16）

liven（up）　v. 使活跃　　　　（03）

loosely—knit　a. 松散的　　　（13）

lounge　n. 躺椅　　　　　　　（11）

louver　n. 百叶窗　　　　　　（08）

lumped　a. 整块的　　　　　　（05）

lux　n. 勒克司（照度单位）　（05）

M

magnitude*　n. 大小，量，量值（05）

physiological　*a.* 生理学的，生理的　（08）

pilaster　*n.* 壁柱，半露柱　（07）

pivotal　*a.* 中枢的，关键性的　（14）

place a veil over　把某事掩盖起来，避而
不谈某事　（14）

plan　*n.* 平面图　（01）

plug　*vi.* 苦干　（15）

polarise*　*v.* （使）极化，两极分化　（13）

polemic　*a.* 引起激烈争论的　（16）

polytechnic　*a.；n.* 工艺的，多种科技的；
工业大学　（08）

pooling　*n.* 集中　（10）

pose*　*v.* 提出；（使）摆好姿势　（13）

post-modernism　*n.* 后现代派　（03）

practitioner　*n.* 实践者；开业者　（03）

pragmatic　*a.* 重实效的，实际的　（05）

preconceive　*vt.* 预想，预先想到　（01）

precondition　*n.* 前提，先决条件　（01）

prescription　*n.* 规定；惯例　（16）

prestressed　*a.* 预应立的　（07）

privacy　*n.* 独处，隐居；隐私　（06）

procurer　*n.* 获取者　（13）

profitable　*a.* 有利的；有益的　（04）

prolong*　*vt.* 延长；拉长　（04）

prophet　*n.* 预言家；倡导者　（16）

propylaeum　*n.* （神殿等）入口　（02）

provision　*n.* 条款，规定　（16）

pull—up　*n.* 折叠椅　（11）

purportedly　*ad.* 有意识地　（15）

purview　*n.* 权限；眼界　（02）

Q

quantification　*n.* 数量；量化　（14）

quantify*　*a.* 确定数量；用数量表示（05）

quasi-global　*a.* 准（半，类似）总体的
（05）

R

radiator　*n.* 暖气炉；散热器　（11）

rationality　*n.* 合理性；理性观点　（14）

reaffirm　*vt.* 重申，再肯定　（13）

realistic*　*a.* 现实（主义的）　（05）

recipient　*n.* 接受者，接受器　（14）

regionalism　*n.* 地方色彩派　（03）

regulatory*　*a.* 调节的，调整的　（16）

reluctance*　*n.* 不情愿；勉强；磁阻　（04）

renaissance　*n.* 文艺复兴（时期）　（03）

repository　*n.* 博物馆，陈列室，贮藏所
（10）

res publica　*n.* ［拉］国家　（13）

responsive　*a.* 响应的，易起反应的　（12）

resultant*　*a.* 作为结果的；合成的　（06）

resuscitate　*vt.* （使）苏醒，（使）复活，
（使）复兴　（13）

revenue*　*n.* 税收，税务局（署）　（08）

revitalise　*vt.* 使新生，使恢复元气　（02）

revival　*n.* 复兴；复活　（04）

revivalist　*n.* 复兴的　（03）

ridicule　*n.* 嘲笑，嘲弄　（03）

rigorous*　*a.* 严格的；严密的；精确的
（15）

rigour　*n.* 严密，精确；严格　（15）

Romanesque　*n.* 罗马风建筑　（01）

rules-of-thumb　*n.* 经验做法，较粗糙
的方法　（07）

S

sculpture　*n.* 雕刻，雕塑　（01）

sector*　*n.* 区，段，部门　（13）

secure　*a.* 牢固的，稳定的　（07）

seduce　*vt.* 诱惑；诱使……堕落（犯罪）
（13）

seismic*　*a.* 地震的　（07）

seminal　*a.* 有重大影响的；开创性的(16)

sensation　*n.* 感觉，知觉　　　　(11)

sensor*　*n.* 传感器，灵敏元件　　(08)

sequin　*n.* 装饰衣服用的金属圆片(09)

serviceability　*n.* 适用（性）；耐用（性）
　　　　　　　　　　　　　　(05)

sewage　*n.* （阴沟处的）污水，污物(12)

sheer　*a.* 透明的；极薄的；纯粹的(04)

shimmering　*a.* 闪闪发光的　　(04)

shutter　*n.* 百叶窗，窗板　　　(10)

simplistic　*a.* 过分简单化的　　(09)

simulation　*n.* 模拟，模仿　　　(08)

sizable　*a.* 相当大的，广大的　(07)

skyscraper　*n.* 摩天大楼　　　(04)

slate　*vt.* 预定　　　　　　　(07)

slenderness　*n.* 高厚比　　　　(07)

slippery　*a.* 含糊的，难以捉摸的(09)

smack　*vt.* 掴，拍，打，猛击　(09)

solar panel　太阳能板　　　　　(08)

sovereign　*a.* 具有独立主权的　(13)

spacing　*n.* 间隔，间距　　　　(07)

specification*　*n.* （设计，产品等）说明书，
　　　　　　　　　　规格　　(06)

spectrum*　*n.* 光谱；领域　　　(04)

speculative　*a.* 思辩的；纯理论的；投机
　　　　　　　　性的　　　　(06)

spillover　*n.* 外溢因素，过剩；溢出（量）
　　　　　　　　　　　　　　(14)

sprawl　*n.*；*v.* （无规划的）漫延(02)

springboard　*n.* 跳板；出发点　(03)

sprout　*vt.* 使萌芽，使生长　　(09)

stance　*n.* 态度；姿态　　　　(03)

statism　*n.* 中央集权制　　　　(16)

statutory　*a.* 法定的，依照法规的(16)

stencil　*n.* 图案，文字　　　　(09)

stock-in-trade　*n.* 惯用手段；存货(06)

straddle　*v.* 跨立于　　　　　(06)

stucco　*n.* 拉毛水泥，灰墁，（拉）毛粉
　　　　　　　　　　　　　　(10)

stud　*v.* 点缀　　　　　　　　(10)

stunning　*a.* 令人吃惊的　　　(04)

stylistic　*a.* 风格的，文体的　(01)

subarctic　*a.* 近北极的，亚北极的(12)

subdue　*vt.* 使比较安静柔和，缓和(11)

subjective*　*a.* 主观的　　　　(02)

subtle*　*a.* 微妙的　　　　　　(11)

suburbanise　*v.* 市郊化，（使）变为市
　　　　　　　　　郊　　　　(02)

succession　*n.* 连续，接续，（生物）演替
　　　　　　　　　　　　　　(12)

suitability*　*n.* 适合，适合性　(06)

superimposition　*n.* 重迭，附加物(09)

supremacy　*n.* 至高无上　　　(03)

surrogate　*a.j.n.* 代用品（的）替代（的）
　　　　　　　　　　　　　　(15)

sustainable　*a.* 可持久的，可维持的(08)

symbolic　*a.* 象征主义的　　　(01)

synonymous　*a.* 同意（语）的　(04)

T

tabula-rasa　*n.* ［拉］擦去了文字的书板
　　　　　　　　白板　　　　(13)

tack　*vt.*；*n.* 钉住，平头针　(09)

take issue(with sb) over(about, on) *sth.*
　　　　　　　不同意，与……争论
　　　　　　　　　　　　　　(14)

talus　*n.* 斜面，山麓堆积，踏磊(12)

taunt　*vt.* 嘲弄；辱骂　　　　(04)

tax　*vt.* 使……耗尽　　　　　(11)

theorisation　*n.* 建立理论　　　(16)

tile　*n.* 瓷砖，贴砖　　　　　(09)

to hand　手边　　　　　　　　(01)

topography　*n.* 地形，地形学，地形测量学
　　　　　　　　　　　　　　(12)

totality　*n.* 整体，总体　　　　(01)

transaction　*n.* 处理；业务，交易(16)

transcript　*n.* 副本；文字记录　(02)

Appendix Ⅱ TRANSLATION FOR REFERENCE

第 1 单元

认 识 建 筑

建筑表现其意义的方式与绘画或雕塑不同，因为它本质上要复杂得多 。它一开始就需要进行分析 。首先，我们根本不能完整地看到一幢建筑：我们所能获得的仅为建筑内外的部分印象 。结果，我们总是不得不将我们所看到的与不能看到的联系起来才能形成一幅清晰、完整的画面 。单是一饱眼福是不可能的，需要边看边想 。为了有助于这种思维活动，我们手里有一种重要的工具，平面图 。它可同时提供建筑内外整体与局部的有关信息 。平面图与剖面图（展示建筑内部结构）一起，以抽象形式，构成一幅合成的建筑图，这是无论多少幅照片都不能表现的 。因此，在学别的知识之前，有必要先学会看平面图，并广泛熟悉建筑学中常用的各种图示手段（剖面图、正视图、三向投影图）。

由图示向建筑实物的转变遇到又一困难 。如今我们往往再也看不到建筑师最初希望表现的形式 。完工之前，一些工程被放弃或改变 。已经完工的部分被拆毁，其他后加的部分却属于另一种风格 。的确，时间改变着一切艺术作品 。而时间对建筑的影响更为明显，因为一幢主要建筑的建造要花很长时间，还因为建筑（总是要为实用服务）必须适应人们不断改变的需求 。因此，我们不能以相同方式去连续地或几乎完整地看 一幢完工的建筑（如索尔兹伯里主教堂，Salisbury Cathedral），看 一幢未完工的城堡，（如布雷萨克城堡，Chateau de Brissac）或一幢不断改变的建筑 （如凡尔赛宫，Palais de Versailles）。在第一种特殊情况中，我们能立即欣赏到建筑师的作品。在第二种情况中，我们只好想象建筑师想要表现的内容。在第三种情况中，我们不得不去发现建筑的连续阶段以便正确理解所看到的内容，而不能将几次建筑活动的结果归于一个建筑师的构想。

最后，绝对不应该忘记，即便最堂皇的建筑也绝不是只作为艺术品而建。如果不注意到建筑的目的，无论是功利主义的还是象征主义的建筑，都是不可理解的。宗教建筑、住宅和宫殿的特殊建筑形式总是反映了某一特定社会，或宗教信仰，或日常生活或权力的履行等方面的需求。与其他艺术家相比，建筑师的独立性较小，他总是在由他所属的社会或他所服务的个人所严格限定的框架内发挥他的创造力。这样的局限性，按不同的年代和社会水平（希腊神庙，城市住宅，便是极为标准的类型）对建筑师的创造力有着不同程度的限制。同时也赋予建筑艺术一个重要的社会意义：建筑是一种奇特的表现形式，是人类需求与梦想的最持久最直观的表现形式。

我们对一幢建筑感兴趣，因而从中我们看到令我们赏心悦目的体积、空间、节奏和色彩的"效应"。在有些情况下（例如，一幢城市住宅或乡村建筑），这些影响非常简单，首先是考虑一幢建筑与周围环境的和谐。在其他情况下（这也最令人感兴趣）这些影响极为复杂，它们可以是一个或多个富于创造的人精心设计的。在这两个极端（没有建筑师参与的建筑艺术和建筑大师的建筑艺术）之间，还有多个层次，但要区别它们则毫无意义。更值得做的是分辨建筑艺术所能采用的各种表现手段。只有这样我们才能增强对所欣赏的建筑的理解力。

这种理解不应等同于美学欣赏，但它又是必要的前提。没有这种理解，同时产生的似乎表达个人观点的鉴赏就只不过是重复以前的观念：罗马风建筑的"贫瘠"，巴罗克式建筑的"矫揉造作"，早期教堂的"平淡无奇"……。因而，我们向读者强调这一点并不过分：忘却这些成见，并以新奇的眼光和开明的头脑去观察以便欣赏每种风格所特有的建筑形式。

观察所有这些现象可得出同一结论：一件建筑艺术的作品太复杂，不能一看就理解，需要同时注意到它的所有要素，需要想象它各个连续的状态（包括那些从未完成的状态），需要了解建筑物对于那些修建它的人意味着什么。这些初步分析必须是在建筑的美学欣赏之前。它可以使人构成一幅建筑的清晰画面，并能区别各种限制条件（结构需要，现存建筑，风格的延袭，客户的要求等）造成的结果和纯粹艺术创造的结果，即纯粹玩弄艺术形式而已。

第2单元

建 筑 评 价

建筑师、客户、城市居民、政府机构或鉴定委员会怎样评价新建筑的设计？如果这些新建筑要耸立在有名胜古迹的地区，这个问题就显得特别重要。人们怎样才能判定计划中的新建筑是给环境增光添彩，还是有损于环境？它是否将促进有利于名胜古迹地区的进一步发展？能够用作评价基础的标准是什么？答案是否存在于坚持某种"正确的"建筑思想？这种建筑思想来源于"专家们"传下来的古典主义的，现代主义的，或后现代主义的观点？这一工作是否需要具备专门的鉴赏能力，还是需要广大公众参与的众口一致，或是两者兼而有之？

根据近来围绕有争议的建筑展开的讨论的性质——在这些讨论中自然而然的意见分歧演变成漫骂式的对抗，显然人们需要更加理智的方法来解决这些问题。持相反意见的双方的分歧常常纠缠在人们强烈坚持的有关美学和政治的信念，以及诸如"时代精神"的需要这类模糊的概念上。局限于兴趣、思想和个性这类主观问题无助于建设性的争论，而且还会忽视怎样维护公众利益这类更加复杂和重要的问题。

纵览提交给有权审批建筑工程的董事会和评审委员会的听证记录中那些松松垮垮的、互相冲突的意见以及后来提出的报告，人们就会了解这一问题的深刻性。任何参加过评阅建筑学院学生作业的人都熟悉常常用于客观评价的主观标准。这种随意性的，带着感情色彩的制定建筑标准的方法已经使城市风貌、郊区的发展、我们周围郊区化的乡村规划支离破碎。决策机构对此负有不能逃避的责任。

应该把当前的困境放到适当的历史背景中加以思考。1945年以后的历代建筑师们在建筑史上第一次未能满足古希腊人建立城市以来整个社会认为是理所当然的两个希望：既能设计出构成城镇建筑群的基本建筑，又能设计出宏伟壮观的、能体现社会最高愿望的里程碑式的民用及宗教建筑。过去的建筑师们就是以这种方式将其建筑设计融入城市的整体规划之中，使新建筑与原有建筑一样漂亮，甚至更加漂亮。这类建筑的著名范例不胜枚举：雅各布·圣索维诺通过把大钟楼改建成一座独立的塔式建筑，将皮亚泽（中央广场）与皮亚泽塔（小广场）连接起来，从而"再创"了圣·马可广场和皮亚泽塔，还有圣·马可教堂新图书馆的杰出设计；杰夫·布隆德尔设计的中世纪的梅斯大教堂的正面（1764）——可惜已遭毁灭——及其相邻建筑；姆勒斯科设计的雅典卫城入口；雷恩设计的牛津和剑桥的建筑等等。振兴当代建筑实践以满足过去的标准是一项刻不容缓的任务。

建筑学是我们大学里讲授的一门人文学科，也是一门应该允许理性讨论的学科。本文的目的不在于判定一座拟议中的建筑的最终艺术价值，因为其艺术价值需要经过仔细的评估并且只有时间才能做出最终的评价，而在于提出一种方法，帮助我们对在各种名胜古迹地区修建新建筑的设计质量进行评价，是一种能决定现有设计方案是给这个地方的美景和特色锦上添花还是造成损害的方法。这一方法提供了一整套标准，有助于辨别规划中的建筑的特色，使这些特色与周边建筑辉映成趣。这些特色一旦明确，就将作为有关居民、评论家、决策机构和建筑师辩论该项设计方案优缺点的共同基准，而且还将为决定是否接受、改进、甚至修改设计或规划打下坚实的基础。

建筑是一门大众艺术。它是城市的砌块，是一项历经数百年才能认识其得失的复杂工程。城市总是在变化、发展、改建、毁坏和重建。所有这一切都是为了适应社会和政治变化、工商业的需要，以及技术革新的节奏。村庄和农村地区也承受着相同的压力。每当要建一座新的建筑时，必须对其进行仔细的审查，不是作为孤立的个体，而是作为构成所有地区日益复杂的整体的一部分进行评价。

第 3 单元

新古典主义中的现代派遗产

古典主义建筑艺术的复兴一直伴随着与现代运动相似的那种改革热情。对立双方的相互关系又进了一步。许多新古典主义艺术家自己的态度可以看作是现代派（同一硬币的反面）的直接产物，两者都因进步、技术和现代感而着迷。正是这种着迷的状况可能会导致新古典主义的毁灭。

新古典主义建筑艺术仅仅是 70 年代初打破现代派垄断局面的一个方面。企图利用历史来给后现代派、地方色彩派，以及新地方色彩派注入活力的做法只不过是将消化不良的历史建筑中的零碎加到原本现代派的结构中去而已。严肃的古典主义复兴者在这一伟大变革中只不过是形单影只的一小部分，甚至起初被当作偏离主流而遗弃。

新古典主义由于真正学术精神的支持而获得一些同行的狂热信服，由于公众的支持而建成一些重要的建筑。这些最终确立了这一小批新古典主义建筑师对当代建筑艺术的发展所作的重要贡献。

既遭孤立又遇敌意，成长于逆境之中，还遭教育界的排斥，所有这些都对古典主义的发展有着深刻的影响。

在古代，以及自文艺复兴至19世纪初，古典主义建筑占了统治地位。甚至在19世纪古典主义仍是两大主要流派之一，并在本世纪前40年又成了占统治地位的流派。

古典主义建筑艺术的最近十五年是巩固时期。自十五世纪以来前所未有，古典主义的实践者和理论家们不得不在从未有过的同行嘲讽的气氛中从零开始证明古典主义存在的合理性。巩固时期的成功是由于公众对现代运动的过火行为越来越反感。因此，毫不奇怪，新古典主义思想体系的基础竟是反对现代运动所表现的一切。

古典主义理论家尤其激烈否认现代派的两条基本原则，即通过前卫派促进艺术发展，以及技术革新至高无上的理论。

然而，对现代派一切方面都持反对态度面临着不分精华糟粕全部否定的危险。实际上，对于更为极端的传统主义者，否认前卫派的重要性已经变成了否认一切向往现代的愿望；否认技术至高无上已经变成一种建筑原教旨主义：1820年以后的任何形式的结构和建筑物都被排除在古典主义之外。战后现代派使古典主义建筑艺术的自然发展进程突然中断，而专注于1820年以前的建筑又使古典主义与此进程割裂开来。

一些前卫派艺术家也会创造出公众认可的作品。然而自二战以来，这种合乎情理的观点已被夸张成一种荒谬的观点，公众对新艺术的任何形式的欣赏都会使这种艺术自动变糟。然而，这并不意味着向往现代，标新立异，甚至追求震撼人心的效果这种愿望在古典主义建筑艺术中是闻所未闻的。可以证明，认为历史是由盲目发展所驱使的一种不可抗拒的技术力量来推动的观点是不正确的。但这不能改变以下事实：自罗马拱以来的古典主义建筑艺术已经适应了新的要求。尽管要做到不赞赏乔治时代各种古典主义建筑形式的美妙很难，但要否认19世纪及20世纪初所建造的古典主义建筑的合法性却是不现实的。

尽管欣赏乔治时代的建筑不能说是一件坏事，弃绝现代概念（在乔治时代并非如此）就赶走了许多卓有才华的年青人。建筑原教旨主义者对真正有用的技术进步不屑一顾，就吓跑了许多建筑项目及其商业利益。如果新古典主义建筑艺术不改变对与现代运动有关的一切不分青红皂白完全否定的态度，它就注定永远只是旁门分支，并且如现代派毁损者所预言的那样最终给淹没掉。作为少数身体力行的古典主义者中的一员，这是我不愿见到的未来。

如果古典主义建筑风格既要发展又要壮大，它就必须兼收并蓄现代技术和建筑艺术，以创造出既新奇又明显是古典主义的作品。它绝不应把硕果累累的过去当作沉重的包袱，徒劳地去阻止进步，而应该把它当作跳板，跃入令人振奋的未来。

第4单元

摩 天 大 楼

人们常把摩天大楼说成是20世纪的同义语。毫无疑问，高层建筑是我们这个时代的标志。结构上的奇迹达到了登峰造极的地步，体现了人类要修建更高建筑的目标。摩天大楼是本世纪最令人惊异的建筑成就。

但是如何设计高层建筑这一问题仍然使实践者感到如坐针毡，不知所措。人们在审美观和风格上摇摆不定的态度就象昼夜交替一样是可以预料的，此刻我们正忙于重新制定摩天大楼的设计规范。在这一过程中，我们不能肯定我们所学到的正确的东西是否正在被错误的东西所取代。

摩天大楼的成功的解决办法和建筑艺术本身取决于摩天大楼所引起的结构、用途、环境、以及公众的作用等问题解决得如何。无论何种风格都必须考虑到这些问题并对此做出反应。建筑学首先是一门表现艺术。

摩天大楼完全改变了我们的城市的规模、外观和概念，也改变了居住其中的人们的观念，这种情况无疑将继续下去。建设者和建筑师应当对关系到高层建筑的设计及其与城市环境的融合的所有因素加以考虑，这一点在今天比以往任何时候都更加重要。

摩天大楼设计的整个历史过程可以分为四个重要的阶段：功能主义、折衷主义、现代主义，以及现在新闻媒介称为的后现代主义。我们对现代主义的称呼并没有改变，只是包含的范围扩大了。很有意义的是，人们在高层建筑发展的早期，在很短时期内就对最重要的结构问题提出了解决办法。由于这些建筑在上一个世纪的最后 20 年里主要集中在芝加哥，很快就得到人们认可并被称为"芝加哥风格"。

从 1890 年到 1920 年的这段时间曾被认为是建筑学发展的黄金时期。在已建成的高层建筑中，几乎没有几座在构思巧妙和独创性方面能与建筑师路易斯·沙利文设计的建筑媲美。作为反潮流派迎着正在兴起的折衷主义派，沙利文认为摩天大楼的设计就是把结构和规划变成内外装饰，其答案不可能在过去的规范中找到。

由于大量借鉴了从希腊的神殿到意大利文艺复兴时期的建筑风格和装饰，折衷主义阶段产生了一些极为杰出的不朽之作。其中的最佳典范显示了娴熟的专业技能，设计新颖，富有戏剧效果，力图反映 20 世纪人们的要求和愿望。由雷蒙·霍德和卡斯·吉尔伯德等建筑师精心制作的设计方案参加了 1922 年举行的有名的芝加哥论坛报大厦国际设计竞赛。这次竞赛要求设计出"世界上最美、最独特的办公楼"，吸引了二百多件参赛作品。最后选中了豪厄尔和霍德的复兴哥特式设计。这一选择无视现代派的思想，延长了折衷派建筑风格的生命力。由少数欧洲建筑师所开创的现代派倡导了一种最好称之为"现代派的"建筑风格，持续了十年时间。这种建筑风格既不是全新的，也不是革命性的。然而它却用现代派的理论结束了折衷派的装饰风格，并成为今天众所周知的"装饰艺术"。

由于当时的部分建设者没有勇气，不愿投资于还没有得到认可的建筑风格，因此具有早期现代派风格（又称为"国际建筑风格"）特点的摩天大楼为数很少。但是第二次世界大战以后，这些早期现代派摩天大楼的后代，如曼哈顿的麦克格罗—希尔大厦，开始构成现代派的共同风格，其平顶玻璃框架结构在过去十年中成为人们批评的焦点。

这些庞大的建筑给了我们严肃的教训。但是把责任主要归咎于审美学是错误的，因为投资模式和社会动乱对这些问题的产生同样负有责任。不幸的是现代美学中的极简抽象派艺术却听任削边去角。由于这是获取最大利润的途径，当然受到建筑商的欢迎，结果优雅高尚的建筑语言很快就沦为凡夫俗子的陈词烂调。许多人对正在逝去的东西感到悲哀，因为正是在一层薄薄的，闪闪发光的玻璃装饰里面的结构形式本身，产生了我们这个时代某些最富有创新精神的设计。

在寻求理想答案的过程中，这些思想不应该被抛弃。毕竟，摩天大楼的历史——也是本世纪的历史——就是探索个性的历史。

第 5 单元

设计中的安全考虑

在目前的设计过程中，安全概念是很复杂的。结构设计的内在危险来自设计者对结构所处的环境、材料的特性和结构自身的性能等的了解有限。在建筑设计和施工过程中，通过采用最佳设计、最佳施工技术、最佳材料、最佳施工专业知识，以及最全面的环境资料来寻求安全性。在设计计算时采用适当的数值确保安全系数。为方便讨论起见，认为对材料特性、施工质量、细部构造等实际控制完全按照设计说明书的要求进行。这一假设对确定设计分析（更恰当地说，综合分析）过程是必要的。安全标准的控制就是在这一过程中落实的。

让我们来看一看极限状态或载荷与阻力系数设计（LRFD）方法用于设计的情况。这些方法看来同样重视满足正常使用要求和最终极限承载状态要求。然而，引起争论的地方在于认为设计的主要目的是生产适用结构，而且按照正常使用要求建成的结构本身实际上就是安全的。因此，问题就出现了：承载力极限状态的确定对于结构的安全性有什么作用？可以说在极限承载状态下的稳定性要求为明确考虑载荷情况提供了一个在正常使用条件下的具体安全系数。对这一安全系数的评估不会产生通常意义的局部安全系数。的确，这部分安全控制方法更类似于主要对结构行为性质产生影响的设计要求。

在设计过程中明确使用数值系数是在回避设计模型及其假定与实际结构及其周围环境之间的差异。这种等级的系数反映出对实际情况的不了解。我们来看一看所谓理想的"绝对安全"的建筑吧。这种建筑兴许是其材料和结构特性完全清楚，而且在使用期限内保持不变；再者这种建筑的环境、荷载和支承条件都了解并且被控制在规定的水平内。设计这种建筑不需要安全系数。

按惯例，设计者假设基本变量最低容许值，在设计的各阶段使用保守分析模型和半综合系数，将安全系数纳入他们的分析中。这种设计方法在质量上是否成功，只有通过对根据其原理修建的所有建筑的故障率和故障性质进行调研才能确定。那就不存在对任何给定荷载条件下的安全系数进行评估的切实可行的方法。

将局部安全系数体系引入设计过程要求掌握大量的、在设计中必须考虑的基本变量数据。这些数据应该使人们能够对每种未知变量进行单独评估。每个系数仅能反映人们对一个给定参数的了解状态。其它许多已知对设计有影响的参数，如模型误差，是不能单独评估的。它们的误差必须通过某种整体的或综合的设计安全系数来加以考虑。这种等级的系数与那些与特殊变量直接相关的系数之所以不同，在于这种值的确定包括评估值。该评估值通过对现行设计进行某种形式的核定而获得。因此，局部安全系数的引入要求满足下列两个条件：大量精心挑选的与每种基本变量相关的数据和明确无误的量化局部安全系数的规划。

出于实际考虑，在得不到某一特定变量的数据的情况下，必须使用直观选择的或通过某种分析方法得到的基本变量的实际值。

纳入某些现代规范或标准的局部安全系数体系与第二个条件并不相符。例如，最低荷载安全值的使用使得局部安全系数方法达不到特定的目的。

改变规范形式的正当理由必须是使其更加自相一致，更适合设计过程的需要，而且能够在将来引入新的资料和方法时不需要修改系数；再者，它还必须更加易于使用。

第 6 单元

论 设 计

由于多种原因，要论述大体上以建筑设计标准为根据的基本规则在近年来日益困难。其原因主要是目前人们对新技术条件下建筑风格的发展有不同的观点；设计人员面对有一大串可以用来解决结构问题的方法，还有大量可供选择的建筑材料。结果常常是建筑群杂乱无章，设计详图粗糙。在过去，选择性非常有限，人们通过长期努力提高建筑学学识水平和精确性来避免设计粗糙。在 18 世纪，这个国家乔治王朝时期的居住工程清楚地表明了这些特性。在还保存有这些工程的地方，两百年后的今天这些工程仍然有很强的适应性和实用性。无疑，乔治王朝式的鳞次栉比的房屋在很大程度上符合阿历克斯·戈登所说的建筑设计应该达到的四个目标。这些目标是：

1. 改善气侯；
2. 利于活动；
3. 增加财富；
4. 带来乐趣。

当然，他还可以加上一条：任何设计必须与投资规模相称。

在发生石油危机的 1974 年，人们的反应是千方百计节省急剧上涨的室内能源开支。戈登倡导了一项设计方案。在这一方案中他提出了如下设计指导目标——使用寿命长，能源消耗低，适用范围宽。其目的在于通过降低建筑物的燃料消耗和维修成本，使其更易于适应不断变化的用途来减少建筑物的周转资金。近来有迹象显示这些原则正在得到人们的考虑，并且现在有些建筑在很大程度上反映了这些约束条件。运用有限选择建筑材料的指导原则对设计大有好处。虽然在过去三年中仿乔治王朝式住房令人惊异地有了小小的复兴，但是这种解决办法提不出任何真正的答案，而且在当今这种微不足道的规模也不具有任何真实的意义。然而 20 世纪 20 年代威尔文花园城最后采用新乔治王朝式建筑风格却有很大的优点，在建筑比例、建筑形式、色彩和细部的理解上显示出很高的学识水平。

曾有一种流行办法显示出这种简洁设计受到人们的高度尊重。它源自讲究轴线和对称性的古典装饰风格，反映了对诸如窗户、前门及山墙等标准细部的理解。或许显得单调甚至不尽恰当，但绝非粗俗不堪。设计人员在这一选定的风格范围内，根据方便设计的矩阵布局画出简略的设计图，也认识到一些（简单的）制约因素，如场地、用途、标准细部以及当时的规范、条例等。剖面图和立面图自然而然地出自总图，由那些在细部基础设计方面技艺娴熟的能工巧匠准确地完成。整体设计、量度、设计说明书、合同以及建造过程几乎都能得到理解和实施。这一切当然不能持久，虽然一些近代大师比如勒·科布西耶、莱特、米尔斯·凡德罗，以及还有一两位不那么知名的人的作品还留有对这些早期设计方法的信心的痕迹。

由于其他许多权威人士已对过去50年来的设计和建筑进行了诸多论述，因此对最近20年来的建筑设计史的进一步探讨必须就此停笔。总之，为受过良好教育的客户服务的学者型的建筑师的影子已经随着双方自信心的丧失一起消失了。现在他们得依靠许多其他专家的特殊技能。深受世界范围的，特别是德国及其邻国的经济崩溃的影响，一个新的建筑世界在本世纪20至30年代已发展起来。其中一个明证就是"国际风格"。我们必须在新的要求范围内搞建筑，旧式设计看来已不再合时宜。官方客户，公众需要，日益增加的都市人口，以及成本核算都对设计产生影响。在更加严格的规则范围内，轻型构架和建筑饰面材料的技术发展显得日益有用。

现在我们的建筑有的新颖时髦，有的还属探索性的，有呈几何图形的，有精雕细刻的，也有毫无特色的，以及组件装配的。形形色色的结构绝技与有待完善的用料革新同时并存。一端是公共建筑，大专院校，声名显赫的的商业大厦（设计上全都各显千秋），另一端是组件装配的建筑，为社会提供诸如学校、住宅、办公楼、厂房及工业建筑等等需要。

我们仍然面临着设计和施工基本方法的这种对分局面。这一局面突出了我们这个时代社会的和技术的目标之间的差异。在建筑领域我们已到达其中一个分水岭——处在两难矛盾之中：

简便住所	高性能住所
坚固型实心墙体	轻便型框架结构
保护隐私	利于社交
低密度	高密度
车辆用道	人行通道

在这种利害犬牙交错的两难中，我们现在必须正确处理好设计和使用性能两个重点之间的关系。

一个可以接受的解决办法似乎是对以前的最佳方案进行辨别和分析，然后再决定是否支持大刀阔斧的改变。很有必要弄清楚深刻的变化对以前的方案的适用性有多大影响，是哪些新的制约因素使其不能再次使用。持续变化的戏剧性效果并不适用于长寿命的建筑这一人工产品。这就意味着要认识到人类对住所的第一要求是便于人类活动，关键是要能躲避风雨。依沙克·维尔斯的格言看来很适合今天的要求：

"建筑艺术再重要也不如其实用性重要，对其雄伟的赞美再多也不能超过对其提供的舒适性的赞美。"

为了更加接近这条哲理，我们就需要发展新的设计方法，以便更有信心地对许多互相冲突的问题找出现在和将来的答案。在寻求连续性的途中没有现成的方案，而目标必须是连续的——一个满意的设计会带来卓有成效的、报偿丰厚的合同。

第 7 单元

砌体新标准，新高度

新的砌体结构设计标准，ＣＳＡ　Ｓ304.1"砌体建筑设计"已经通过投票和修订，预定于下月出版发行。由此基本承载能力普遍提高30％，有时达到100％。

除了更有效地利用钢筋混凝土的强度和砌体建筑固有的巨大抗压强度之外，新的砌体建筑设计标准规定：允许大幅提高砌体承重墙体的高厚比。即：或者可以按标准墙厚增加高度，或者可以使墙体比目前更薄。这些变化势必影响承重砌体建筑的设计，特别会影响静荷载相对较低的单层建筑的高墙设计。

承重墙的高厚比通常利用高度与厚度的比例 h/t 来表示。按照传统，设计标准规定出最大高厚比。对于经验设计方法，这种标准最大高厚比 $h/t=20$ 也仍然是一种选择。有关风压和地震区的极限值必需满足。考虑到墙体开孔允许的高厚比可以降低。

经验设计方法很受建筑师和工程师的欢迎。计算方法简单，省时。在很多情况下，采用更复杂、更耗时的工程分析方法进行设计并无明显益处。然而，经验设计方法对于钢筋混凝土砌体建筑并不适用。这种情况，加上新的设计标准明确允许更薄的墙体，使得工程分析设计成为更吸引人的选择。

更高、更薄的墙体

工程分析方法的另一益处来自目前单层砌体建筑普遍使用的轻质屋顶系统。这样的屋顶经常要求牢牢紧固，以避免上升风力将屋顶刮离墙体。通常，为了紧固屋顶，钢筋必须锚固在墙体内几米以下。由此，墙体已经得到部分加固，无需花费太多就可继续加固墙基以使墙体全面加固。有鉴于此，就有可能利用钢筋抵抗风压引起的墙体平面变形，同时紧固屋顶。

按照新的设计标准，只要计算出的强度足以承受实际荷载，高厚比极限 $kh/t=30$ 就适用于所有配置钢筋或未配置钢筋的墙体。此处，k 意指有效高度系数，根据墙体支撑情况，其数值为 0.8～1.0。新的标准可使墙体高度达到按经验设计方法计算出的墙体高度的两倍。例如，利用标准的 20cm 砌块（实际厚度 $t=0.19$m），最大墙高为

$$h = 30t \div k = 30(0.19) \div 1 = 5.7\text{m}$$

至

$$30\,(0.19) \div 0.80 = 7.125\text{m}$$

之间。这一最大值明显高于按经验设计方法计算的

$$h = 20\,(0.19) = 3.8\text{m}$$

在大多数情况下，宽间距配置钢筋可以满足强度要求。当静荷载（如屋顶、管道设施、雨、雪等）较轻时，常常有相当大的储备承载能力。

为了利用钢筋砌体建筑固有的抗变形能力，有关超薄墙体（kh/t 超过 30）设计的规定是设计标准的全新特点。为了利用这种设计方法，轴向荷载必须低于截面轴向承载能力的

10％，而且必须限定钢筋的最大用量以便确保延展性能。在此基础上，常可获得大大超过40的墙体高厚比（h/t）。例如，这就意味着，一幢利用20cm砌块的建筑，墙高7.6m或更高是可能的。

实践与实惠

对于结构设计者，计算墙体高厚比和计算承载能力的设计标准与钢筋混凝土的设计标准几乎相同。尽管需要一段时间熟悉了解，大多数结构设计者在这一领域都有着丰富的经验，要实现这种转变不应有什么困难。对于超薄墙体，考虑功能与强度控制而直接计算变形的方法虽然新，却是标准的分析方法。尽管比起经验设计方法这种结构设计方法也许花费稍高一点，整个建筑成本将会大大降低。甚至可节省占地面积。

超薄墙体的设计要求较高的砌体建筑抗压强度。这样的强度在现有产品范围内可以获得。但是，由于这些产品不标准（如砌块强度大于15MPa），测试和质量控制就更为重要。例如，施工图应该确定，与采用30cm砌块无配筋墙体或利用半露柱结构相比，采用20cm砌块的砌筑墙体按1.2m间距配置钢筋的最佳经济效益。采用宽间距配置钢筋，并且仅在需要的网格内用灰浆固定钢筋有助于降低成本。

采用配置钢筋的砌体建筑修建薄墙体或超薄墙体可以降低建筑成本，满足固定屋顶的要求。并且，由于配置钢筋，提供了更牢固的结构，更能抵抗意外荷载。对于建筑外层的修建，几乎没有什么影响，只是由于结构的要求，工艺会有所改进。导致类似设计方法的有关规定在过去十年里已经存在于《通用建筑法规》（广泛应用于美国西部）。这些规定已经产生了在经济和技术两方面都很成功的设计。

未来发展

由于变形常常制约着墙体设计，需要改进之处是增大墙体的刚度。应用预应力混凝土的经验和以前对预应力砌体建筑的测试结果都表明，应用预应力钢筋混凝土有可能设计出甚至更薄的墙体。采用预应力钢筋混凝土可以延缓变形裂缝的产生，从而大大降低变形。尽管新的设计标准允许预应力砌体建筑，却未给予充分指导。然而，由于测试表明$h/t=60$左右的高厚比是可能的，在特殊工程中可以考虑采用这种方法。随着在澳大利亚、瑞士、英国和美国出现类似的发展情况，广泛地采用预应力砌体建筑应该不会为期太远。

第8单元

绿 色 建 筑

从根本上讲，"绿色建筑"不是一个轮廓清晰的目标，而是一种存在于心灵的感受。它寻求改变我们的生活方式使之与我们这颗脆弱的星球保持更为持久的平衡。这最终意味着我们的生活方式将会发生急剧变化。但眼下对我们工程师而言，它意味着我们必须应用我们的智慧、知识和创新能力去研究与我们的星球更为和谐的技术手段。这种思路肯定需要对涉及所有潜在问题的解决办法采取一种现实的态度。同时也要求对常规解决办法和标准重新进行评价。

例如，试想设计一个适当的室内环境时采取绿色建筑的思路。常规办法是利用"黑箱子""制造"出一个完全人造的气候，用上一切想得到的能量和资源。但是，没有这些设备，人类大部分基本的环境需求仍可得到满足。大自然可以提供主要部分，机械设备提供辅助支持。因而，大部分照明可以借助日光，致冷利用周围空气，供热利用人体和办公设备。这些自然资源还可以由其它自然手段来补充：太阳能供热，利用风压或日照产生的空气升力通风，利用水的蒸发降温。这些都是古老的原理。现代计算机分析模拟方法使我们能够更好地理解并充满信心地去应用这些原理。

舒适标准是问题的另一方面。通常以为我们需要 500 勒克司照明度和 22℃左右的温度，尽管这种过于简单的方法并不反映我们心理和生理的充分需求。空调系统可以控制空气温度，但是由于空调系统不能充分辨明个人需求和愿望，它们常常令居住者不满意。如今，应对舒适重新定义，以使房间温度能反映出每日和季节影响，能够按个人愿望进行调节并提高个人对周围环境的控制能力。

建筑环境的绿色思路中第三个因素是建筑物本身：建筑形式、立面和建筑材料。三者共同调节气候，缓解和控制自然的变化。因而，外墙可以吸纳日光，并传到室内。外墙可防止过强光照，提供遮荫、通风和冷却功能。冬天它可保持室内温度，还可保持与外部世界的视觉联系。在建筑内部，空气流通可通过屋顶形状、暖气管道和四周装有百叶窗控制的天井调节。如此设计的建筑可以结构更简单，更紧凑。室内条件也可更稳定。即使室外是严寒酷暑，室内也可温度适宜。室内条件有更大的灵活性。如果未来环境需要，被动致冷，自然通风的建筑可以附加空调装置。但是与此相反几乎是不可能的。由此可以降低投资成本、管理成本、能源消耗和排污量，并且降低非永久性能源的使用。居住者有更大的主动控制能力，受机器支配更少，环境更合人意，从而达到了真正目的：居住者感到更舒适。

纽约市 22 层楼高的奥地利文化中心堪称绿色建筑思想的实例。由阿特利尔·雷蒙德·亚伯拉罕（Atelier Raimund Abraham）设计的这幢建筑采用了太阳能板，热泵，高隔热标准，居住情况传感器和日光传感器来创造一个高效节能的环境。

英国考文垂的电报电话培训中心由麦克科马尔·贾米森·普里查德（MeCormac Jamieson Prichard）设计。教室屋顶采用了波浪形状以形成由空气升力推动的横向通风效果，足以去除由信息技术设备所产生的较高室内热量。

由迈克尔·霍普金斯（Michael Hopkins）和帕特纳斯（Partners）设计的诺丁汉内陆税务中心有 40000m² 自然通风的办公区域及 1994 年底完工的附属居住区域。它的建筑设计、结构和环境几方面高度结合的形式赋予建筑既赏心悦目，又能遮荫，又能调节温度的特点。玻璃楼梯塔为自然通风提供了日光和风力两方面的辅助。这一建筑首次获得建筑研究中心环境评估最高分。

由索尔布鲁奇·赫顿建筑事务所设计的 GSW 中心是一座与 50 年代旧楼房连接的 23 层大厦。西面的双重立面构成热气通道，诱发自然通风，从而完全消除了空调需求。

最近在埃塞克斯动工的安格利尔工业大学的新建 6000m² 资料中心建筑说明书要求有环保意识的、低能耗建筑。在 ECD 合伙公司的一份设计中，关键元素都采用了自然通风和暴露的高热容量结构的一体化设计。窗户设计与并列室内光格相结合使建筑周围的日光得到最大量的利用。人造光源与窗户开启都由计算机控制。

第9单元

装 饰 美 学

自1966年美国建筑师罗伯特·文图里说出"越少越生厌"这句话以来，现代人对装饰品和装潢的态度一直经历着根本性的变化。文图里改变了建筑师路德维希·米斯·凡·德·罗厄让人熟悉的名言，并指出现代建筑学已变得过分简单化，已经与生活失去了联系。尽管他的观点在那时带有异端邪说意味，但有一小部分建筑师却接受他的观点，其中包括当时耶鲁建筑学院的院长查尔斯·莫尔。莫尔首先表示了他的反叛，他在室内墙上画图，而不管甚至忽略该图在那儿是否具有装饰功能。1967年评论家雷·史密斯把它们称作超大图形。60年代末毕业于耶鲁大学受教于莫尔的学生激进地在自己住所的墙面上，从地板到房顶画上紫色对角线条状图案，在墙角画上大大的黄色点状图案——所有这一切都旨在解除功能主义的理论和设计原则的控制。

也许最早使用超大图形装饰的是文图里1962年为费城的大饭店设计的整修方案，但那时并不叫这个名字。饭店名称用4英尺高的字母拼写在一面墙上，然后反射在对面墙上的镜子里。特大型文字叠映在一个小小的就餐空间极大地扩大了餐厅里的空间感。这样做的目的主要是作为空间试验，而不是装饰。这种做法随后演变成越来越多地用画和图案来进行装饰，如艺术家威廉姆·塔普利的房间就采用了复杂的图案来装饰。大多数超大图形都用于室内装饰工程。但是到1970年，它们不断出现在建筑物的外墙上。这些画在墙上的巨幅壁画使都市"顷刻之间"就焕然一新。

从这些早期采用画、色彩和超大型图案的尝试中，一场真正的运动在建筑学领域内发展起来了，其精髓是装饰品：装饰品有时是平涂的，有时完全是三维的，它们被装饰在建筑物的室内和室外。朴素的白色墙壁消失了，代之而起的是丰富的、复杂的色彩组合，或者是凸出的壁柱、剪影和其它简单地用钉钉在墙上的装饰品。巨大的花或假柱极其夸张，毫无条理可言，但却频频出现在建筑物外墙上。主要的公共场所正被设计成几乎像舞台布景一样，其装饰性图案让人一看就会既熟悉又吃惊，使人对历史和文化轶事浮想联翩。传统的柱子和三角饰仍然存在，但已被分解变形，常常出乎意料地与其它建筑诸元并行不悖；传统的砖木结构变成了诸如不锈钢和霓虹灯一类的华丽的现代材料，令人惊叹不已。

装饰工艺，尤其是玻璃装饰工艺，熟铁装饰工艺和绘画风格——这些长期以来都不属于建筑设计的主流现在却承担了更加重要的建筑任务。字画艺术家，其技艺本已逐渐被人淡忘，只能在被遗忘的农家墙上才能隐约见到，但现在再次复出。他们制成金丝镶边或将整个房间变成梦景。家具设计者不断创作充满智慧和想象的家具：椅子的形状象蝴蝶，桌子精雕细刻让人想起18世纪的家具。一群构成了称作"造形和装饰运动"的艺术家抛弃了画布，而在整面墙上画满纯粹的装饰画，或在房间里面放上充满想象的雕塑。他们中的许多艺术家用瓷砖、色布、珠子、金属片，甚至野鸡羽毛来进行装饰——这些材料常常被认为仅用于装潢而与艺术无缘。这两个领域之间的传统区别越来越模糊不清，因为许多造形和装饰派艺术家也制作屏风、椅子、桌子、床和灯。这些东西随时能产生潜在的用途同时也能引起联想。

这个运动正以有时被称作"后现代主义"的方式改变着当代建筑的面貌。但"后现代主义"这个名称是评论家查尔斯·金克斯 于1975年让它流行起来的，很快就被美国建筑师罗伯特·斯特恩采纳。其实它是一个靠不住的术语，暗指整个现代运动正在被抛弃，全然不同的东西正在取而代之。这完全不是事实。正如评论家艾达·路易斯·哈克特贝尔非常贴切地指出的那样：现代主义的高潮已经结束，弗兰克·洛伊·怀特、米斯·凡·德·罗厄、勒·柯布西耶等大师的时代也已经终止，我们正清楚地——或者我应该说模模糊糊地——向其它东西迈进。事实上我们一段时间以来一直在这样做。不管获得的是现代主义的结晶或是继承者，但绝不是后现代主义所宣扬的彻底决裂。本质上将产生一次20世纪的革命，我们称其为现代建筑学。

只要看一看大多数作品就会明白现代运动之前不可能设计出这样的作品。现代主义的简单形式和技术手法依然存在，只是隐藏在表面下，但是仍然显而易见，仍然相当有用。装饰主义非常反对现代主义的明显缺陷，但并不是完全拒绝现代主义。为了对那些试图把他称为后现代主义者的人进行回击，罗伯特·文图里坚持他的公司只从事现代建筑。他是正确的。

第10单元

论 园 林

最好的园林远不只是将各种美丽的花草树木种在一起。成功的园林都代表了各种要素经过精心组合成的一个整体，用途从纯粹的装饰作用到严格的功能作用不等。路径、池塘、花盆、格架、棚架、喷泉和栅栏在创造一个让人心醉的、和谐的花园中起着极为重要的作用。如果用人们装饰居家使之"适于居住"的精力来建造园林，就能使之成为一个令人愉快的地方。在那里你可以找到属于自己的东西，可以进行沉思，可以逃避快节奏的工业社会的压力。

实际上，人工园林的独特风格比纯粹的花草树木更能决定园林的式样。具有时代特征的园林——维多利亚式、法国式、伊丽莎白式、美国殖民时期园林——都要求恰当地处理好建筑和设计上的各个方面，使这些特色能够一目了然。的确，只要简单地在某种式样的凉亭，凳子或棚架上加点什么立刻就能"识别出"园林的特色。同样，那些具有"人文特征"的园林，如英国的乡村花园、中国的沉思花园（指古典园林——译注）或意大利的水上公园，选择了恰当的栅栏、桥和装饰物就形成了风格，使人产生与环境永恒一致的感觉。

在世界上，园林建筑能树立园林的名声。在南卡罗来纳州的查尔斯顿附近的木兰花公园里，一条造形别致的、有格子棚架的步行桥称作长桥，是这座公园的标志。它设计独特，穿过一座柏树环绕的湖泊的一角，很快就映入人们的眼帘。这座桥带点法国风格，白色桥身，与深色水和披挂着铁兰的高大柏树对比鲜明，有助于创造出一种浪漫的气氛。这也许就是它比世界上其它园林建筑更容易成为图片和绘画对象的原因。

　　尽管一些园林建筑作为园林的组成部分不用装饰看起来也很不错，但另一些建筑却需要用一些花草树木进行点缀。英国人尤其喜欢培植攀缘玫瑰、紫藤、忍冬、爬在墙上的常春藤、篱笆眺台和凉亭。这种做法有时十分成功，整个建筑物完全掩映在藤蔓纵横、红花绿叶之中。

　　当然，也有单靠花草树木产生戏剧性的效果从而形成独特风格的园林。在马里兰州的巴尔的摩附近有座拉迪尤剪型树木公园，这里的日本紫杉被修剪成一幅围猎狐狸的风景，形成了古怪离奇的精彩场面，使这个公园因此而闻名遐迩。在公园的入口处，由灌木修剪成的五只猎狗、一名猎人骑着一匹马穿过草坪，追逐一只灌木修剪成的狐狸。这种现实主义的像实物一样大小的图案构成一景，将人们引向公园的其它部分，那里的修剪造型更令人称奇叫绝，妙趣横生。

　　建造一座美丽的园林，园艺师和建筑师的作用非常重要，但他们的努力如没有第三方的重要作用——艺术家的帮助也达不到目的。如今最好的园林似乎都包含了园艺师、建筑师和艺术家的智慧。有时这三种技能体现在一个人身上，但更常见的是集中了许多人的智慧。例如，位于美国旧金山附近的美丽的菲洛利美国国家花园就是园艺师伊沙贝拉·沃恩和风景画家布鲁斯·波特合作的结晶。波特进行场地和特色的总体设计，沃恩完成花木的挑选和栽培规划。

　　印象派画家克洛德·莫奈是一位艺术家，但他在设计自己位于法国杰维利的花园时表现出了园艺师和建筑师的技能。在他家的入口处，他亲自设计并完成了非常简洁但又让人感到吃惊的花台。他的粉红色的拉毛粉饰的房子装有颜色大不相同的绿色百叶窗。作为补色，他种植了几大丛粉红色天竺葵，并用粉红色和白色的玫瑰花台点缀其间，再用灰叶石竹来给这些凸出的花坛镶上边。几团精心挑选的色彩醒目的花与附近的建筑物融为一体，是这座特殊花园成功的关键。

　　园林也能是艺术作品的宝库。这些艺术品不一定是现实主义的，但必须是引人注目的装饰品。园林艺术开始时用石头和枯木来表达象征意义。古代的中国人在他们的花园中用巨砾来代表神兽。他们给这些石头系列命名为"龟石"、"鹰石"和"龙石"来代表与它们相似的实物。从石头和枯木所表现的象征主义出发，园艺师们开始追求现实主义。从解剖学的角度讲雕塑越逼真，这座雕塑的价值就越高。古希腊和意大利是雕塑艺术的佼佼者，他们在园林风景布置里将神和英雄的雕像安放在基座上。

　　如今，艺术界兜了个圈子又回到了原位，再次强调象征主义和印象主义。人们要求艺术家埃斯特班·维森特解释他艺术中的现代风格和业余爱好园艺之间明显的自相矛盾时，他说得好，"如果不接触自然，你就不能创造艺术。"并说："任何与自然有关的东西也必然与艺术有关。"

　　最好的园林似乎是结合了园艺师、建筑师和艺术家的天赋。从某种程度上讲，这三种为园林做出贡献的人都是艺术家，因为有许多园林和园林建筑的典范都称得上是艺术作品。

家具布置的美学设计

　　房间能够做到既有用又漂亮，虽然有时由于特定的限制为了一个方面而必须牺牲另一个方面。每当遇到这种问题时，发挥创造能力就能找到一个令人满意的解决办法。例如：没有隐蔽起来的散热器可能严重干扰人们对美的欣赏。人们需要它们来取暖，但它们的存在又会损伤房间的美感。这时一个简单的办法就是在两侧放上书橱，然后在散热器上放一个金属铁栅，再在上面放一个书架，这个"问题"就会变成这个房间中一个非常吸引人的饰件。也许所有的问题不会这么容易就解决了，但尽力用创造性的方法去解决这类问题比撒手不管更有意义。家庭的美感取决于如何运用设计原理。

　　在某种程度上，人们的自然直觉决定着房间家具的放置。即使那些并不精通艺术基本原理的人也会把沙发靠客厅长的一面墙摆放，因为沙发放在那个位置看起来"顺眼"。但是再精心地设计一下，就会产生巧妙的美感，使得房间更加漂亮。

和谐

　　房间的陈设布置设计溶合了各种因素，以使整个房间表达一个特定的主题或格调。"整体大于各部分的总和"这个古老的原理完全可以运用到房间的布置上。每一件家具和每一个因素都有助于整体，但结果必须是富有魅力和独特个性的整体。房间的美取决于各部分的相互关系，家具和陈设必须一看就觉得应该放在这个房间，彼此应该协调一致。

比例

　　因为比例是一个空间关系问题，所以房间和可以利用的墙面的大小将决定使用家具的种类和数量。家具应与房间的大小成比例。小房间应摆放小型家具并且数量应尽量少，大房间则应摆放体积较大的家具，通常这样才能达到最佳效果。墙面空间由于摆靠在它旁边的家具和其它附件而隔断。所以每个墙面家具和陈设的安排都必须考虑空间分隔问题以使其看起来赏心悦目。悬挂在墙上的画或其它装饰品应该与家具和墙面和谐一致。

　　家具的组合比例也很重要，一张小巧精致的桌子放在大而沉重的椅子旁边就显得微不足道，如将这张桌子放在一件更精致的家具旁边就会显得美妙绝伦。

平衡

　　几乎所有的房间中，都有一些家具比另一些家具厚重。较大的，更重要的家具应摆放在房间四周以使房间各部分平衡。但是室内建筑物的附件如窗子或壁炉也有"重量感"，因此应在对面墙边摆放较大件的家具以达到平衡。

　　我们常常可以运用色彩来使房间各部分达到平衡：一小片鲜艳的色彩或醒目的图案具有增重效果，常常能够平衡大片较暗的色彩。因此将椅子套上鲜艳的椅套可以平衡一扇大窗户上的色彩暗淡的窗帘。

家具的组合平衡也很重要。大多数房间需要正式的或非正式的平衡。但是，一般说来，现代风格和更加随意的传统风格适合于非正式平衡。一间庄重的传统房间可以用对称布置的家具组合来表现出典雅考究。房间的格调取决于人们想在多大程度上利用每种平衡。过多的不对称会导致杂乱无章，太多的对称又会使房间变得呆板，令人望而生畏。

强调

如果在设计中确定起主导作用的兴趣中心，那么大多数房间会变得更兴趣盎然。大房间可以有一个以上的起主导作用的中心，但小房间通常有一个或者两个中心就足够了。

在决定兴趣中心所用的家具及其摆放的位置之前，应该仔细研究每一个房间。也许壁炉，大窗户，两扇窗或其它建筑构件都能用来作为突显兴趣的地方。家具、陈设、色彩或图案都能突出一壁大墙面的重要性。比如，墙壁嵌上色彩更鲜彩的壁画，或者用不同质感的墙纸来装饰立刻就会引人注目。一件又大又重要的家具，一幅大的画或一组画可以使这个地方更加突出。

一些特殊的活动、业余爱好或兴趣可以为在房间中选择兴趣中心的位置打下有意义的基础。乐器或某种收藏品能通过摆设的方式而显得引人注目。这样一个兴趣中心常常能确立房间的个性特征，为房间的整体布置设定一个主题。

节奏

家具和陈设品的线条，色彩和质感会使人们的眼睛向一定的方向移动。眼睛以舒缓优雅的方式移动比以跳跃的、颠簸的方式移动常常更赏心悦目。我们已讨论过产生节奏感的不同方法，所有那些方法都可以用来设计陈设布置图。令人赏心悦目的节奏感取决于设计中各要素的良好组织。

重要陈设的线条如果与房间的建筑线条一致那么会更加吸引人。长方形家具的线条与墙壁平行或垂直会显得更得体。将家具放在对角线上常常让人心烦意乱，除非是折叠椅或者是躺椅。线条的连续性有助于眼睛平稳地移动，这样与椅背同样高的桌子就不仅更方便使用而且与椅子相比通常更有吸引力。画和其它装饰品的陈设应能使眼睛的移动平稳舒缓。

重复是一种产生节奏感的良好手段，但是运用必须谨慎，太多会产生单调、一成不变的感觉；而要提高人们的兴趣感则需要一定程度的对比。

第12单元

园林建筑学理论

园林建筑学包含五大组成部分：自然形成、社会作用、方法论、技术和价值。无论建设的规模或重要性如何，这五个组成部分总是缺一不可的。在涉及到人和土地的专业中，社会和自然因素必然渗入到各个方面。其解决办法，规划和设计方法应适用于各种层次。这就始终要求具备良好的判断力。

让我们先看一下已知的自然因素与园林规划与设计两者的关系问题。在区域范围内，一片景观的开发或用途改变所造成的重大影响必须在制定政策、允许该项规划和设计实施之前，就得到清楚的了解和评估。自然因素的调查对于理解变化可能给生态系统带来的影响是至关重要的。调查内容包括地质、土壤、水文、地貌、气候、植被、野生生物，以及这些因素之间的生态关系等。对视觉品质的分析也具有同样的重要性。所以，土地使用政策的制定要建立在对园林的易损性或抗损能力的认识的基础之上。在其它情况下，某一时期某一地貌在演变过程中所产生的自然景观，如发生在科罗拉多大峡谷和其它地方的情况那样，形成了一种天然资源，应该作为公共事业得到保护和管理。对于较小规模的园林建设，土壤和地质条件在决定建设成本和建筑形式中可能起关键性作用，如什么地方最适合于建设，什么地方不适合。在主要目的是为人们活动和植物生长建立舒适场所的地方，日照、风力和雨量是设计的重要因素。由此可见，在园林的规划和设计过程中，场所或地域的自然因素都在诸多方面相互发生作用。

社会作用也同样用于各种规格的园林建设中。在场地规划和园林设计中，应考虑到各种变量，如人们在使用和评价开阔地和公园时的文化差异，年轻人和老年人的生理和社会需求等，因为设计的要旨就是要反映社会价值和人类需求。在决定投资修建园林供人们娱乐和选择其美学标准时，应考虑到人们对环境的认识、他们的行为模式、以及户外活动的趣向等。重要的是设计者应当了解环境对行为的影响，也应当充分意识到人类利用和控制环境的基本需要。

技术是完成设计的工具，也是制定政策所依赖的手段。随着新材料、新机器和新技术的发展，某些技术总是在年复一年地发生变化。技术在三种园林建筑中的作用是明显的。园林建筑中的具体技术领域包括植被、栽培和生态顺序、土壤科学、水文学和污水处理、小气候控制、地表排水、腐蚀控制、道路铺设、维护保养等等。

设计方法包括识别园林建设中的各种冲突，明确因园林而产生的各种问题的一整套方法。它是一种操作程序。在这个程序中，所有相关的因素和变量都能得到评价，从中产生出解决问题的方案。计算机制图，分析技术，标识体系等在这个程序中都可以用到。此外，完全有理由推荐霍普林（Halprin）提出的那项开创性的研究方法。他提出采用像在音乐和舞蹈设计中一样的评分技术作为一种展示和使设计过程看得见的手段。按照霍普林的看法，这可以使更多的人参与设计和作出决定并促成新一代方法的产生，用这些方法来规划和设计大规模的复杂环境与区域，从而得到更加富有人道主义特色的解决办法。

这些要素结合在一起的目的是形成一个基础。以此为根据园林规划和细部设计能够反映人类的行为模式（人）和特定的环境特征（景）。因为这二者在文化、地区和相邻关系上都会变化，所以没有万能的解决办法，也没有先入为主的解决办法。如此看来，分析社会和自然因素对全面理解问题尤为关键。对问题的全面理解又会产生独一无二的、恰当的设计形式和规划关系。

设计过程的目的是为了逐步发展适合人们需要的形式和相关内容。该过程可以与创造了世界上壮丽自然景观的地貌的原始的造形过程相媲美。这里，有形的地表形态——谷地和山脊、清水满盈的盆地、凹凸不平的山顶等等——代表着地质结构和侵蚀介质间相互作用的进化阶段。我们所看见的形态是由于无机物质对长年累月的风化等强制条件作出的反应的结果。从北山腰到南山腰、从草地到近北极高原、从河谷到怪石嶙峋的山坡，植被的变化确切地反映了自然地理变迁所造就的一系列环境状况。野生生物的分布反过来又受到植被品种和分布范围的支配。生态模式的每一个方面都是因因相果的。所有这一切都不可逆转地融合为一个自行维持和进化的生态体系，代表着自然力量及其在进化过程中的某一特定时刻的坚定意志。这种类比也许有缺陷，但正是这种造形力量的坚定意志与引起变化的内因相结合，才应当是园林规划者和设计者所奋斗的目标。

第 13 单元

城市的意义

半个世纪的规划活动改造了旧的建筑环境，但是却没能获得公众的好感。最近 20 年来人们对现代派的城市规划已明显地不再抱有幻想。曾经被人们捧为大胆创新的，体现所谓整体观念的规划并不足以成为长期的解决办法。战后建筑开发最突出的缺陷是没有空间感。现代派的城市规划把城镇划分为一个个互不相同、互无联系的小区，因而使社区生活出现两极分化。

人们的不满情绪有增无减，这促进了新的建筑规划观念的形成：即把传统的城镇作为新开发的样板。新一代的规划设计专家仔细研究了旧有的模式后，在城市规划中纳入邻里思想，把公共设施、商业网点和居住等诸多功能融为一体。传统城市规划模式的采用使一些陈年的问题又冒了出来：在处理建筑与城市之间，建设新的村镇与自然景观之间，建筑形态与公有户外空间之间等关系时，怎样解决好继承与改革的问题。

尽管传统城镇越来越受到公众的支持，而一些批评家却认为传统模式在今天行不通，因为它们无法解决当代社会问题和技术发展所带来的问题。可是，这些批评家没有注意到当今最有活力的大都市事实上都是传统设计的遗产，而这些"异物"并非像现代派所描述的那样是"空地好盖楼"思想的体现，而是对建立"公共王国"思想进行有益的尝试的结果。新传统主义者提出技术问题并不是因为敬畏科学，而是有其实际的考虑，那就是怎样利用技术使其为城市生活服务而不是颠倒过来让生活为技术服务。因此，应该正确地利用科学来为人们取暖，帮助我们的日常生活，处理商业事务——如果这些仍然属于健康的城市生活范畴的话。

对汽车问题的处理也许最能体现对待技术的新态度。新传统主义者设法把汽车控制在区域外围使用，为居住区行人留一方净土。这将最大限度地减少对汽车的依赖。然而，更重要的是为居民创造一个能享受公有户外空间的城市环境。在阿斯科特的贝尔维迪亚村，德米特里·波菲利建了一个他所谓的"安居核心"。这种建筑和空间的布局形式不仅仅是为了长远使用，而且是为了能逐步将其改造成为更大的地区都市中心。在佛罗里达的温莎城，安德烈斯·杜利和伊丽莎白·普拉特尔—齐贝克一道整理了城市发展的各种要素，提出了一项建筑计划，限制个人居住癖好而提倡突出街道、广场、绿地以及街道的立视效果。

这样的规划思想在更著名的由利昂·克里尔设计的庞德贝尔总体规划中也反映了出

来。这一总体规划展示了协调城市环境必需的所有综合配套设施，公共地段四周是公用设施，住宅区都面向中心绿化带，商业区总是近在咫尺。

这些新的城市规划实践中特别重要的一点是在新建城镇边沿设定"硬界"，使其成为独立的整体，不再无计划地向四周田园扩展。新传统主义者认为对城市全貌的总体规划至关重要。这一行为必须源于对构成我们的环境的各个要素的全面理解。现代派却故意模糊了城市各种不同设施的界限。柏林的波茨坦默-普拉茨地区就是一个恰当的例子。战后该地区形形色色，光怪陆离的建筑物在一片荒郊野地上争先恐后地冒出来，结果这个地区被弄得松散混乱，空隙丛生。希尔默和萨特勒在这个地区的总体规划中大胆地重新使用了传统模式的街道、广场、综合考虑其用途，建立了一套他们认为任何规划方案中都必不可少的公共场所体系。

在本文中提到的这群规划专家之外，有人认为高科技是灵丹妙药，建筑师则是这种万灵药的获取者。然而，新传统主义者却选择了一条更加现实的道路；即利用集体的经验和判断力，不为传统的工业形象所动，也不加入会受良心谴责的反传统大合唱。他们认为，要想使我们的城市有更加光明的前景，人类就应该学会充分利用传统城市模式中一切好的东西。

第 14 单元

城市和区域规划的评估方法

自从评估研究出现在社会科学和行为科学的议事日程上以来，人们一直在探索评估私营和公营事业两方面的决策者们不断变化的目标的方法。城市和区域规划者在分析、规划和实施过程中都非常依赖目标与评估方法之间的相互作用。15 年前，不同背景的决策者和分析家对现有的很多评估方法都提出了批评，认为它们花费大、费时多、忽视官方和规划实施对象的需要，而且不易实施。评估方法的最新发展已不再强调所谓纯粹理性的预期评估方法，而注重规划活动的实施和监控阶段。

分析各种评估方法之前，我们先考察一下效率和公平这两个概念，它们是规划评估和政策分析的传统目标。米勒称它们为"经济的油和水"。米勒还注意到：过去各种研究都倾向于强调效果——不论是局限于设计标准范围内还是指更广泛意义上的外部效应或外溢因素，情况都是如此。近来，公平观念越来越受到重视。规划者已更加注意这样的事实：公众的决定可以在当地人口中重新分配成本和利益。

米勒总结了理论研究中处理效率与公平的三种主要方法。这些方法倾向于：（1）只注重单方面目标；（2）只在某一特定层面上选用一个目标作为约束条件；（3）建立一个多元目标效用函数以对各种目标进行利弊权衡。成本-效益分析（CBA）和规划平衡表（PBS）分别属于前两种，而多变量分析，如目标-完成情况模型（GAM）或协调性分析，则属于后一种。

经济评估方法源于私营部门，吸收了福利经济学的原理来解释投资决策所产生的越来越多的社会影响。成本-效果分析（CEA）与成本-效益分析（也称为社会成本-效益分析）已成为最常见的量化评估的代表，不过，成本-效益分析更流行。

成本-效益分析（CBA）有两个基本过程。这些过程给决策者提供作出选择所必须的信息及选择本身；这种选择代表最佳投资和最低操作费用。成本-效益分析范围更窄，通过一份成本核算表就能见分晓的方式，它帮助决策者在互相排斥的选择对象中作出选择以获得明确的利益。成本-效益分析在其技术根据以及基础理论两方面均受到人们的批评。

成本-效益分析，在技术方面受到的批评可以归纳为五个方面：量化、折扣率、风险和不定因素、模糊因素和外部效应，以及公平分配。量化关心的是成本与效益的计算是否精确。舍尔夫对运用货币价值来为未进入交易市场的商品定价持有异议；米萨对诸如噪声与健康一类的模糊因素的量化也提出了疑问。市场-影子价格的使用也引起了争论。在某些情况下，市场过程不能充分显示社会价值和影子价格，比如劳动价格。对选择折扣率计算方法的争论主要集中在对下面几个问题的不同假设上：预测利润和预测损失、公共工程和私营工程以及大规模工程对国际国内资金流动和投资资本的影响。对风险与不定因素的解释应采用什么方法也是争论的话题，这就迫使分析人员要么选用计划风险，要么对其影响置之不理。模糊因素与外部效应对资金量化的可转移性与成本-效益分析在环境问题和其它发展问题中的效用提出了质疑。此外，希尔认为成本-效益分析没有充分解决分配问题和政治问题（如有的话），而这些却是一个工程最终是否成功的关键所在。最后，研究人员对成本-效益分析中的公平分配问题的重视程度也意见不一。批评意见既有来自支持这一评估方法的经济学家，也有来自反对福利经济学的基本原则的社会学家。

希尔对成本-效益分析理论基础中的更根本性的缺陷也提出了批评。他断言这种方法是为私营部门设计的，即使在最好的情况下也只能与公营事业的需要相似。成本-效益分析难以表达动态效果。舍尔夫指责经济效益派使用"理论"、"客观"等概念没有坚实的基础。在他看来，支持发展经济的人用抽象的数学表达式掩盖了某些原本武断的决策。这种家长式作风体现为不尊重公职人员，将导致无视政治因素，是一种危险的疏忽。

尽管有这么多缺点，成本-效益分析在一定范围内仍然是有活力的。但是，它在公平与效率之间，在可用数量表示的结果与不可捉摸的结果之间，在理性的理论与无理性的从业者之间都无法达成妥协。

第15单元

决定性的补救办法
——规划无效现象探源

从错误中学习是城市区域规划的一条准则。从理论上讲，反馈过程应该能促使人们对业已证明无效的政策立即进行纠正或摒弃。从长远角度看，国家级的、广泛而严格的评估之后理当归纳整理规划失败的各种原因，使政府、专业人员，甚至广大居民都能更好地了解规划活动的各种可能及政府的局限。无论是单个的规划，还是整个规划体系都需要这种监控，在每种情况下，实践都不可能与理论完全一致。

就单个规划而言，复审过程即使有也都随意性大，不那么正规化。规划机构的复审和修正工作也不正规，而是按照政治上的优先考虑来进行，或对既得利益集团（包括其它政府机构）的大声抱怨作出反应。后一种情况往往代表规划活动的结局，其优点为：可以解决早先在规划准备阶段避而不谈而在政治上有争议的问题。多数规划组织都没有财力和时间，也不愿意对规划绩效进行系统的、连续的评估。不论是出于有意还是疏忽，总之，规划活动成了典型的"杂乱无章"的增量过程。由第三方作出的评估，通常包含对政策的有效性作专业分析，有时范围更加广泛、更加仔细周到、更加公正。遗憾的是，地方规划很少能得到详细的、独立的评估。即使在对规划政策进行相当严格的分析的地方，正如摩尔和罗德1977年对英国区域规划政策的评估那样，结果也不尽如人意，与其说令人信服，不如说是在随机应付。在上述摩尔和罗德的评估中，政策难以界定，互相矛盾，又不断地变化翻新，加之经济体制的开放性，成问题的指标，冒昧的假设，以及令人怀疑的统计方法，所有这一切加在一起使得评估结果难以令人信服。

由此可见，规划绩效评估并非易事。首先，弄清评估项目就不容易。政策、策略及某些具体的规划方法或隐蔽或间接，或特别，各不相同，还存在无效政策的难题。而且，当某些特定的目标成为数家机构争相采纳的测评方法的对象时，要把相关的一套政策与特定问题区分开来也不容易。正因为如此，即使在一个具体的规划文件中，同一个目的也可能涉及几个政策。其次，必要的资料也难以得到，最好的时候也只能用不能令人满意的代用指标。最后，因果关系的衡量还会在开放的复杂的社会中造成无法克服的困难，在各种政策相互强化或相互对立的地方，或在反应明显滞后的地方，情况尤其如此。

规划体系或规划本身的绩效监控似乎引起了更多的注意。商业部门、社团组织、政府部门、官僚部门，以及学术界都不厌其烦地对规划的准备过程及决策程序提出批评，并热衷于提出改进意见。政府通常采用谨慎实用的系统评估方法，强调收集有关资料，比如审批规划申请所需的时间等，其目的是改进现有规划机制，偶尔也有更激进的大修大补。

在更深层次上，许多勤于认真思考的人怀疑规划体系是否能达到其特定目标——虽然这并没有妨碍规划人员奋力工作，而是因为城市政策本来就太复杂，很难获得成功。分析家们很快找到了资本主义国家妨碍规划成功的原因。这方面的文献大多使用了所谓的批评性语言，从公平社会的固有观念及其在城市形态方面的相应表现着手，但是却提不出实际的东西来帮助改进自由民主混合经济体制中的规划体系。大卫·哈维认为"规划人员似乎注定要永远遭受挫折"；迈克·迪尔和艾伦·斯科特则认为城市规划的反应性和姑息性本质并不仅仅是技术、分析或人为失误的结果，而是一种社会逻辑的必然产物。这种逻辑给一切政治行为的范围和有效性设置障碍。

评估规划体系的部分问题表现为：都市和区域规划只涉及政府权限范围要关心的诸多问题之一。其它需要关心的问题包括增加商品生产、服务项目、国民收入以及在国际贸易中最大限度地增加相对优势，从而确保社会和经济的高度适应能力，保护个人选择自由和责任感。这些目标可能会互相冲突，但必须在其冲突范围内寻求妥协。任何不面对这些冲突的评估只能反映部分问题，对体系改进工作不会有多大指导作用。而且，对一个规划体系完全合理的评估还应考虑到被规划社区的行为、分析和信息的诸多局限性以及规划人员和决策官员的局限性。

实际上，狭义分析法可能是唯一实际的选择。与全面分析方法相比，它能提供更加敏锐的观察力。因此，受欢迎的可能是各类这种评估方法：单独看它们可能都不完善，但由于源自各种学科领域，因此，可以各自的方式帮助人们对问题有更加深入的理解。比如：规划者可以从有关冲突调停、官僚政治决策和私有财产发展规划等诸如此 类的文献中学到许多东西。

第 16 单元

功能分区的两种模式

从经济理论的角度看有两种相互竞争的功能分区模式被当作政府的调节措施。一种是以亚瑟·皮古教授的《福利经济学》为基础发展起来的皮古模式；另一种是科斯模式，以罗纳德·科斯 1960 年获得诺贝尔奖的论文《社会成本问题》为依据。皮古模式指的是"外部效应"（也称相邻效应或外差因素）这一概念。在现代福利经济学里，外部效应是一种市场缺陷，产生于两种情况：甲方因乙方的活动而遭受的经济损失得不到补偿，如工厂排放的烟雾影响附近的房舍；甲方创造的利益被乙方无偿享用，比如玫瑰花园被过路人自由观看。前者被称为消极外部效应，后者被称为积极外部效应。皮古的传统理论视污染为典型的消极外部效应。这种得不到补偿的成本和利益造成经济的无效率。皮古派经济学家的理由是：市场只对私人成本和私人利益作出反应，因而边际价值和边际社会成本是不一致的，而这一点却是帕雷托经济效率的条件。因此，他们认为国家或政府应该干预市场以纠正经济无效问题。皮古模式被看成是干预性的，认为政府或国家对土地市场的调节有积极的作用；而科斯模式对这种调节的代价不断地提出怀疑。科斯派在其论述这两种方法的比较的经济文献里，讲到皮古派认为政策制定和执行是零交易成本，将政策作为似乎是外生的或独立存在的来对待。科斯派坚持认为在还未规范化的市场操作过程中发现问题时不宜急于制定政策。一些学者甚至认为：从经济效率的角度看，让市场自行调节更为有利。在规划领域里，皮古模式赞成功能分区，科斯模式反对分区。

从经济学角度考虑分区而形成的这种二分法普遍存在于美国文献里。英国文献尽管不这样讨论分区，然而在有关"规划"（城镇规划、城乡规划或城市规划）的更广泛的理论探讨背后仍然存在着这种辩论的基本内容。在英国，规划经济学的多数传统文献，如威廉·利恩的《土地经济学面面观》和《土地使用规划经济学》都接受皮古派规划学说。在英国文献里与"皮古派-科斯派"辩论对应的是规划界对有关问题的传统二分法。这些问题是：规划与市场、规划与价格机制、自由意志规划（如哈耶克提出的论点）、用产权代替现行规划调节政策，以及各种反对规划的非经济论断。在英国规划文献里，对弗里德里希·范·哈耶克的影响或它对这种影响的观点反映得更强烈。这可能是因为他的一些引起激烈争论的文献的缘故。他在这些文献里对英国 1947 年城乡规划法案中的某些严厉条款进行了攻击。英国对"产权"的表述的主要特征是不必要地把产权当成是与"发展控制"或其它调节措施迥然不同的东西，而没有把"市场"与"规划"当成产权的替换模式，也不把它们看作是竞争规划。

　　索伦森和戴在其对外部效应的讨论中广泛引用了哈耶克的著作（尽管这些著作对外部效应这一概念提出了质疑），却只字未提科斯1960年关于这一概念的颇有争议的论文，从经济学家的角度看这也许令人感到非常奇怪。同样，B·J·皮尔斯也引用了皮古关于外部效应的著作，也未提科斯。但他却引用了受科斯1960年的论文启发并在那之后发表的有关产权的著作，如哈罗德·登姆舍茨和史蒂文·陈的著作。其实克洛斯特曼赞成规划的经济学论据也采用了标准的皮古概念，而未按照惯例提到科斯的对立理论。格雷厄姆·哈利特的《城市土地经济学》作为教科书也只简短地提到科斯对外部效应的分析而且没有把它与分区规划联系起来。菲利浦·库克的《规划与空间发展理论》——规划理论的主要著作——没有提及科斯，表明科斯的理论在英国学术界没有多大影响。K·G·威利斯的《城乡规划经济学》是使读者详细了解这位移民预言家的理论的唯一著作。其中在讨论M·E·阿夫伦对功能分区所作的经验主义考察时也很少提及科斯的学术影响。因此，在英国学术界，约翰·伯顿给史蒂文·陈的《社会成本之谜》的长篇后记（皮尔斯的论文里引用过）似乎是科斯经济观最清楚的说明。科斯在英国规划文献里没有引起重视可能两个原因：其一，英国缺乏明确的分区体系，而美国却很普遍；其二，英国有中央集权下的福利保障。在美国各规划学院中能够更加强烈地感受到科斯理论的影响或对其作出的反应。一部分原因是他们采用了威廉斯·菲谢尔的著作《分区法则经济学》作为通用参阅文献；另一部分原因是罗伯特·埃利克森的文章的影响，《郊区发展对策》的影响尤其显著；还有一部分原因是明确的，法定的分区体系在美国得到了广泛采用。

Appendix Ⅲ   KEY TO EXERCISES

UNIT ONE
Reading Comprehension
Ⅰ. 1. T   2. T   3. T   4. F   5. F

Ⅱ. 1. The plan, the cross section

    2. attribute, the intention of

    3. a framework

    4. unique embodiment

    5. An urban dwelling, rural architecture, effects

    6. same

    7. incomprehensible

Vocabulary
Ⅰ. 1. b   2. c   3. a   4. e   5. d   6. f

Ⅱ. 1. contrived   2. aesthetic   3. indulge   4. constraints

    5. preconceived   6. composite   7. manifest   8. conferred

Writing
buiding totality,   transformation,   constraints,   appreciation

UNIT TWO
Reading comprehension
Ⅰ. 1. 1—2   2. 4   3. 3   4. 6   5. 5

Ⅱ. 1. B   2. A   3. D   4. C   5. D   6. A

    7. D   8. B   9. A   10. C

Vocabulary
Ⅰ. 1. d   2. e   3. f   4. a   5. b   6. c

Ⅱ. 1. A   2. C   3. B   4. D   5. C   6. A

    7. B   8. D

Writing
judgment differences historical context suggest process

UNIT THREE
Reading Comprehension

I . 1. T   2. T   3. F   4. T   5. F

II . 1. A   2. D   3. C   4. B   5. C   6. A   7. C   8. B

Vocabulary

I . 1. c   2. e   3. f   4. b   5. a   6. d

II . 1. fervour   2. obsession   3. supremacy   4. ideology

　　 5. oblivion   6. liven   7. crusading   8. stance

Writing

1. E   2. A   3. F   4. B   5. D   6. C

UNIT FOUR

Reading Comprehension

I . 1. 1—4   2. 5—9   3. 10—11

II . 1. D   2. A   3. C   4. D   5. B   6. C

　　 7. A   8. B   9. D   10. C

Vocabulary

I . 1. b   2. a   3. c   4. f   5. e   6. d

II . 1. A   2. C   3. B   4. B   5. D   6. C

　　 7. A   8. B

Writing

　　 a) Accomplishment of skyscraper

　　 b) The question of how to design skyscraper

　　 c) A brief history of skyscraper

　　 d) Lessons from skyscraper

UNIT FIVE

Reading Comprehension

I . 1. 5   2. 1   3. 4   4. 2   5. 3

II . 1. D   2. B   3. A   4. C   5. A   6. C

　　 7. D   8. B

Vocabulary

I . 1. e   2. d   3. a   4. c   5. b   6. f

II . 1. A   2. C   3. D   4. B   5. A   6. B

　　 7. C   8. D

Writing

Para. 1 The concept of safety in design is complex.

Para. 2 Consider the limit state or the Load and Resistance Factor Design(LRFD)approach to design.

Para. 3 本段第一句或：The explicit use of numerical factors does not reflect the real world.

Para. 4 There is no practical way of evaluating the actual factors for any given load case.

Para. 5—7 The practical factor of safety systems in some modern codes or standards do not completely comply with the necessary conditions to be satisfied.

Para. 8 The format of code must be changed.

UNIT SIX

Reading Comprehension

I.1.4 2.1 3.2 4.3 5.5—7 6.8

II.1.B 2.A 3.C 4.D

5.B 6.C

7.A 8.D

Vocabulary

I.1.f 2.c 3.a 4.e 5.d 6.b

II.1.A 2.B 3.C 4.A 5.D 6.B

7.C 8.D

Writing

1. When design becomes a specialist group exercise, the adoption of an acceptable and adaptable design method becomes highly desirable.

2. The prolification of design methodologies has tended to make the theoretical activity an end in itself.

3. The working sequences of the workshop are specified.

4. Two particaular problems emerge.

5. AIDA is introduced.

6. Future events are projections of present development.

UNIT SEVEN

Reading Comprehension

I.1.F 2.F 3.F 4.T 5.T

II.1.A 2.A 3.C 4.B 5.C 6.D 7.C 8.A

Vocabulary

I.1.c 2.e 3.f 4.b 5.d 6.a

II.1.C 2.B 3.A 4.C 5.D 6.B 7.A 8.B

Writing

structural, masonry, provisions, slenderness,
empirical, reinforced, compressive, stiffness

UNIT EIGHT

Reading Comprehension

I.1.F 2.F 3.F 4.T 5.T

II.1.C 2.B 3.B 4.A 5.C 6.A 7.C 8.C

Vocabulary

I.1.g 2.c 3.a 4.b 5.d 6.e 7.f

II.1.B 2.B 3.B 4.C 5.A 6.C 7.C 8.A

Writing

attitude, equilibrium, prime, environment,
criteria, expectations, facade, climate

Unit Nine

Reading Comprehesion

I.1. (2) 2. (3) 3. (1) 4. (4) 5. (5)

II.1.B 2.A 3.D 4.D 5.C 6.B 7.A 8.A 9.B 10.C

Vocabulary

I.1.b 2.a 3.d 4.c 5.e 6.f

II.1.A 2.B 3.B 4.A 5.C 6.A 7.A 8.C

Writing

Because American architect Robert Venturi found that "Less is a bore", the modern attitude towards ornament and decoration has been undergoing a funda-mental change, some architects thought modern architecture was too simple so that it lost touch with life. They developed a new movement in architec-ture, which canbe called ornamentalism.

They threw away the functionalist theory and design rules. They used varieties of way to decorate the inside and outside of the buildings such as supergraphics, sprouting pilasters and other embellishments, which are different from traditional ornaments. The embellishments which are different from traditional ornaments. The embellishments are sometimes fragmented, distorted and often ironically juxtaposed to other architectual elements.

They used different decorative crafts, such as glasswork, wroughtironwork and brushwork, which have been excluded from the mainstream of building design.

This movement is changing the appearance of contemporary architecture, so some people called it postmodernism. But it is not a whole rejection of Modernism, but a reaction against the more obvious failures of Modernism. This is ornamentalism.

Unit Ten
Reading Comprhension
    I . 1. period   2. structure   3. decoration 4. plantsman   5. artist
    II. 1. A   2. C   3. B   4. D   5. A   6. D   7. D   8. B   9. A   10. D

Vocabulary
    I . 1. b   2. e   3. d   4. c   5. a   6. f
    II. 1. B   2. D   3. A   4. C   5. A   6. B   7. B   8. A

Writing
On Garden

Garden is a pleasant place for you to find privacy, to meditate and to escape the pressures of fast-moving, machine-oriented world. But best gardens are not beautiful plants alone. They generally represent a careful integration of diverse elements, ranging from the purely ornamental to the strictly functional.

Whether a garden is successful or not is determined by the following elements: garden accents, structures in the garden, plant decoration, plantsman, architect and artists.

The garden accents can establish the style of a garden, such as the charac-teristic of period, ethnic. The successful structure can make a garden famous. Equally the plant decoration can obtain the same aim. However, only people can carry out these garden design. The plantsman develops the planting schemes and selects the plants. Architects do the overall garden design. The artists complete the artwork in the garden. Sometimes these three skills are embodied in a single person.

In the garden design, people emphasize symbolism and impressionism. In general, best garden should be artistic and has its own distinct characteristics.

Unit Eleven
Reading Comprehension
    I . 1. harmony   2. proportion   3. colour
        4. setting up the centers of interest   5. rhythm

Ⅱ.1.A 2.B 3.B 4.D 5.C 6.D 7.D 8.D 9.A 10.A

Vocabulary

Ⅰ.1.b 2.c 3.a 4.e 5.d 6.f

Ⅱ.1.A 2.B 3.A 4.A 5.B 6.A 7.C 8.B

Writing

1. beauty 2. sacrificed 3. instincts 4. aesthetics
5. harmonious 6. scale 7. size 8. repetition

Unit Twelve

Reading Comprehesion

Ⅰ.1. social process, technology, values
　2. geology, topography, ecological
　3. cultural variation, physical
　4. analytical, notion, Scoring
　5. planting, soil, sewage

Ⅱ.1.B 2.A 3.A 4.B 5.C 6.B 7.A 8.B 9.C 10.A

Vocabulary

Ⅰ.1.e 2.a 3.b 4.c 5.f 6.d

Ⅱ.1.A 2.C 3.B 4.D 5.A 6.D 7.C 8.B

Writing

1. relevant 2. Natural 3. site 4. suit 5. components (factors)
6. methodology 7. Technology 8. judgement

UNIT THIRTEEN

Reading Comprehension

Ⅰ.1.3 2.2 3.6 4.1 5.4—5

Ⅱ.1.D 2.D 3.B 4.A 5.C 6.B
　7.A 8.D 9.C

Vocabulary

Ⅰ.1.c 2.e 3.a 4.f 5.b 6.d

Ⅱ.1.A 2.B 3.D 4.C 5.B 6.C
　7.A 8.C

Writing

Modernist planning has failed to capture the public's sympathies because it divided and polarized community life by zoning towns into distinct and unrelated sectors.

A new generation of architects and planners take traditional towns as models and introduce into urban design the idea of neighbourhoods with a diversity of functions.

Though supported by the growing public, the new traditional towns have caused some criticism. what the new traditionalists concern themselves about is how technology can be correctly harnessed to serve our daily life rather than the other way around.

The new traditionalists seek to limit the use of cars to peripharal areas, creating pedestrian neighbourhoods and quarters that will ultimately reduce the reliance on antomobiles.

The new attitudes have yielded quite a number of promising results.

A conclusion is therefore drawn that humanity must learn to make use of the good that is engrained in traditional urban models.

UNIT FOURTEEN

Reading Comprehension

I. 1.7 2.2—4 3.1 4.8 5.5 6.6

II. 1.B 2.B 3.D 4.C 5.A 6.A
    7.C

Vocabulary

I. 1.f 2.e 3.d 4.c 5.b 6.a

II. 1.C 2.A 3.D 4.B 5.C 6.B
    7.D 8.A

Writing

Various evaluation techniques have been sought to deal with the changing goals of decision makers. Among these methods stand out cost-effectiveness analysis (CEA) and cost-benefit analysis (CBA), which have emerged as the most common manifestations of quantitative evaluation. Although CBA is more prevalent than CEA, it has been criticised on technical grounds as well as on more fundamental issues concerning its theoretical underpinnings.

Technical criticisms of CBA may be summarized under five major headings: quantification discount rates, risk and uncertainty intangibles and externalities, and distributional equity. more fundamental shortcomings in the theoretical basis of CBA were pointed out by Hill and Self. The former asserted that this method was not devised for the public sector and that CBA causes difficulties in expressing dynamic effects. The latter argued that the entire school of economic efficiency uses rationality and objectivity without any firm basis for doing so.

In conclusion, CBA remains a viable method despite all its shortcomings.

UNIT FIFTEEN

Reading Comprehension

Ⅰ. 每段第一句。

Ⅱ. 1. D　2. C　3. B　4. A　5. B　6. A

7. C　8. D　9. C

Vocabulary

Ⅰ. 1. c　2. b　3. d　4. f　5. e　6. a

Ⅱ. 1. A　2. C　3. B　4. D　5. D　6. C

7. A　8. B

Writing

Feedback can resuilt in timely amendment or abandonment of ineffective policies. Therefore it is necessary to gather and analyse data of planning failures. The present
situation of planning is that few plans are subject to rigorous detailed performance evaluation. Consequently, planning becomes a disjointed process. A number of evaluation methods
are analysed but generally they are ineffective and impractical due to such factors as interest conflicts and political or economical considerations.

On the other hand, performane evaluation of plans and planing systems is actually difficult. There are numerous constraints too complicated to make the evaluation realistically
feasible. The situation has attracted growing attention among all parties concerned.

In all the options discussed, narrower forms of analysis are recommended as the only
practical one. Though individually incomplete, they may well offer sharper insights than
those designed to grasp the complete picture.

UNIT SIXTEEN

Reading Comprehension

1. A　2. D　3. B　4. B　5. C　6. D　7. C

8. A　9. B　10. D　11. A　12. B

Vocabulary

Ⅰ. 1. e　2. c　3. a　4. a　5. f　6. b

7. d

Ⅱ. 1. B　2. A　3. A　4. A　5. D　6. C

7. B　8. D

Writing

There are two competing paradigms of zoning: the Pigovian paradigm and the Coasian paradigm. The Pigovians hold that the state or goveernment should intervene in the market to correct the economic inefficiency caused by uncompensated costs and benefits, while the Coasian paradigm doubts about the cost of such regulation.

In the planning area, the Pigovian paradigm is for zoning whereas the Coasian paradigm is against zoning. This dichotomy can be found in American literature, but hardly in British literature, where most traditional texts on the planning economics adopt Pigovian justification for planning and the Coasian paradigm receives little attention. There are probably two reasons: absence of an explicit zoning system and existance of statist welfare system in Britain. In the United states, the impact of the two paradigms can be strong felt because explicit statutory zoning systems have been widely adopted.

图书在版编目（CIP）数据

建筑类专业英语. 建筑学与城市规划. 第 3 册/李明章主编. —北京：中国建筑工业出版社，1997（2006 重印）
高等学校试用教材
ISBN 978-7-112-03028-6

Ⅰ. 建…　Ⅱ. 李…　Ⅲ. ①建筑学-英语-高等学校-教材②城市规划-英语-高等学校-教材　Ⅳ. H31

中国版本图书馆 CIP 数据核字（2006）第 082452 号

本书按国家教委颁布的《大学英语专业阅读阶段教学基本要求》编写的专业阅读教材。本册包括建筑风格、新古典主义和现代主义、高层建筑原理、安全设计、砖石工程新工艺、绿色建筑、未来城市、分区规划、装饰美学、园林设计等内容。全书安排 16 个单元，每单元除正课文外，还有两篇阅读材料，均配有必要的注释。正课文还配有词汇表和练习，书后附有总词汇表，参考译文和练习答案。语文难度大于第一、二册，并配有科技英语写作的简要说明与写作练习。供本专业学生四年级上半学期使用，也可供有关人员自学英语参考。

高等学校试用教材

建筑类专业英语

建筑学与城市规划

第三册

李明章　　　　　主编
王天发　　　　　编
娄作友　潘龙明
黄天琪　　　　　主审

*

中国建筑工业出版社出版、发行（北京海淀三里河路 9 号）
各地新华书店、建筑书店经销
北京建筑工业印刷厂印刷

*

开本：787×1092 毫米　1/16　印张：14　字数：340 千字
1997 年 6 月第一版　2019 年 3 月第十一次印刷
定价：**39.00** 元
ISBN 978-7-112-03028-6
（33359）